The Nature of Work

Also by Paul Thompson (with Eddie Bannon)

Working the System: Workplace Organisation
and the Labour Process in Telecommunications

The Nature of Work

**An introduction to debates
on the labour process**

Paul Thompson

**MACMILLAN
EDUCATION**

First published 1983
Reprinted 1984, 1985, 1986, 1988

Published by
MACMILLAN EDUCATION LTD
Houndmills, Basingstoke, Hampshire RG21 2XS
and London
Companies and representatives
throughout the world

Typeset in Great Britain by
Styleset Limited
Salisbury, Wiltshire

Printed in Hong Kong

ISBN 0-333-33026-9 (hard cover)
ISBN 0-333-33027-7 (paper cover)

To Betty and John
   Elsie and Reg

Contents

Contents

Preface

My interest in the labour process first developed in political activity with shop stewards and shopfloor workers in the motor industry on Merseyside in the early 1970s. The experiences of the restructuring of work and pay began to be put to academic use in subsequent years of part-time research at Liverpool University. At first most of the innovative writings on the changing nature of work and class derived from Italy and France. All that changed with the publication of Braverman's *Labor and Monopoly Capital* in 1974, and the explosion of interest in the labour process that followed in its wake.

My research became increasingly directed towards tying together and evaluating the new debates, comparing them with older sociological traditions. This book draws on the knowledge I gained in those years, although its scope, aims and content are very different. I owe a considerable debt to Tony Lane for his encouragement and support through that period. Richard Hyman, too, was kind enough to give me some very useful advice which helped me to revise a number of my ideas about labour process theory and its limitations.

In working on the present book, my thanks go to Theo Nichols for a set of fair and useful comments on the whole manuscript, and to Dave Robertson and Lynne Segal for looking at particular chapters. I have continually drawn on the advice and knowledge of Mike Jones, the discussions between us contributing considerably to the development of my own ideas. In addition, the critical attention of Hazel Davies to the style of the manuscript has greatly added to its readability. My editor at Macmillan, Steven Kennedy, has also been an invaluable source of help in improving its form and content. Responsibility in all respects remains, of course, my own.

Thanks also go to Jean Pearson for work on the bibliography and index; and while most of the typing of the manuscript was my own, Tricia Houghton was kind enough to help with some of the chapters. Most of all, I would like to record my debt to Jill and our daughter Jane who have tolerated what often appeared to be endless periods of work on the book and its forerunners. Without their support such efforts could never have been completed.

Liverpool   PAUL THOMPSON
December 1982

Glossary of Labour Process Terms

The aim of this glossary is not to produce a set of definitions for the complete range of sociological and Marxist concepts, but rather to deal with those terms used throughout the text which have specific relevance to the labour process.

alienated work   Work performed under conditions in which the worker is estranged from his or her own activity in the act of production, through the sale of labour power and the subordination of skills and knowledge to the capitalist, or other external social forces.

automation   A form of production in which all manual intervention by the worker is eliminated, in some cases to be replaced by supervision, monitoring or control of machinery. It includes a number of types such as continuous process, numerical control and automated assembly; and is distinguished from *mechanisation*, which concerns the operation of tools or machinery through sources independent of the worker's manual dexterity.

capitalism   A mode of production based on the generalised production of commodities for exchange and profit.

collective worker   At a certain stage of capitalist production, manual and intellectual workers are combined together in association by the machine system. The term is used to stress the partial interchangeability of functions, and the potential for genuine co-operation in the labour process in a socialist society. See also *homogenisation*.

control system   Mechanisms by which employers direct work tasks, discipline and reward workers, and supervise and evaluate their performance in production. See also *subordination*.

deskilling   Incorporation of the crafts, knowledgable practices and elements of job control held by workers into the functions of management, or operation of machinery.

division of labour   This is not the existence of different jobs, but the simplifying and fragmentation of tasks into smaller parts, so as to cheapen and control the costs of labour. Marx also uses a distinction between this *technical* division and the *social* division of labour, related to wider societal processes through which workers are allocated to different branches of production. This has relevance to the analysis of relations between social hierarchies of race and sex, and hierarchies in work.

fetishism   The process in production whereby the workings of the market, exploitation and private ownership *appear* as natural and inevitable rather than social relations capable of transformation.

forces and relations of production   A distinction between skills, machinery and other physical properties of production, and the social relations of ownership, command and control. These are held by Marx to act constantly on one another, enabling a critique to be made of those who believe that science and technology are neutral.

Fordism   A term used by some labour process theorists which extends the technique of factory production — based on the assembly-line — developed by Ford into a category referring to a general stage in capitalist production.

homogenisation   Controversial term used by Marx and other labour process writers to refer to the equalisation of types of work under the impact of *deskilling* and related trends.

intellectual and manual labour   All human labour involves mind and body, but this concept is used to describe the separation of *conception* and *execution* that is built into the design of jobs, reflecting the objectives of capital.

job enrichment   One form of work humanisation by employers. It is often used as a generic description of a number of different processes of enlarging, aggregating and rotating tasks.

labour market   The means of allocating and pricing jobs in the economy as a whole, and within particular firms (an *internal* labour market).

labour power   The capacity to work which is transformed into *labour* that produces value for the capitalist through the creation of commodities.

labour process   The means by which raw materials are transformed by human labour, acting on the objects with tools and machinery: first into products for use and, under capitalism, into commodities to be exchanged on the market.

large-scale industry   A term used by Marx to distinguish between the mature factory system in which the labour process is transformed by the uses of science and machinery, and previous stages such as *manufacture* (dominated by the introduction of the division of labour), and *co-operation* (characterised by the concentration of workers into the same or connected processes by the capitalist).

reproduction of labour power   The wider means of ensuring the continuity of wage labour through the organisation of the fundamental material and social needs of human life — food, clothing, leisure, etc. This is a crucial part of connections between the labour process and institutions such as the family.

reserve army of labour   What Marx described as a relative surplus population of unemployed workers, or potential workers — such as the sporadically employed, housewives and migrants — who form a necessary part of the working mechanisms of the capitalist mode of production.

subordination of labour   Marx used these terms in a more precise way than that of *control*. The *formal* subordination of labour is established when workers and their skills are subsumed in a labour process under the control of the capitalist. This is ultimately transformed into *real* subordination through the incorporation of science and machinery within the expanded scale of production — which, in turn, allows a qualitatively new and more effective means of domination of labour.

Taylorism   Management control strategy named after F. W. Taylor. The first systematic theory and practice of management, its defining characteristic has been the attempt to separate mental and manual labour, subjecting both to exact measurement. Taylorism spawned a more general movement known as *scientific management*.

valorisation   The process of creating surplus value. The labour process only becomes distinctively capitalist when it is combined with valorisation.

worker resistance   A widely used term by labour process writers to refer to informal *and* organised worker opposition to management and employers in the labour process. It is more specific to work than the often misleading application of the concept of 'class struggle'.

Introduction

Every member of the Amalgamated Society of Engineers was a time-served man, and in the union there was a standoffish attitude: a sort of pride of craft, and a pride of union. The members really believed themselves to be the aristocrats of labour, and they dressed differently and better than other workers.

As a shop-steward I used to attend the Clyde Workers' Committee meetings which were held in the Templars' Halls in Ingram Street. It was a very open meeting all about industrial questions and action in the workshops, and everyone put forth their own point of view. It was a strange looking meeting, too — a couple of hundred engineering shop stewards, all with their bowler hats, blue suits and rolled umbrellas, discussing the next policy to pursue.

(McShane, 1978: 42, 89)

Harry McShane's description of skilled engineering workers in the early part of this century provides an example of the relationships between the nature of work and forms of social consciousness and behaviour. It was not greater pay alone that made skilled workers an aristocracy of labour. Craft work profoundly shaped their self-image and action inside and outside the workplace. Their knowledge of the job and degree of control of working conditions made them the backbone of emergent movements for workers' control of production.

Such movements were not confined to Britain: 'highly specialised workers of the machine and tool industry with a high level of professional ability . . . were materially most susceptible to . . . workers' self-management of production' (Bologna, 1976: 69). Nor have sectors of skilled, craft work entirely disappeared from modern industry. Jobs like tool-making are being eroded in terms of their numbers and skill (Coventry Machine Tool Workers' Committee, 1979), but the following description still evokes a continuity with the past:

> The atmosphere, while still being informally friendly had a faint air of professionalism about it. Right from my first day there, it was made clear to me that toolmakers were craftsmen, and as such inherently superior to all other workers except for a few other small and highly skilled trades. The ethos which has been graphically described as the 'aristocracy of labour' was very present. At the centre of this ethos lay a very strict adherence to high standards of workmanship.
>
> (quoted in Fraser, 1969: 26)

However, mass production and assembly-line work are more likely to be characteristic of post-war industry. It is difficult to imagine a meeting of motor shop stewards sitting in suits and bowler hats! Neither is Beynon's (1975: 640) graphic description of young car workers much related to a craft work ethic: 'Attracted there by the money, soon they found there was nothing else. They didn't like the line, the last thing they wanted to do was to screw on wheels. They left jobs unfinished; they plagued the foreman; they threw bombs of bostic into scrap bins'. The effects of such work systems on productivity, absenteeism, labour turnover and industrial conflict were of sufficient concern for the US government to set up a task force to investigate the problem. Meanwhile other commentators called, rather improbably, for the abandonment of the assembly line.

With the recent emergence of the new, microprocessor technology, we have a further revolution in the organisation of work, and consequently in wider attitudes and behaviour. Not only does the microprocessor offer the possibility of incorporating a much wider range of human skills and intelligence into machinery at a minimal cost; for the first time it brings the techniques of the assembly line — standardisation, speed-up, task fragmentation — into the office on a large scale.

The word processor

'a process of having word originators (executives, etc.), select formula clauses from pre-coded, pre-organised clause books . . . Once selected, clause codes . . . variable inserts, are either dictated into recorders or jotted down on "to-be-typed" forms. Automatic typewriters repetitively type the "canned" clauses, and the typist manually keyboards in the new or variable data . . . benefits are word originator and typist efficiency and more work produced from the same number of hours on the job. In addition, less training is required of all the people involved.'

(article from *Administrative Management*, quoted in Braverman, 1974: 345)

Behind the glossy advertisements showing futuristic electronic equipment lies the reality of more routine tasks and less skilled jobs. The changing face of the office is complemented by the erosion and blurring of industrial skills such as those in printing. Here the new technology allows the journalist to perform a number of tasks that were once the province of highly skilled printers. Not surprisingly there have been a number of drawn-out disputes over the introduction of new technology in Fleet Street. But the effects of the latest technological developments go far wider than the workplace and trade union strategies. The education system in particular is facing a major upheaval as the labour market is restructured and the demand for apprenticeships is drastically reduced.

Factory, office, newspaper: there are different examples of working environments and their influences. Yet from the 1950s a prominent theme within social science has been of the worker no longer interested in work, part of a society increasingly preoccupied with problems of consumption and

leisure. The dominant methods of workplace investigation —
attitude surveys, studies of the formal characteristics of
organisations, and of occupational groups — have largely failed
to give any real prominence to underlying changes in the
nature of work and its attendant social relations. New technology, with its massive potential to transform and replace
human labour, has provided a further context for assertions
concerning the declining importance of work.

In the past decade, however, there has been a resurgence of
interest in changes in the nature of work and work experience.
A body of research mainly Marxist in origin, has developed
under the heading of 'labour process theory': the central
argument of this research has been that the degradation of
work remains central to understanding the functioning of
modern capitalist societies. This is not to suggest that the
workplace is the only source of influence on people's ideas
and behaviour. Merely that for all the talk of 'post-industrial'
societies, most people's lives remain structured by work.

There is a further problem in mainstream social science.
Conceptions of *work in general* tell us little about changes in
social relations, skills and machinery. Work tends to be *described* in terms of the various structures and tasks connected
to levels of economic and technological development. It therefore tends to take the above components for granted.

A labour process perspective locates the basic activity of
transforming raw material into products through human labour
with a given technology, within the specific dynamics of a
mode of production and antagonistic class relations. Work is
not just something that a society organises to meet social
needs, or people carry out in order to survive. It is a framework within which those who own and control economic
resources seek to ensure the appropriation of the *surplus*. The
way that economic surplus is appropriated will strongly condition working arrangements.

Labour process perspectives are therefore distinguished by
their ability to place work activity within the total system of
production. Take the previous example of the word processor.
Like all machinery based on the microchip, it is not an abstract
'invention', but machinery designed for a social purpose. In
this case the purpose is to increase productivity and efficiency,

partly through building into the technology a more complete division between the mental labour of 'word originators' and the manual labour of typists. Nor is this shaping of science and technology new. Referring to the introduction of assembly lines by Ford, Drucker comments: 'if we actually analyse this new so-called technology, we shall find that it is not a technology at all. It is not an arrangement of physical forces. It is a principle of social order. This was true of Ford's work . . . He made not one mechanical invention or discovery; everything mechanical he used was old and well-known. Only his concept of human organisation for work was new' (quoted in Beynon, 1973: 18).

Drucker is a noted management writer, yet he has touched on a vital part of labour process theory. This is the distinction between the physical forces and social relations of production. That has always been a basic Marxist concept, yet like many others its application to the study of work was largely lost. With others it has now begun to be recovered. The purpose of this book is to describe and evaluate the new writings on the labour process, much of which has not been made accessible or available to a wider audience.

In Part One, a *background* to the debate is provided. Chapter 1 examines the main features of the treatment of work in the various branches of social science. No single chapter can hope to deal with these trends in detail. Instead the aim is to indicate the main points of continuity between the various theories and concepts, and the discontinuities with those used in labour process theory. Beyond that, signposts are provided to the sources of more detailed exposition and critique. It is not my intention to argue that there are no overlapping ideas and research between the two traditions; rather that a comparative examination can lay the basis for a synthesis on some issues in a new sociology of work. Chapter 2 puts the labour process concepts used throughout the book such as deskilling, subordination and division of labour in their original context of the writings of Marx. Marx's ideas were themselves rooted in the context of the nineteenth-century English factory system. By combining theoretical material with empirical examples from the period, the chapter seeks to show their continuing relevance, as well as areas of ambiguity and weakness. Finally it goes on to show how and why Marx's attention to the labour process was abandoned in the subsequent evolution of trade union practices and political events.

Part Two looks at the contemporary labour process debates themselves. In Chapter 3, the central feature is an exposition of the main analysis that rediscovered the conceptual tools of Marx on work — that of Braverman. His contribution is discussed alongside supportive and parallel research concerning work under monopoly capitalism. The breadth of Braverman's analysis ensures that it raises most of the major themes necessary to the debate: the impact of science and technology on skills, managerial strategies of control; relations between production and society; and the changing class and occupational structure.

Braverman's distinctive theories on these questions have raised a host of critical comments, as well as further research using his analytical framework. Nevertheless, labour process theory cannot be contained within the parameters of that debate, both because of what it omits and what others have contributed. Therefore subsequent chapters in Part Two of the book deal with the key *themes* in more general terms. Chapters 4 and 5 take up the two central questions at the heart of the early debate. Is the autonomy of workers being increasingly subordinated by decreasing the level of skill in production tasks, while increasing managerial control over their execution? In Chapter 4, 'The Degradation of Labour?', the focus is the historical variations in relations between skills, labour markets and worker resistance. Particular attention is paid to the contemporary impact of new technology. In Chapter 5, 'Forms of Control and Resistance', the emphasis is on the available means of managerial control open to capital. Capital has to coexist with worker initiative and organisation. Therefore careful consideration has to be given to evidence on how much autonomy workers can exert or be given without endangering existing patterns of ownership and control. This includes a discussion of modern schemes of job enrichment and work humanisation.

Chapters 6 and 7 turn to areas that are neglected or underdeveloped in the main body of labour process theory. Chapter 6 deals with the theme of 'Legitimation and Consent in the

Workplace'. The conventional idea of managerial control is limited in important ways. A small but growing number of writers are beginning to examine how workers control *themselves* in the context of practices deeply embedded in the capitalist labour process. This means taking up issues of ideology and culture, and how they influence the relations between consent, coercion and resistance in work. In Chapter 7 the focus is shifted to a further area of analysis inadequately dealt with through orthodox Marxist categories, namely that of the social division of labour in society as a whole. 'The "Other" Division of Labour' discusses the effects of the wider divisions on the nature of the labour process. By focusing on gender relations, evaluation is made of the extent to which patriarchal forms influence work allocation, tasks and rewards; and also the suitability of Marxist concepts like the industrial reserve army and deskilling.

Part Three consists of one final chapter (Chapter 8) which seeks to extend the debate to some of the major, and often more difficult, *consequences* of theoretical questions that remain unresolved in the labour process sphere. It begins with a short summary of the evaluative arguments in the book. This provides a context for an examination of two issues. The first concerns the *distinctiveness* of the capitalist labour process. All the discussions of historical and contemporary work trends fail to answer this question satisfactorily. The chapter attempts to begin some answers through a comparative analysis of the labour process in Eastern Europe. Secondly, there are many unresolved issues concerning the relations between the nature of work and the possibilities for social change. A close examination of potential lessons arising from labour process research necessitates a highly critical response to the asssumptions built into aspects of orthodox Marxism. Finally, Chapter 8 looks at the implications — primarily in Britain — of changes in the labour process for workplace practices and union strategies. Aside from the longer term changes, new technology and economic restructuring in the recession are producing a sustained challenge to traditional patterns of worker organisation and job controls. The effects and responses are examined briefly.

PART ONE

The Established Traditions

1
The Sociological Study of Work

The slogan of the 1933 World Fair was 'Science Finds, Industry Applies, Man Conforms'. Within the social sciences the conceptualisation of the changing nature of work has often corresponded with this mechanistic notion. Scientists and technologists are seen as making independent discoveries which constantly renew the productive apparatus, while managers put the results to their most efficient use, and workers react and adapt to the changes. Meanwhile industrial sociologists theorise about the best combination of conditions for productivity, progress and harmonious relations.

It is a framework of ideas normally standing in sharp contrast to a labour process theory emphasising the social construction and conflictual character of work relations, science and technology. Yet the contrast is not with any single set of ideas in the social sciences. There is a bewildering variety of disciplines which claim work as their province. Industrial sociology coexists with organisational theory, management sciences, industrial relations, the social psychology of work, the sociology of occupations, to name only the major ones.

The origins of the sociology of work lie in the attempts of the classical theorists to come to terms with the nature of industrialisation. Marx, Weber and Durkheim all wrote about work, not as specialists, but within wider general theories (Esland and Salaman, 1975). Their respective theoretical influences have remained strong, though increasingly filtered through narrow specialisms.

A particular concentration on the sphere of work as such is normally dated from the emergence of plant studies like those of Western Electric in Chicago in the 1930s by Mayo (1945). In this period sociologists, psychologists and even anthropologists combined to study workplace behaviour, primarily in the context of helping management to understand variations and restrictions of output.

Dissatisfaction and further developments in the post-war era have led to rival schools of thought and further specialisms. Some researchers have maintained an emphasis on studying *workplace behaviour* directly, shifting the focus to the relations between forms of technology and the social organisation of work. Others have diverged to examine the rules underlying the functioning of *organisations*, with direct applications to patterns of control; or in a parallel shift away from direct work relations to an emphasis on *industrial relations*; the framework of bargaining and conflict between capital and labour. A further alternative has been to stress the more general features of class and class imagery, noting the interrelations with the world of work.

The purpose of this chapter is not to provide an historical account of the development of various specialisms and schools of thought (see Rose, 1975), nor to make a full examination of the theories and the contrasts between them (see Salaman, 1981).[1] The aim is to look at the major systems of ideas and concepts that link the sociology of work together, so that a contrast is provided to concepts used in labour process theory in the rest of the book. While the fragmentation of the social science treatment of work is an important problem in its own right,[2] there are sufficient conceptual and methodological overlaps — concerning understandings of skill, technology, the division of labour, and the organisation of work — to make such a comparison necessary and worthwhile.

There is a newer sociology of work influenced by labour process theory, but the traditionally influential body of ideas can be examined through a series of *debates* on key issues that have taken place. Before this, however, it is worth noting that the parallel debates took place in a context of general models of industrial society in the post-war period. The most influential of these was presented by Kerr and others in 1962.

They argued that the following interrelated factors were basic to the dynamic of post-war societies:

1. Industrialism has replaced capitalism.
2. Technology demands rising levels of skill and responsibility.
3. A growing proportion of technological and managerial personnel is transforming the class structure.
4. New wealth and leisure is created.
5. The decline of overt protest characterises industrial relations.
6. Humanistic managers and professionals are replacing capitalists.
7. Classes and hierarchies have been shown to be 'eternal' in Western and Eastern Europe, as part of a process of industrial convergence.
8. Power is diffuse. In a pluralistic industrial society, the working class has been fragmented and conflict institutionalised.
9. The state is omnipresent, and bureaucracy necessary.

There have been a number of major recent critiques of Kerr,[3] yet the themes persistently recur in a variety of different theoretical contexts. It is to these that we now turn.

Workplace Behaviour

The major schools of industrial sociology have always been more interested in the behaviour of workers than in the nature of work. Who owns, controls and designs work has largely been taken as given, as have the consequences of these social relations on forms of technology and the division of labour. The focus has been on the reactions of workers, manifested particularly in the long-running debate on the reasons for 'restriction of output'. This emphasis has been reinforced by the well documented connection between sociological investigation in the workplace and managerial sponsorship and concerns (Baritz, 1960; Bendix, 1963).

Origins of industrial sociology

These factors have led to a belief that industrial behaviour can be explained and changed *within* the workplace. The result has been a well established tradition of 'plant sociology', isolated from any wider environment but carrying the advantage of a direct and immediate connection with shop-floor life. The previously mentioned Western Electric studies, which largely set this tradition underway, were themselves a reaction to *Taylorism*.

Connecting his ideas on the organisation of work with his experience on the shop floor of a steel mill, F. W. Taylor developed the theory of 'scientific management'. The application of scientific techniques for controlling and measuring work were aimed at eliminating inefficiency. This inefficiency was rooted on the workers' side in a rational attempt to control and limit output, thus maximising rewards. On the management side it derived from their lack of knowledge, and thus control, of the productive process.

By appropriating that knowledge from the workforce and locating it in separate managerial functions, and developing a payment and selection system that appealed to workers' self-interest, a profitable and efficient partnership could be created.[4] That, of course, was not how workers saw it. They saw the hated stop-watch and time and motion man. Nor was the apparatus of work study developed by Taylor and his followers in the USA and Europe in the 1920s only unpopular with the unions. Some employers were sceptical of its value and fearful of the resistance provoked. Many social scientists condemned it in forthright terms.

Until recently it has been the convention to describe Taylorism as a partly failed and superseded system. Rose is typical in his description of the contribution of Taylor: 'The sheer silliness from a modern perspective of many of his ideas, and the barbarities they led to when applied in industry, encourage ridicule and denunciation' (1975: 31). Workers were not mechanisms whose willingness to work could be switched on and off by payment systems, without reference to individual difference and social needs. 'Taylor's worker is a monstrosity: a greedy machine indifferent to its own pain and loneliness once given the opportunity to maim and isolate itself' (Rose, 1975: 62).

It was not suprising that later perspectives on workplace behaviour described themselves in terms of *human relations*. Associated primarily with a long period of observational research in the Western Electric plant from 1926 to the early 1940s, the Human Relations Movement had a more sophisticated explanation of workplace organisation and action.[5] The factory was presented as a social system where the culture and conditions of the work-group affected and often restricted output.

But this was not due to Taylor's 'economic rationality'. For Mayo and his co-researchers, the worker was motivated by a compulsion towards sociability, too often restricted by working conditions. The problem lay in the social system of the factory itself. This system contained two interrelated aspects, its *technical* and *human* organisation. The former process does not necessarily provide a basis for co-operative working relations. However, the human or informal organisation can secure harmony.

Hence managerial intervention within factory life can modify social processes, improving efficiency and meeting social needs. On this basis recommendations were made to Western Electric's management on improving social skills of supervision, creating better working conditions, counselling programmes, and the like. As one commentator favourably remarked: 'The Human Relations Movement demonstrated in numerous studies how the style of supervision and composition of different groups affected their work performance and satisfaction' (Argyle, 1972: 2).[6]

Post-war plant sociology

A reaction to and critique of human relations theory reached its peak in the immediate post-war period, when the familiar charges of managerial bias, insularity from wider socio-economic factors, and neglect of workers' organisation and conflict were effectively made. However, new research remained focused on the plant and within the most basic conceptual

framework established by previous studies, i.e. the separation
of technical and human organisation.

This time the emphasis was reversed, with technological
influences taken to be the central determinant of attitudes
and behaviour. Some studies continued in the tradition of
examining work-group behaviour, for instance in Sayles's
analysis of 300 primary groups in thirty plants. Degrees of
conflict were linked to group patterns established by plant
technology. In terms of the factory as a whole, 'the social
system erected by the technological process' (Sayles, 1958:
93) is referred to, although a recognition is retained of worker
motivations in initiating action.[7]

A shift towards technological determinism is also apparent
from studies emphasising work attitudes. The 1950s were
notable for the strengthening of trends towards mass production, which stimulated sociological interest, such as Walker
and Guest's *Man on the Assembly Line* (1952). Based on
single-plant interviews with 180 workers, mass production
was presented as: 'a code of law governing. . .behaviour and
way of life in the factory' (1952: 2). With the machine as the
unalterable 'commanding feature' of factory life, the workforce had to be the factor to be adjusted. For despite the
noted dislike of machine-paced work, it was reforms of the
human organisation that were stressed. This was to include
job rotation and enlargement to overcome 'psychological
starvation' and the 'loss of bonding' resulting from the new
patterns of technology and management associated with mass
production.

The more influential research of Blauner (1964) can be
situated within a similar framework.[8] Once more the emphasis
is on attitudes, although with greater theoretical attention
given to the question of alienation. Blauner's findings were a
useful check on prevalent trends asserting widespread job
satisfaction (Brown, 1954), or concern with leisure and consumption rather than work (Dubin, 1956). In restoring technology, the division of labour and alienation as central concerns, a clear distinction was made with Marxist theory.
Blauner contrasted Marx's stress on the homogeneity of work
with his own view that work is subject to structural differentiation related to changing technologies.

Four basic types of work technology were distinguished: craft, machine-tending, assembly line and continuous process. In itself this was unexceptional, coinciding with conventional divisions into single units, small batch, large batch, continuous process and mass production (Woodward, 1958). What is distinctive in Blauner's argument is the assertion that technologies were evolving towards the continuous process type, as manifested by industries like chemicals.

This was seen as leading to a reduction in alienation, 'automation' completing a 'U-curve' of stages of technology and work satisfaction within capitalist development.[9] Blauner argued that 'The worker in the automated factory "regains" a sense of control over his technological environment, that is usually absent in mass production factories' (1964: viii). Such experiences were held to lead to 'social integration' and identification of belonging and function within the enterprise. So even if Blauner distanced himself from some of the prevailing orthodoxies, the difference is not substantial. The worker may not always be satisfied and integrated, but the future trend will lead in that direction. The emphasis on the emergent 'utopia' of automation was a characteristic feature of writings in this period (Kumar, 1978).

One problem with the research on technological influences was that it failed to elaborate a view of the relations *between* the technical and human aspects of work organisation. The most influential attempt to do this was through the concept of *socio-technical* systems associated with the work of the Tavistock Institute in Britain.[10] Though based strongly on a long-term research programme in the mines in the 1950s (Trist and Bamforth, 1951), the perspective is most commonly linked to Woodward's studies of the relations between technology and management organisation (1958 and 1965).

In a survey of firms, she found that styles of management and formal work organisation were determined primarily by technology: for example, lengthening lines of command as technological complexity increased. This attacked the orthodox human relations perspective in that it emphasised the formal work organisation and its constraints on the previously favoured ability to manipulate informal practices and managerial styles. Yet a space was still seen for varying managerial practice within technological constraints. This was explained succinctly by Rice: 'any production system requires both a technological organisation — equipment and process layout — and a work organisation relating to each other those who carry out the necessary tasks. The technological demands place limits on the type of work possible, but a work organisation has social and psychological properties of its own independent of technology' (1958: 4).

Not all early post-war research went in a technological direction. Some developed what Rose calls a neo-human relations school (Maslow, 1958; Argyris, 1957; McGregor, 1960; Likert, 1967; Herzberg, 1968). Like Woodward and some of the other previously mentioned studies, they were concerned to look at workplaces as *organisations*, rather than the older idea of factory social systems. But even this search for the pyschological characteristics of organisations was partly in the plant sociology tradition, with its emphasis on modifying styles of management and conditions of work in an effort to improve satisfaction and efficiency.

They remained in the framework of anti-Taylorism, believing that workers were not primarily motivated by economic self-interest, needing to be tempered by the harsh hand of managerial discipline. Although each theorist saw the alternative in a slightly different way, the overall emphasis was on inherent social needs for self-fulfilment, status and belongingness, which although arising outside work, could be satisfied within it. The new theorists differed from the old partly in being more critical of existing managerial practices, seeing a 'clash between the individual's psychological aspirations and needs and contemporary organisational structures and management styles' (Brown, 1980: 158). A further difference lay in the recognition that workers brought needs with them to work. Taken together, it meant that workers were not seen merely as passive factors to be 'adjusted'. Managerial practices needed changing, and proposals for participatory leadership, group decision-making, decentralisation of organisational power and job enlargement became popular among some managers.

Other researchers were also trying to modify human relations theory, although from the traditional concerns of work-groups and restriction of output rather than the psychology of organisational behaviour. Two of the more prominent and useful studies, both using participant observation methods, were by Lupton (1963) and Roy (1973). Production norms were related concretely to work-group culture in an attempt to explain that restriction of output did not arise out of an irrational failure to comprehend managerial logic. Instead it needed to be seen as a means of surviving work, maintaining earning power and jobs, and as a response to managerial authoritarianism.

Technology, work organisation and alienation: a critique
Conventional critiques of orthodox plant sociology — insularity, managerial bias, assumption of industrial consensus — all express partial truths. But it is necessary also to make a critique on its own terrain, in terms of the concepts used to explain work relations. The basis of the weaknesses of these studies of workplace behaviour lies in an inadequate treatment of work as a system and a process.

To understand this we have to return to the recurrent theme of industrial sociology, namely the relationship between technical and human organisation of work, and examine it in greater depth. 'Technical' is normally taken to mean technological hardware — what Marx called the instruments of labour. The human organisation itself is normally divided into a division of labour and a social organisation of work. Within the latter, formal components deal with the structure of command and co-operation, while informal aspects refer to the work-groups and their behaviour patterns.

From Taylorism onwards, the technological side has been taken for granted as a neutral form. The arguments have been about the most effective means of human organisation, though recognising in some cases the technological influences upon it. Taylorism dealt with the social organisation, but its principles and methods — particularly the separation of conception and execution and the fragmentation of tasks — had direct relevance to the division of labour and the design of work, including technology.

In this context it has been quite wrong to describe Taylorism as silly and outdated, given that, 'it dealt with the fundamentals of the organisation of the labour process and of control over it' (Braverman, 1974: 87). As Braverman explains, work organisation has long since incorporated Taylorist principles, which often become the province of industrial engineers rather than managerial personnel. He quotes Peter Drucker, a management consultant, to explain this split:[11]

> Personnel Administration and Human Relations are the things talked about whenever the management of worker and work is being discussed . . . But they are not the concepts that underly the actual management of work in American industry. This concept is Scientific Management. Scientific Management focuses on the work. Its core is the organised study of work, the analysis of work into its simplest elements and the systematic improvement of the workers' performance of each of these elements . . . And it has no difficulty proving the contribution it makes; its results in the form of higher output are visible and readily measurable.
>
> (quoted in Braverman, 1974: 280)

As admitted in numerous textbooks on industrial behaviour, studies deriving from a human relations tradition have focused on styles of management and the relations between formal and informal aspects of social organisation, leaving the fundamentals of the labour process relatively untouched. Braverman argues that this has led to a concern only with the 'habituation of the worker', the best means of adjustment to the existing labour process.

While the worst studies lean in this direction, the idea is slightly misleading. What has happened is that orientations deriving from a human relations approach have run *parallel* to the substance of work organisation:

> most present technology was born and developed in a strictly Taylorist spirit . . . Only, in general, when a new technology has been developed, and is put into production, is there any recognition of the social problems embodied in it. At that stage, the techniques of the social sciences can be applied: job enrichment, job enlargement, or the use of semi-autonomous work groups.
>
> (Rosenbrock, 1979: 2)[12]

Even the best concepts from traditional industrial sociology do not grasp the interaction between social relations and technical organisation within the labour process as a whole. A good example is the socio-technical systems idea. Different social arrangements of manpower are regarded as compatible with the *same* technology, establishing a greater degree of organisational choice. But the effects of the social relations of ownership and control *on* technology remains unacknowledged. This is in contrast to some of the newer sociology of work, in which the social design of jobs has been recognised as being influenced by principles of scientific management, existing patterns of production and strategies for controlling the workforce (Davis and Taylor, 1972; Dickson, 1974; Fox, 1980; Reeves and Woodward, 1970).

The growth in the 1950s of studies exploring technological influences merely tended to add a touch of determinism to an already existing concept of the neutrality of technology. For instance, Blauner says three factors shape technology; the state of mechanical and scientific processes, the nature of the product, and the economic and engineering resources in particular firms (1964:6). No mention was made of the workplace conflict that may shape technological change; nor was there any notion that machinery embodies social purposes. The consideration of such factors is separated out into the sphere of social organisation.

Even when people and technology are combined, the traditional fetishism of social relations is retained. Argyle put this neatly when referring to 'man-machine systems', 'in which the best combination of men and machines is designed, where both men and machines do what they can do best' (1972:32). Many of the studies of the influence of technology on work have in fact been predominantly about *attitudes towards* types of technology (Blauner, 1964; Walker and Guest, 1952). When technology itself is defined, it has often been in narrow and superficial terms: as the hardware of tools and equipment, and as taken-for-granted broad classifications such as mass production, continuous process and small batch (Sayles, 1958; Blauner, 1964; Woodward, 1965). Beneath the formal definitions, the underlying labour processes have seldom been examined.[13]

Furthermore, the view of science and technology as neutral

tended to be accompanied by an assumption of linear progress of production systems, the end product of which would be a humane, continuous-process system. This perspective has been particularly associated with Blauner. There have been justifiable criticisms of the notions that automation leads to the integration of the worker into the enterprise (Mallet, 1975; Gallie, 1978) and to more skilled and satisfying work (Nichols and Beynon, 1971). But assumptions of rising skill and responsibility, combined with the blurring of manual—white collar distinctions, have been widely held (Kerr, 1962; Crozier, 1971; Argyle, 1972), even among critics of Blauner (Gallie, 1978).

It is hardly suprising, then, that an understanding of alienation has been weak. The most conventional criticism of this kind of industrial sociology has been that of ignoring prior orientations to work which strongly influence rewards expected and satisfaction experienced (Goldthorpe, Lockwood, *et al*; 1968; Wedderburn and Crompton, 1972; Cotgrove, 1972; Gallie, 1978). But while this point is partly true, the major weaknesses still lie within the analysis of the workplace. Given the mistaken view of the direction and consequences of changes in production systems, the objective features of alienation were inevitably misunderstood and underestimated. Marx's concepts, developed in his study of the labour process, could be safely described as having an anachronistic ring (Faunce, 1968).

In addition, the methods of definition and identification of alienation became increasingly suspect. It was assumed that alienation could be measured subjectively through survey techniques, even when related to objective features of work (Walker and Guest, 1952; Blauner, 1964). Yet the survey content has generally been based on 'sponge' questions (i.e. those that 'soak up' a meaningless variety of responses), which fail to make clear what aspects of the job — pay, skill, security, relations with workmates — are being linked to 'satisfaction' (Fox, 1971; 1980). To add to this there is the other problem that respondents may simply be reproducing expected social attitudes in a context where individual worth is still measured through work status.

This methodological orientation tends to slip into definitions of alienation based on subjective feeling states (see Seeman, 1959). As Salaman comments:

> Very often the lack of any proper theoretical conception of the nature of work in modern society, or of the interests that determine the design of work and organisation, or of the forces in society at large that determine the development of appropriate and realistic expectations, entirely invalidates these exercises in a — theoretical, management-biased empiricism.
>
> (Salaman, 1981: 87)[14]

Industrial sociology has not successfully linked together the voluminous literature on restriction of output and the debate on alienation. In fact it is remarkable that there has been no solid explanation of the *source* of the continual battle over output. Various studies have referred to workers' irrationality, managerial inefficiency and monetary motivations, but this has been abstracted from any analysis of the nature and purpose of production under capitalism. Rather work has been linked, as a general phenomenon, to the need to produce goods and supply individual satisfactions.

The capitalist economy is a backcloth that is occasionally acknowledged, as when Rice (1958) refers to socio-technical systems needing 'economic validity', while Herzberg promotes his consultancy techniques by noting the need to optimise the return of investment in people (1968).[15] Yet it is the struggle for profitability that impels capital to transform and control the labour process, shaping and stimulating workers' own battle to satisfy economic and social needs. Without this insight, restriction of output simply appears alongside lack of motivation, difficulties of communication and conflict between groups as pathologies departing from the norm of harmony.[16]

Organisation, Hierarchy and Control

A number of industrial studies in the post-war period began to show an interest in workplaces as *organisations*. These included attempts to examine the constraints placed by technology on the goals and structures of management (Woodward, 1970) and the effects of size of company on organisation and worker attitudes and behaviour (Ingham, 1970). Preceding and consolidating this trend were more general studies of the characteristics of organisations, which are reflected in more specific studies of work (Etzioni, 1961; Crozier, 1964).

This has been presented as a drift from plant to organisational sociology (Burawoy, 1979), Zimbalist pointing out that 'The study of the workplace was largely neglected during the 1960s' (1979: xi). Why, therefore, take it up here? Despite the shift in emphasis, key aspects of organisational theory have strongly influenced analyses of work, particularly pertaining to the division of labour, hierarchy and control.

In general terms, emphasis has been given to the relationship between organisations and their working environment, so as to determine what kind of organisation is best for the enterprise. This has involved looking at what appear to be persistent features of organisations — hierarchy, control, division of labour — in an attempt to describe systematically the rules underlying organisational behaviour. We have already seen how the social relations of work tend to be separated into the sphere of work organisation. Unfortunately more attention has been paid to the way people are organised than to the way in which a particular organisation of production structures social relations (Fox, 1971).

Furthermore, the organisation of work into particular skills, crafts and tasks is taken to be synonymous with the existing distribution and nature of occupational categories. The division of labour becomes identified with occupational roles separated from the socio-economic forces that created them (Freedman, 1975). This sharply contrasts with labour process theory, which begins from the analysis of the separation of work into constituent elements as a means of cheapening parts and ensuring managerial control.[17]

An additional component of organisational sociology has been to associate the forms of hierarchy and control with specialist functions within the organisation structure. Authority relations, therefore, are seen as a technical factor deriving from this aspect of the division of labour. Capitalism and its production relations are thus dissolved into an imperative towards bureaucratic hierarchy. While the extension of bureaucratic patterns into all areas of society is an important phenomenon, treating it as a general theory results in concealing its specific roots in capitalist development: 'With the subsumption of industrial sociology under organisation theory, the distinctiveness of the profit-seeking capitalist enterprise is lost' (Burawoy, 1979: 5). In consequence, specific and detailed knowledge of labour processes are seldom prominent.

Perspectives on the division of labour are often based on underlying Durkheimian theory. Like many nineteenth-century writers, Durkheim believed that industrialism and the associated rise of a whole new set of tasks and roles was a progressive force. Progression lay mainly in the basis the division of labour provided for new forms of social solidarity and co-operation. The idea that workplace organisation could be based on a 'web of rules' and consensus of values has influenced contemporary sociology, as in the concept of a harmonious socio-technical system (Salaman, 1981: 126—30).

Durkheimian influences can also be seen in the work of Mayo and the human relations school, but this time deriving from the qualifications Durkheim made to the division of labour as a source of integration and fraternity. He recognised that excessive specialisation could result in a disruptive loss of meaning — anomie. Human relations theory noted the varieties of lack of attachment of workers to the organisation and, like Durkheim, believed that a sense of belonging and function could be re-created by altering work-group values and managerial skills. However, in contrast to the concept of alienation, the concept of anomie fails to recognise that fragmentation of work and hierarchical control are objective features of the capitalist organisation of production.

Bureaucracy and capitalism

The more specific influences on organisation theory derive from the legacy of Weber. He argued that bureaucratisation was endemic to industrial societies. The search within the capitalist system for the the most intensive and efficient

methods of working was said to result in a process of rationalisation whereby jobs could be systematically ordered, routinised and subject to centralised managerial control (Weber,
1964). Such a hierarchical division of labour, however, was
not simply a product of capitalism, but of a universal necessity for rational authority and organisation. Furthermore,
these tendencies were held to increase with the growing complexity of organisations.

These concepts have been central to much of modern
industrial and organisation sociology. The inherent rationality
of bureaucratic hierarchy and its implications for control are
taken up by Tannenbaum: 'Organisation implies control . . .
Control processes help circumscribe idiosyncratic behaviours
and keep them conformant with the rational plan of the
organisation' (1967: 3). Similarly, the identification of
authority structures with technically necessary specialisms
has served to strengthen the view, most succinctly put by
Kerr *et al.* (1962), that there is an 'inevitable and eternal'
separation between managers and managed.

With the growth in size of modern enterprises, Weber's
views concerning the bureaucratic consequences of scale and
complexity have been taken up in plant studies by Ingham
(1967) and Scott (1963). Making the link explicit, Crozier
sounds a hymn of praise to the modern organisation: 'The
large corporation . . . seems to be a uniquely powerful instru-
ment for carrying on economic activity. This organisational
construct has come to embody collective rationality for all
industrial and post-industrial societies' (quoted in Kumar,
1978: 272). In addition, some writers have taken the growth
of large-scale production and bureaucratisation to confirm
that alienation is an inevitable function of industrial development (see Faunce, 1968).

The most systematic recent critique of Weberian theories
of work and power has been made by T. J. Johnson (1972) and
1980). He argues that the Weberian categories ignore the dual
nature of bureaucratisation, as a necessary feature of co-
ordination on the one hand, and as a means of control and
surveillance by capital on the other. But the argument that
the impetus to bureaucratisation arises from the necessity

for capital to control the labour force is not new. The critique of Weber was made prominent by Marcuse (1964) and other members of the Frankfurt School[18] who asserted that bureaucratisation was not an abstract rationality, but a product of certain tendencies in capitalist development. More recently, Edwards (1979) has given an empirical basis to this view in an historical account of the shift from personal to bureaucratic control of the labour force in US industry. This is seen as a specific response by employers to problems of discipline and integration in the labour process.

Another dimension of the Weberian legacy is the emphasis that has been given to professional managerial strata as the guardians of a rational division of labour within the hierarchical enterprise and society (see Hughes, 1963; Halmos, 1970; Bell, 1974). According to Blau and Schoenherr, rational decisions require 'that the recommendations experts make on the basis of their technical competence govern as much as possible such decisions of organisation as to whether to shut down a plant and lay off its workers' (quoted in Salaman and Thompson, 1981: 15). On the surface the existence of professions based on complex bodies of knowledge may seem to contradict the tendency to fragmentation and centralised control. But this forgets the parallel trend towards the separation of conception and execution of tasks, of which many professionals have been beneficiaries (Esland, 1980).

The presentation of these strata as a neutral technocracy ties in with the inflated role given to managers in running modern capitalism. As Anthony (1975) points out, managerial control of a neutral system of production was often posed as an equivalent to emergent state planning of the economy. This type of thinking about the role of management was not new. Early plant sociology was saying similar things, although perhaps in a more blatant form: 'management is capable, trained and objective. Management uses scientific knowledge, particularly engineering knowledge, for making decisions. Political issues are illusions created by evil men. Society's true problems are engineering problems' (Mayo, quoted in Baritz, 1960).

Radical perspectives

Not all sociologists have accepted what Salaman (1981) calls a naive and one-sided interpretation of Weber's views. There has been some recognition, particularly in Gouldner (1954), of the negative effects of bureaucracy, and of the possibility that informal patterns could be functional to organisational goals. The importance of the unofficial rules of workshop culture towards maintaining work commitments has also contributed to a non-mechanistic concept of organisations (Roy, 1973). In addition there has been an emphasis on the development of bureaucracy as a form of managerial philosophy and control, rather than simply rationality (Crozier. 1964; Merton, 1957; Blau, 1972).

Some modern followers of Weber's 'economic sociology' use labour process perspectives to criticise some of his ideas; notably that the dispossesion of workers' powers in production by a capitalist bureaucracy is a necessary, technical requirement of industrialism (see Hill, 1981: 7—11). This neo-Weberianism has been complemented by interactionist theory which emphasises organisational models as a product of negotiation and social construction (see Salaman and Thompson, 1973, for a representative collection of articles).[19] An important part of this thinking has stressed alternative, non-bureaucratic forms of organisation, in which choices are dependent on factors like power relations and control strategies (Child, 1973; Perrow, 1972).

These modifications have established some useful points, but they do not provide an alternative to the dominant mechanistic frameworks of Durkheim and Weberian theory. For example, what if informal patterns are *not* functional to work organisation? Indeed, there is considerable evidence that autonomous shop-floor organisation is an aspect of contested 'rationalities' concerning the frontier of control between capital and labour (Beynon, 1973). Conflicts and inequalities cannot be explained solely by reference to patterns of organisation. Moreover, there has been little attempt to analyse the origin of forms of work, technology and social relations. While there may be differences within Weberian theory, there are also strong overlaps to the dominant mechanistic trends within industrial sociology. Weber was aware of Taylorist seientific management and regarded it as part of the general movement towards the rationalisation of industrial society (Albrow, 1981: 290). The classic description of bureaucracy as a tight specification of procedures and responsibilities runs parallel to the fragmentation of work and the separation of conception and execution. Only a recognition of these kinds of convergent concepts can explain *how* plant sociology was able to drift into organisational pastures without making a substantial break from established theoretical frameworks.

Class, Work and Industrial Society

A common point of criticism regarding both plant sociology and organisational studies has been their insularity from wider non-work factors. While there were assumptions that modern society was, as Nisbet summarised, 'urban, democratic, industrial, bureaucratic, rationalised, large scale, formal, secular and technological' (quoted in Kumar, 1978: 112), they were seldom given explicit consideration. However, there were trends in industrial sociology that broke from the predominant patterns of technological determinism, insularity and organisational formalism.

Certain studies adopting an industrial relations perspective have shown that levels of strike activity varied despite technological constancy between plants (Turner, Clack and Roberts, 1967), and that the variety of work experiences and conflicts can counteract tendencies towards bureaucratisation of enterprises and trade unions (Eldrige, 1971). But too often industrial relations writing has betrayed an equivalent formalism, whereby excessive emphasis has been placed on the formal mechanisms of collective bargaining. Trade unions become part of organisational systems inexorably leading to an institutionalisation of conflict (Dunlop, 1958). Any breakdown of this orderliness, such as unofficial strikes, wage drift and restrictive practices, therefore tended to be seen once more as pathological problems (Flanders, 1970; Clegg, 1972).[20] The nature of work itself was seldom placed on the agenda. Indeed, the underlying reasoning was based on a mistaken assumption that industrial conflict was limited to the realm of distribution. Because these conflicts were temporarily reconcilable and subject to institutionalisation, those conflicts located in the conditions of production of the surplus were correspondingly neglected (Hill, 1981: 259–60).

Orientations to work

The major alternative was provided through attempts to look at orientations *to* work, integrating themes concerning the changing nature of class and industrial society'. At the core of this approach was the view that people's experience of work was primarily shaped by factors external to the work situation. The most prominent of these studies, that of Goldthorpe, Lockwood *et al.* (1968), argued that a new type of affluent worker was coming into being, attached particularly to the advanced mass production industries and relocated housing and communities.

Such 'privatised' workers were outside the proletarian traditions of cohesiveness of community and comradeship at work. Instead, the impetus of consumer society and the emphasis on provision of family needs created a context where workers' commitment centred on the instrumental regularity of the pay packet, regardless of the limits of work satisfaction.[21] The question of the wider framework influencing work attitudes was taken up in other studies, each establishing aspects of prior orientations to work. Dubin (1956) had already emphasised the supposed shift of the search for satisfaction towards the home and consumption, and this was reinforced by Cotgrove (1972).

Others sought to confirm the existence of instrumental attitudes (Ingham, 1967; Wedderburn and Crompton, 1972)[22] while more recently Gallie has developed the concept of socio-structural patterns from a comparative examination of French and British chemical workers. He argues that attitudes towards and integration into work depends on the 'specific nature of aspirations and wider conceptions of society current in the working class sub-cultures of the specific society' (1978: 35).

Studies of this nature, using an 'action frame of reference' that takes into account people's own perceptions as shaped by society-wide experiences and ideology, were not wholly new. In the USA, Chinoy (1955) produced a sensitive account of the contradictions between the illusory values of the 'American Dream' and the more mundane realities of car workers' lives. Later, Gouldner (1955) stressed the effects of community ties and social origins on the work outlook of groups involved in industrial action in a gypsum mine.[23]

However, the theoretical framework developed, particularly by Goldthorpe and Lockwood, established a more significant and general trend *away* from the sphere of *work*, and *towards* the wider question of *class* and class imagery (see Bulmer, 1975, for a discussion of these issues). It is beyond our scope to deal with the full range of critical discussion on Goldthorpe and Lockwood, particularly concerning the theory of class and the methodological limits of the action approach (see Daniel, 1969; Westergaard, 1970; Mackenzie, 1974). Attention will be focused on the issue of work. Goldthorpe and Lockwood, together with similar studies, confirmed a shift from production and a denial of the centrality of work experience as a source of shaping consciousness and conflict. Yet the concepts and methods for analysing work were both superficial and distorted.

It was propounded that the work situation produced only slight involvement and attachment to fellow workers. Lockwood, in a further article, asserted that the modern worker 'is unlikely to possess a strongly developed class consciousness because his involvement in work is too low for strong feelings of any kind' (1975: 22). Alienation is admitted, but of a very passive kind, related only to a general detachment from the job. Reflecting the search for consumer satisfaction, workers were held to develop a 'pecuniary model' of society which sustained the willingness to put up with boring work and co-operation with management.

The Marxist usage of alienation was specifically criticised for not being a directly sociological concept, and as untenable, ideological rhetoric limited by a narrow concern with the nature of work. But the Goldthorpe and Lockwood study contains *no* examination of the objective structures of work, and work experience is merely *assumed* to be understood through survey responses. For example, even accepting the existence of a trend towards instrumental attitudes, there is a failure to consider seriously whether if it is connected to changes in the work process itself, rather than to external factors. Furthermore, Burawoy argues that the idiom in which workers express their attitudes is no necessary guide to behaviour. There is no effort to

> distinguish between coming to work, on the one hand, and working on the other — that is between the delivery of labour power and its transformation into labour. The cash nexus is an essential ingredient in bringing the worker to the factory gates [but] does not not play the same role in the labour process.
>
> (Burawoy, 1979: 139)

Martin and Fryer (1975) make a similar point when referring to 'two vocabularies' which coexist and reflect the difference between immediate work experience and assimilated ideology. In addition the survey questions themselves often show little understanding of the social relations embedded in the labour process. For instance, it is hardly suprising that most workers will reject statements saying that team work is impossible because employers and workers are really on the opposite side. Given that co-operation and antagonism between capital and labour necessarily exist side by side in work, such statements are transparently untrue.

With these points in mind, it becomes necessary to emphasise the importance of studying the actual process of work, the informal work-groups and the less obvious acts of resistance and conflict. This is more difficult than survey methods, but studies like Beynon (1973) on Ford show that the image of detached but satisfied workers bears little resemblance to the patterns of everyday shop-floor life. As Bulmer (1975) points out, it is remarkable how little action there is in 'action approaches'. Such an orientation would also reveal the continuing centrality of work to specific aspects of working-class experience.

Post-industrial societies
In stressing the non-integration of workers and the continuance of class-based inequalities, Goldthorpe and Lockwood,

Gallie and others differ from the model established by Kerr *et al.*, Dahrendorf (1959) and similar 'industrial society' theorists. This model of convergent industrial societies had as its basis the idea of the decomposition of capital and labour and the 'end of ideology': skilled, responsible and satisfied workers took on increasingly white-collar and middle-class characteristics, with signficantly reduced conflict. Kerr stated: 'In the mid-twentieth century, workers do not destroy machines. The protest today is more in favour of industrialism than against it . . .The industrialists need not shake in their boots before the raised fists of the new industrial workers' (1962: 7).

Yet in other ways prior orientations to work theorists confirm that model. There is the broad acceptance of an expanding economy free from structural conflict and work deprivation. Like industrial society analyses, Gallie stresses the stages in technological development, upgrading skills and ending the age of mass production with the emergent sector of advanced automation. He says that automation has 'reversed the trend towards an ever-increasing division of labour', and 'blurred the clear-cut distinction between manual and non-manual labour' (1978: 7).

Despite differences of interpretation concerning its consequences, a diverse number of commentators tie in these supposed developments to the key role of a neutral science and technology. Giddens (1973), for example, in agreeing with Dahrendorf that Marx was wrong in supposing the elimination of the skilled worker, points to scientific knowledge as the primary force of production in 'neo-capitalist societies'. In this machine-created world, engineers, scientists and technicians occupy the pivotal place. Thus the theories emphasising the shift away from work converge with those of industrial and neo-capitalism to lay the ground for the eventual emergence of concepts of *post-industrial* society, dominated by professional and scientific labour and the ethos of service and technocracy (Bell, 1974).

The argument is not that we have a world without work, but that the development of scientific-technological labour finally buries the Marxist notion of a bi-polar class structure and gradual proletarianisation. For Bell, Marxist class theory is 'warped' because of the erosion of industrial work, and he repeats the well-worn idea that 'the US has become a white collar society' (1974: 131). The variety of post-industrial society theories came to the fore at a useful time for conventional sociological theory. As Kumar (1978) points out, substantial evidence had been building up on the dark side of this 'triumph of industrialism', with its rational, bureaucratic organisation of society.

With the re-emergence of social and industrial conflict from the late 1960s came ideological confrontation. The near-contempt expressed for work in Terkel's (1977) book of interviews finally seeped through to official thinking, when a US Government Special Task Force reported that worker dissatisfaction was being shown in low productivity, strikes, absenteeism and lack of committment generally (*Work in America*, 1973). Meanwhile, academic studies had begun to question the skill-upgrading thesis (Braverman, 1974) and the extent and progressive nature of automation (Fox, 1974; Nichols and Beynon, 1977).

But just as post-war capitalism Mark I was being brought into question, it suddenly ceased to exist! In its place was Mark II — post-industrial society — which would go beyond the accumulated problems of its predecessor. Evidence for this proposition was little better than for the previous model. The increased weight given to professional and service work 'is assumed from its merely quantative expression in the public records' (Kumar, 1978: 200). The nature of such work, its place in the labour process and its interrelations with manual occupations are given insufficient attention. Such an emphasis only came with the new labour process theory examined in later chapters.

Conclusion: Contrasts and Continuities

In terms of theories and concepts — the treatment of alienation the character of science and technology, the skill composition of the workforce, the origins of hierarchy in work — the various strands of industrial sociology normally stand on the opposite side to Marxist labour process analysis. But it would be foolish to erect a 'Chinese wall' between the two traditions. There are continuities as well as contrasts in a number of senses.

First, there are a number of excellent studies which, whatever their defects, give us considerable insight into the world of work. In this category would come Lockwood's classic, *The Blackcoated Worker* (1958). Through an attempt to construct a typology of work relations and class identification, many of the basic features of the world of work are highlighted in this book including: 'The size of the factory, the organisation of the workgroup, its relations to supervisors and management, the degree to which workers have control over the work process, the extent to which the job facilitates or prevents communication between workers' (256—7).

However, it is significant that many of the best studies, often unintentionally, have to confront and explain actual struggles, thus providing a historical and active dimension to theories and methods missing in conventional analysis. Warner and Low exemplify this in *The Social System of the Modern Factory* (1947). Part of the 'Yankee City' research series, the book situates a 1933 Massachusetts strike against a backcloth of long-term technological and economic change. It focuses on shifts in ownership and control of tools and production away from the immediate producers, the decline of the local economy and the rise of international cartels, and the changing nature of shoe-making from skilled handicraft to fragmented and hierarchical mass production.

Even if workers' concerns are then misleadingly re-interpreted as a search for lost community, the study is similar to a later one by Gouldner (1955) in presenting the case study of a strike. For Gouldner the strike acts as an impetus to add to the interesting descriptive material an examination of managerial strategy, changing technology, and the environment of economic market and social community. The second sociological contribution exists in spite of the narrowness and fragmentation of its specialisms.

Indeed, it is the narrow focus that often generates insights requiring Marxism to 'selectively incorporate sociology's partial truths' (Burawoy, 1979: xiii). Burawoy refers in particular to some of the empirical detail of plant sociology. But a similar case could be made out for Gallie's study of the relations between cultural traditions and workplace consciousness; or the important debate about class imagery among British social scientists (Bulmer, 1975). A reverse movement is also taking place, whereby sociology incorporates aspects of Marxism, and this constitutes a third factor of continuity.

Thus in recent years labour process theory has begun to make a significant impact on sociological debates. Evidence can be seen in theories of work, organisations and industrial relations within a radical Weberian tradition (Esland and Salaman, 1980; Hill, 1981) and in the debate on deskilling collected together in Wood (1982). Such material has added to the existing analysis by Marxist sociologists on industrial themes, particularly Beynon (1973), Lane (1974), Hyman (1975) and Nichols and Beynon (1977). But as Hill points out, 'The influence of new perspectives is strong even among people who do not support them, because they have successfully structured the agenda of what is held to be worth discussing' (1981: vii). These trends have created the basis for a 'new sociology of work' which can combine the best of both traditions.

A final reason for avoiding a complete separation of theoretical frameworks is that Marxism has not constituted a unitary tradition. In fact it is remarkable how many sociologists thought their own notions of a neutral technology's reshaping work and class were confirming Marx's methods, while refuting his theoretical conclusions. An example is provided by the US sociologist, Mayer 'The proletariat has not absorbed the middle class but rather the other way round. . .In the sense that class structure here described reflects modern technology, it vindicates the Marxist thesis that social organisation is "determined" by technological forces' (quoted in Goldthorpe, Lockwood *et al.*, 1968: 9).

Goldthorpe and Lockwood themselves refer to 'The Marxist claim that the development of the forces of production is the ultimate determinant of patterns of stratification' (1968: 6). By renewing Marx's theory of the labour process, recent writers have made it more difficult for such misconceptions to flourish. To enable an accurate comparison of theoretical traditions to be made, it is therefore necessary to trace the rise and fall of that original analysis.

2
Marx and the Idea of the Labour Process

In modern studies of work, concepts such as deskilling, fragmentation and hierarchical control play a prominent part. Disconnected from and unrelated to an economic and historical context, they make little more than a fleeting, descriptive sense. Marx's writings, particularly in *Capital, Volume One*, provide such a framework. Marx argued in general terms about the nature of work relationships inside a capitalist mode of production. In addition he combined these theoretical categories with an attempt to chronicle the major changes in the economy and the labour process. To understand the latter, it is necessary to start with the general framework.

The General Character of the Labour Process

Work has always been necessary to satisfy the various social needs that exist in human society. In production the purpose is to create goods that serve those needs, i.e. commodities that have a use value. Contact with human labour has been the only means of producing use values, yet as a totality a labour process is an activity between man and various components of 'nature'. Marx therefore identified three simple elements of the labour process, independent of any particular social formation:

1. Purposeful activity of man, directed to work.
2. The object on which the work is performed, in the form of natural or raw materials.
3. The instruments of that work, most often tools or more complex technology.

The latter two elements are referred to by Marx as the *means of production*. Taken all together, the components of the labour process form the general preconditions of all production. Furthermore, it is made clear that the human and technical aspects of the labour process interpenetrate. This is indicated in Marx's famous analogy of the architect and the bee. Although the bee works in a complex and productive way, the architect consciously constructs the operation — an exclusively human characteristic. Hence, 'Man not only effects a change of form in the materials of nature, he also realises his own purpose in those materials' (Marx, 1976: 284).

Whether it is a skilled worker adapting tools for a new use, or employers organising the design of machinery for a particular goal, man is shaping the means of production. So when Marx makes the following comment he is not being technologically determinist: 'Instruments of labour not only supply a standard of the degree which human labour has obtained, but they also indicate the social relations in which men work' (Marx, 1976: 286). He is arguing that technology, or any other productive force, embodies relationships between people. Technology in particular provides a manifestation of the relations between social classes.

For instance, when capitalists began to bring together independent craftsmen in a workshop under their control, the nature of production changed, even when the same commodity was being introduced. The forms of co-operation and division of labour inevitably bore the imprint of capital in its search for greater productivity and profit. In turn, this affected the nature and uses of tools, machinery and the means of production in general.

This analysis of the components and interrelationships of the labour process parallels Marx's general usage of the concept of forces and relations of production. Once again, they are meant to be seen as mutually conditioning. Micro-processor technology, for example, will quite clearly have a considerable effect on relations between workers and managers, between workers themselves, and indeed on life outside the factory in terms of leisure and family. Yet such technical innovation itself is a partial reflection of the existing social relations and struggles between labour and capital. Hence the numerous advertisements stressing that the new machines will not go on strike, get tired, become sick, or take time off to have a family.

The effect industrial conflict can have on technical innovation is one example of the way social relations themselves can be a productive force. Moreover, social relations do not have to be inside production to affect it. The sexual division of labour embodied in housework is part of the social relations necessary for efficient capitalist production, in that housework reproduces some of the conditions that enabled the 'labourer' to work. In summary, 'Production, then, is both a material and social process, an activity whereby people transform both their circumstances and themselves. Each of its facets, in Marx's view, conditions and constrains the other' (Corrigan, Ramsay and Sayer, 1978: 2).

The Capitalist Labour Process

The description of the labour process and its attendant concepts does not make clear the conditions under which people work in particular socio-economic formations. The specific features of capitalism derive from the fact of the capitalist purchasing the various components of the labour process — the means of production and labour power — setting one to work on the other. Marx used the term *labour power*, rather than simply work or worker, to indicate that the worker's physical and mental capabilities exist in a *relationship* to capital. The capacity to work is transformed into a means of producing value for the capitalist.

The production of commodities with a use value is not the sole goal of the capitalist. He needs to exchange those commodities for a price greater in value than the costs incurred in production. The process of production must therefore combine the labour process with the creation of value. Hence the labour process becomes inextricably linked to the struggle for profitable production. In purchasing its components, the capitalist must not only provide the right materials, but seek to exert control over the conditions under which the speed, skill and dexterity of the worker operates. Hence, when Marx referred to the labour power of workers as *variable capital*, it was not just an economic category. Only living labour could create value, and the surplus *varied* according to 'the relative strengths of the combatants in the production process' (Nichols, 1980a: 35).

To ensure profitability, it is vital that in the work of transforming the product into a commodity for the market, no more time is consumed than is necessary under the given social conditions. As the old saying goes 'time is money', and *labour* time is the key question.[1] It is not enough to create value that is an exact equivalent of the payment for labour power. Production must be extended into *surplus* value, which although created by labour power, becomes the legal property of the employer. The labour process becomes distinctively capitalist, therefore, when it is combined with what Marx called *valorisation* (the process of creating surplus value).

However, as we shall see later, in the early period of industrialisation the specific character of the labour process was not greatly different from when the worker worked for himself. The capitalist had little choice but to take labour power — skills and the organisation of work — as he found it on the market. But there are still two new preliminary features. First, the work was under the control of the capitalist in general terms. Second, the product was his property and not that of the immediate producer. From this point the goal of capital became the subordination of labour on its own terms. Marx established a further conceptual framework to show how this was done.[2] When the labour process was first subsumed under the control of the capitalist, it involved only a *formal subordination of labour*:

If changes occur in the traditionally established labour processes, after their takeover by capital, they are nothing but the gradual consequences of that subsumption. The work may become more intensive, its duration may be extended, it may become more continuous or orderly under the eye of the interested capitalist, but, in themselves, these changes do not affect the character of the actual mode of working.

(Marx, 1976: 1021)

Lacking the means to increase the productivity of labour on a technological basis, economies could only be achieved through such methods such as increasing the length of the working day. A shift towards the *real subordination of labour* could only be ensured by a development of the productive forces, and introducing and using machinery, science, and the expanded scale of production associated with large-scale industry. As Marx said, 'With the real subordination of labour under capital, a complete (and constantly repeated) revolution takes place in the means of production, in the productivity of the worker and in the relations between workers and capitalists' (1976: 1035).

The search for a constant increase in profitability implies an equally constant search for reductions in cost price. As one nineteenth-century agreement between woollen unions and the Bradford Dyers Association stated, the union accepted 'The right of the Association to organise its equipment and to regulate its labour with a view to the lowest cost of production' (quoted in Goodrich, 1975: 57). The application of science and technology to the production process became the major means of directing the labour power of workers on behalf of those who owned and ran the factories. These trends acted to deepen Marx's concept of *alienation*. Time and again in *Capital* he describes the social relations of alienated work and their destructive effects on the worker. For example:

In this process, then, the social character of their labour comes to confront the workers, so to speak in a *capitalised* form: thus machinery is an instance of the way in which the visible products of labour take on the appearance of its masters. The same transformation may be observed in

the forces of nature and science . . . they too confront
the worker as the *powers* of capital. They become separated
effectively from the skill and knowledge of the individual
worker.

(Marx, 1976: 1055)

Furthermore, the new situation in the 'modern' factory
allowed employers to develop much more effective and
sophisticated methods of increasing the *intensity* of labour,
rather than its mere duration.[3] Marx's analysis of the factors
governing the capitalist labour process still remained on a
relatively abstract level. However, he also produced a parallel
and more empirically rooted explanation of the historical
development of changes in working methods and relationships.[4]

From the workshop to large-scale industry
The first factories in Britain appeared in industries developing
in the seventeenth and eighteenth centuries. Often these
pioneering establishments were based on large-scale workshops
that had replaced the domestic unit, for instance in woollen
manufacture. At this stage there was more emphasis on
reorganising work than on mechanising it. Mechanised
factories and the beginnings of assembly-line production
needed further technological and economic change, and
this was not to reach its peak until the heyday of the factory
system in the mid-nineteenth century.

The features of such changes were identified by Marx as
constituting particular stages in the development of the
labour process, from *co-operation*, to *manufacture* and then
to *large-scale industry*. Combining his economic theory with
reference to contemporary records like the Reports of Factory
Inspectors, Marx was able to reveal the transformations taking
place in skills, forms of authority and work organisation.
Using other historical documentation, notably the fine collection gathered by Maxine Berg,[5] both the practice and concepts connected with these transformations can be established.

Co-operation refers to a form of labour in which workers
were brought together in the same or connected processes,
and the means of production were concentrated in the hands
of an individual capitalist. The fact that production is then

based on the 'plan' of the employer establishes a capital relation. In this context the directing authority becomes a function of capital rather than the artisan or 'little master' of the workshop. Naturally that plan came up against the existing skills, power and rewards of the workforce. Thus in creating the beginnings of an industrial army, a command structure founded on *despotic* authority was required by capital.

Nevertheless, the period of co-operation only established these relations in primitive form, acting to pave the way for the emergence of manufacture and large-scale agriculture. In the early period of the industrial revolution employers relied heavily on handicraft and domestic production. Therefore machinery and division of tasks were insignificant, and in spite of despotic authority, the real power of capital over labour tended to be limited by the means at its disposal to subordinate the worker. The movement from the cottage to the workshop was aimed at changing this situation. Lacking the technical means of control, the employers' purpose was to establish *direct* authority over work. This could not exist while domestic production — based on sub-contracting or the 'putting out' system — persisted. As Friedman notes with regard to the silk ribbon-weaving industry, 'A great advantage of the trade from the weavers' point of view was the degree of direct control they exercised over their hours and pace of work' (1977a: 152). Marglin's (1976) research on the origins of management shows that the shift from cottage to workshop and then factory was not only a result of technological efficiency. Employers directed their efforts at ending the internal contradictions of the 'putting out' system with respect to control, using the discipline and supervision of the workshop to reduce costs.

The division of labour

Having established the workshop, capital needed to extend its capacity to control and cheapen those costs. As the pace of industrialisation quickened, hand technology became more prominent, but this still rested largely on the skill and strength of the worker. Employers' attention turned to the possibilities surrounding the *division of labour*, i.e. attempting to combine handicrafts under one roof, or splitting the tasks into partial operations. Leading political economists like Adam Smith and Charles Babbage were extolling the benefits of increased productivity and the perfection of methods using these techniques.

Recognising this, Marx argued that this period (roughly 1550—1770) constituted the phase of *manufacture*, characterised by the struggle to consolidate the division of labour. That division enabled capitalists' authority to be extended, and combined with the external competitive market forces to constrain workers' power. This led Marx to make his well known comment that 'anarchy in the social division of labour and despotism in the manufacturing division of labour mutually condition each other' (1976: 477). In production itself, discipline was backed by other forms of coercion: 'Elaborate and severe systems or fines were imposed by employers on workers who arrived late of left early, and for faulty work' (Friedman, 1977a: 87). Attention was directed particularly to attack the old guilds which tended to restrict the number of journeymen and apprentices that could be employed.

In terms of the effects of the manufacturing division of labour on workers, two major features should be noted. A hierarchy is created based on skill, training and wages, including a substantial class of unskilled labourers. Furthermore, work itself begins to be revolutionised, resulting in a much greater specialisation of tasks that subordinates the knowledge, judgement and will of the worker. The economist Ferguson commented: 'Manufactures, accordingly, prosper most where the mind is least consulted and where the workshop . . . may be considered as an engine, the parts of which are men' (quoted in Marx, 1976: 483). It was this combination of specialisms that led Marx to use the concept of *collective worker* to describe the interdependent organisation of labour prior to the use of extensive machinery.

The systematic organisation of labour within the shop structure was, as historian Eric Roll noted, a transition between handicraft production and modern mass production. Fitters, for example, in the early days of the nineteenth century were still highly skilled craftsmen using complex manual skills backed by a degree of technical knowledge. But subdivision took place, systematising fitting work so that 'To each fitter or group of fitters only one article or group of similar articles were assigned' (quoted in Berg, 1979: 33)

At the time, these changes were best theorised by Charles Babbage, who echoed later themes of 'scientific management' when he emphasised the advantages of dividing tasks between and within mental and manual labour; each part of the process, having been separated, was then cheaper. He envisaged three 'classes' involved in the production process. The entrepreneur and his technical aides would design the machinery, operative engineers would execute their plans based on a partial knowledge of the processes, while 'a multitude of other persons, possessed of a lower degree of skill, must be employed in using them' (quoted in Berg, 1979: 50).

Once again, however, the reduction in skill and control of the workforce is relative to the period: 'Since hand skill is the foundation of manufacture and since the mechanism of manufacture possesses no objective framework which would be independent of the workers themselves, capital is constantly impelled to wrestle with the subordination of the workers' (Marx, 1976: 489). Indeed, there was considerable resistance to the deskilling involved in the division of labour. Workers responded to the dilution of their skills by forming exclusive craft unions, taking up issues ranging from the length of the working day, fighting against speed-up and job loss as a result of mechanisation, and falling piece rates. The forms of organisation reflected the hierarchy of labour powers: they excluded the unskilled, women and children. When machinery was introduced, it was often opposed, sometimes through calls for taxation on the machines, and in some cases — for instance the agricultural 'Swing' riots — by machine-smashing.[6]

Mechanisation and its effects

The more perceptive of the defenders of the factory system recognised that the strength of worker resistance was rooted in the existing nature of the labour process. In his *Philosophy of Manufactures*, Andrew Ure attacked those like Babbage who believed that the division of labour was sufficient to ensure capitalist control. Only the introduction of the self-regulating power of machinery could succeed in 'training human beings to renounce their desultory habits of work, and to identify themselves with the unvarying regularity of the complex automaton' (quoted in Berg, 1979: 66). Employees would become 'factory hands' instead of the 'cunning workman', prone to 'irregularities of many kinds'. He accurately noted that: 'The principle of the factory system then is, to substitute mechanical science for hand skill, and the partition of a process into its essential constituents . . . skilled labour gets progressively superseded, and will, eventually, be replaced by mere overlookers of machines' (quoted in Berg, 1979: 67).

Marx used the views of commentators like Ure in support of his distinction between manufacture, and large-scale industry, with a labour process transformed by the uses of science and machinery in pursuit of cheapening labour and increasing surplus value. Although Marx's distinction between the phases of the labour process were not entirely accurate, as we shall see later, the period of the mid-nineteenth century closely approximated to most of the features of modern industry that he identified.

Where Marx differed from the political economists on whom he drew for numerous examples was in the conceptual framework for understanding the transformation of the labour process in modern industry. Indeed, although 'modern' was intended to refer to the second half of the nineteenth century, much of the debate has considerable relevance to understanding the nature of work today. Despite Ure's reference to 'the union of capital and science, to reduce the task . . . of work people to the exercise of vigilance and dexterity' (quoted in Berg, 1979: 67), he and other political economists asserted that science and machinery were independent forces, determining the future development of production on the basis of technical necessity and efficiency in the common interest of capital and labour.

Machines were regarded as neutral and held to determine human relations. Marx quoted Ure to the effect that: 'In these spacious halls the benignant power of steam summons

around him his myriads of willing menials' (Marx, 1976: 545).
It was both pointless and harmful for those 'menials' to resist
the nature and impact of technology. The Society for the
Diffusion of Useful Knowledge argued to workers that: 'The
word *Machine* seems to convey to your minds some contri-
vance necessarily attended with mischief to the Poor, whereas,
in truth, the word Machine means the same as tool or instru-
ment' (quoted in Berg, 1979: 73). Furthermore, it was held
that value was a result of capital and science being applied
to production, causing the radical economist Thomas Hodg-
skin to comment: 'By the common mode of speaking, the
productive power of this skill is attributed to its visible
products, the instruments, the mere owners of which, who
neither make nor use them, imagine themselves to be very
productive persons' (quoted in Berg, 1979: 81).

It was these attitudes that Marx attacked as fetishism,
whereby social relations involving people are represented as
relations between unalterable *things*. These representations
are not a sleight of hand; they reflect people's actual *experience* of work. Although commodity production is based
on definite relations of ownership and exploitation, this is
hidden by the workings of the market whose characteristics
appear natural and inevitable. The detachment of the social
nature of labour from the conditions that produced it is also
reflected in the appearance of technology as an external and
unalterable power over workers. But, contrary to the view
that the productive forces were untouched by capitalist
social relations, Marx commented that: 'It would be possible
to write a whole history of the inventions made since 1830
for the sole purpose of providing capital with weapons against
working class revolt' (Marx, 1976: 563). He gives numerous
examples of the origins of machinery, in particular various
self-acting tools, in the service of capital. Such was admitted
by many employers' spokesmen. For example, hand tools
were usually designed for the immediate user, like the hand
mule of Crompton. In contrast the impetus for the development of the self-acting mule came from the cotton industry
employers in an effort to undermine workers' organisation.
Ure stated that this situation 'naturally led to an anxious
desire on the part of the proprietors of cotton-mills, that

some means should be devised to enable them to dispense with the labour of the "spinners" ' (quoted in Council for Science and Society, 1981: 16).

Only with this generalised mechanisation, notably the creation of machines by machines, did large-scale industry develop an adequate technical basis for the further expansion of labour productivity. The workforce experienced a number of immediate effects of machine production, many of which profoundly altered the form and content of their work. Although new 'perpetual motion' machinery presented the opportunity of prolonging the working day, legal and trade union resistance accelerated a growing trend towards *intensification* of labour. Furthermore, given the physical repetitiveness of tasks, extending the duration of work would eventually become incompatible with increased intensity. Methods to ensure the latter included speed-up, piecework payment and improvements in machine operation.

The other major effect was a further reduction in skills. A leading industrialist stated that in the interests of factory discipline it was necessary to 'make machines of men as cannot err'.[7] While this overstated the possibilities, there were a number of clear examples of the trend. With the use of labour-saving, hydraulic riveting machines in boilermaking, one skilled worker was able to do the work of nine craftsmen, with eight unskilled labourers or boys taking their place.

A similar combination of displacement of labour and de-skilling took place in engineering. James Nasmyth, one of the leading industrialists in this sector, gave testimony that he had reduced 1,500 of the workers in his employ by such means, commenting: 'All that the mechanic has to do now, and which any boy or lad of 14 or 15 is quite able to do, is to sharpen his tool, place it in the machine in connexion with the work, and set on the self-acting motion, and then nine-tenths of his time is spent in mere superintendence' (quoted in Berg, 1979: 156).

Industrialists and economists, however, talked of the introduction of machinery as elevating the intellect and doing away with the monotony of toil. Like similar references today to automated plant, this tends to confuse the reduction of hard, physical labour with gains in skill and intelligence:

Fifty years ago there existed a class of engineers known as millwrights, who, so far as regarded scientific knowledge were no doubt quite uneducated, but who were nevertheless, men of great intelligence, whose work-boxes contained the tools of nearly every trade, and who could handle these tools with skill and dexterity. Before the days of easy communication, they used to be sent to great distances in charge of works both extensive and intricate, and generally executed them with a thoroughness and intelligence that left nothing to be desired. Through the subdivision of labour, however, this class of highly skilled mechanics has become well-nigh extinct.[8]

Part of this sub-division therefore involved an increasing separation between the mental and manual aspects of labour. As early as 1824, William Thompson noted that: 'The man of knowledge and the productive labourer come to be widely divided from each other' (quoted in Rosenberg, 1981: 22). Hence the often repeated refrain from management and workers alike that they are paid to work, not to think.

It follows that these conditions extend the progressive alienation of the productive process from the worker:

> In the factory we have lifeless mechanism which is independent of the workers, who are incorporated into it as its living appendages . . . By means of its conversion into an automaton, the instrument of labour confronts the labourer, during the labour process, in the shape of capital, of dead labour, that dominates and pumps dry, living labour-power.
>
> (Marx, 1976: 548)[9]

Because workers are no longer responsible for parts of the living mechanisms of work, the control and supervision over them, which Marx called factory despotism, also increase correspondingly. This brings back into focus the concept of the real subordination of labour, which can only become a reality at this stage of development of the labour process.

The other major focus of Marx concerning the effects of changes in this period was directed towards the *composition* of the workforce. Instead of the hierarchy of specialised workers in the period of manufacture, the new conditions tend to *equalise* types of work through the process of deskilling and homogenisation of tasks. One consequence of the resulting greater potential for interchangeability was the employment of more women and children as the factory system expanded and machine work replaced heavy physical labour. Often, they would be used to undercut and dilute the skill of the existing workforce.

Even where a direct replacement was absent, women tended to work in formerly male preserves that had already been degraded in terms of skills and rewards: such as the case when women became the predominant part of the labour force in cigar making, being used to strip, sort and pact the tobacco (Oakeshott, 1979). Nonetheless, it should be noted that the work still involved a five-year apprenticeship, and there were elements remaining of complex and skilled tasks.

Within the trend towards homogenisation of labour, Marx still recognised divisions. First of all, the concept was meant to refer primarily to workers engaged in forms of machine-minding, not to all categories. For instance, it was clear that a minority of workers still belonged to a craft category, employed in satellite positions to the labour process. Joiners, fitters and mechanics came into this category, and despite being largely peripheral to the process of production, remained in part, scientifically educated. In addition there were divisions of authority embodied in distinctions between head workers and assistants, and of function between machine workers and attendants.

It was clear that Marx believed the above changes in work completed the trend towards the collective worker. Capital, having separated workers from their own subjective forms of co-operation and initiative, creates an *objective socialisation of labour.*[10] That is, workers are combined together in association by the machine system, work only taking place in a large-scale collective labour process existing as an objective reality *prior* to the entry into work. The use of the concept was not meant to imply that the capitalist organisation of work was to be regarded in a favourable or neutral light. Rather, its necessarily collective and partly interchangeable character raises the possibility, once freed of capitalist relations of producton, of a co-operative labour process in a socialist society. This process would be dominated by the associated producers themselves, allowing individual talent, freed from narrow specialisms, to flourish.

Finally in this section, a comment is necessary about the concept of 'real subordination of labour', the intention of which is not to dismiss the importance of worker resistance and struggles. Indeed, Marx deals at length with 'the struggle between worker and machine'.[11] He pointed out that there had been a long tradition of opposition to machinery *per se* before workers learned to distinguish between an understandable *Luddism* and the form and use of the instruments of labour by capital.

Workers' struggles were directed to issues of wages and hours, but also to the dilution of skills and the control of working conditions. An example of the latter were attempts by engineers to 'throttle' the use of machinery, restricting its use as a device to save labour and speed up work. The political economist, F. W. Hirst, commented: 'The masters have fought far more against interferences in regard to machinery and the claim of trade unionist officials to "boss" their workshops than against the demand for an eight hours day' (quoted in Berg, 1979: 201).

The concept of real subordination was therefore meant to indicate the new and more powerful mechanisms for control embodied in this stage of the labour process. Capital was given a greater opportunity to appropriate 'the knowledge required to design and enforce the way in which each individual worker functions as a appendage to the machine' (Brighton Labour Process Group, 1977: 12). But the thrust for control was always tempered by worker resistance, modifying and multiplying the variety of means used to subordinate labour. This example indicates some of the problems of how to understand the interpretation and use of Marx's concepts, and this is one of the themes of the following section.

Theory and Reality: a Reflection

The changes in technology and work organisation, which

Marx linked to specific periods of 'manufacture' and 'modern industry', were not in practice so clearly separable. Berg (1979) argues that they were actually overlapping and integrated processes. Nor was the transition between the periods solely that result of technical transformations. Generalised economic expansion and the results of an increased scale of production were also influential. Kumar (1978) goes further. Using historical studies, he points out that Britain was an industrial society more in intent than accomplishment.[12] Substantial numbers of people were still employed in agriculture and domestic service. Some factories were little more than glorified workshops.

Marx and the political economists were writing about economic and technological trends, sometimes without acknowledging their often embryonic and contradictory features. Marx had described the period of manufacture as being characterised by the division of labour and hand technology, yet the early forms of machinery required new specialisms and skills in engineering and metals. Similarly, although modern industry did include considerable deskilling, new skills were created in a double-edged process, even if they became subject to the same changes at a later stage.

Methods of work organisation from the early or even precapitalist periods sometimes survived in later circumstances. There were still artisans, and other skilled workers used informal job practices and craft unionism to maintain their degree of work control, consequently limiting changes in technology and labour process restructuring.[13] Employers, too, sometimes avoided fully mechanised factory organisation of work. A minority continued to use 'outwork' or subcontracting. In the former case, although employed by capitalists, work was done at home by workers using craft methods. Sub-contracting involved employment becoming the responsibility of foremen or even of head skilled workers, who also arranged payment and methods of control and organisation (Littler, 1980; Dobb, 1963; Stone, 1973).[14]

Such arrangements may have been a result of pre-industrial tradition, reinforced by workers' resistance to change, or a preferred form of control by employers, enabling them to avoid problems of management and labour organisation

(Salaman, 1981: 37). A case in point is the shoemaking industry, which remained largely unmechanised in Britain despite the availability of American techniques. Though sub-divided, the work was done in the homes of male workers, factories not becoming the norm until the last decade of the century. Workers' craft traditions and an economic return sufficient to satisfy the owners limited the pace of change.[15] Even when the sewing machine was introduced, it was only the women who were taken into a factory framework; the main work was still done by men as a home industry. Further use of machinery did bring the sub-division inside the factory, although even then the editor of the *Shoe and Leather Record* noted that 'trade union tyranny prevents the machinery being run to its full capacity',[16] as workers sought to control and restrict output in order to protect their craft and their employment prospects.

The sewing machine provides a link to another major example of an industry existing outside the factory system at its peak in the late nineteenth century: the sweated trades like dressmaking and tailoring done by women in the home or in small workshops. Like many of the new instruments of labour, the sewing machine made work lighter and required less physical hand labour, but it also replaced existing craft work. It enabled employers to expand the sweated system rapidly, based on a variety of sub-contracting arrangements (Alexander, 1975).

Marx recognised the coexistence of such domestic industries, but overestimated the tendency to convert them rapidly with other types of manufacture and handicrafts into the factory system.[17] Not only is this an instance of a failure to grasp the variety and pace of change in labour processes, but it also indicates the limits of the concept of homogenisation of the workforce. When writing of the tendency in modern industry to equalise machine work, Marx argued that 'in place of the artificially produced distinctions between the specialised workers, it is natural differences of age and sex that predominate' (Marx, 1976: 545).

But there was nothing natural about the sweated system being based on female labour that was degraded, unorganised and underpaid. The construction of the labour process reflected the wider social division of labour and sexual hierarchies. Furthermore, the displacement of women workers into the *reserve army of labour*, identified by Marx as an important feature of the development of capitalism, was also closely linked to the pre-existing sexual division of labour. Once again, this was insufficiently recognised.[18]

As the nineteenth century drew to a close, international competition from newly industrialising countries like Germany and the USA did give an added impetus to the extension of mechanisation and other features of modern industry. Pockets of hand technology in printing, shoemaking and other industries were eliminated, while new machinery allowed employers to attack the power of skilled workers in the already mechanised industries such as engineering. Even in these instances, however, qualifications need to be made. Berg notes, for example, that in the transition from wood to iron shipbuilding, the new, heavily capitalised industry actually expanded the number of skilled crafts in the production process.[19]

Aside from the features of the labour process directly connected with technology and work organisation, methods of *control* were also more varied than allowed for in the concept of factory despotism. While the extension of technical and bureaucratic means to subordinate labour is not in doubt, this still left considerable room for different 'control strategies'. We have already seen how direct control was precluded by sub-contracting and outwork in some circumstances. But even in the mature factory system no systematic theory and practice of management existed. Therefore new forms of control were inevitably slow, uneven and subject to struggle, particularly with skilled workers (Littler, 1980). Nor can the techniques for control be easily located in specific periods of labour process development.

In addition, there is another dimension to control that the despotism concept tends to hide or underplay. This is what Burawoy refers to as securing control and profitability through organising the *consent* of workers inside the relations of production.[20] Even in the nineteenth century, mechanisms for creating consent ran parallel with coercive measures connected with increasing the intensity to work. Part of this

process was the creation of a new breed of workers appropriate
to the discipline of the factory system. A number of historians
have shown how this necessitated an emphasis on transforming
the workers' character, both inside and outside the workplace (Pollard, 1965; Thompson, 1967):

> The widespread concern with sexual morals, drinking habits,
> religious attitudes, bad language and thrift was an attempt
> on the one hand to destroy pre-industrial habits and
> moralities, and on the other to inculcate attitudes of
> obedience towards factory regulations, punctuality, re-
> sponsibility with materials and so on.
>
> (Salaman, 1981: 31)

Marx was not alone in underestimating the variety of processes involved in industrialisation. As Kumar (1978) points
out, sociologists and political economists necessarily had to
try and treat the changes taking place as if they were part of
a clear *system*, so that the main features could be identified.
He adds that: 'It was not until the coming of systematic
"scientific management" at the turn of the century, sym-
bolised by the organisation of the assembly line, that one
could truly say that industrialism had arrived in the factory'
(Kumar, 1978: 135).[21]

What was remarkable about Marx's analysis was just how
many of the trends he identified came to figure so prominently
in future developments. The legacy he left was not a complete
body of theory without flaws, but rather a series of conceptual tools with which to unlock the problems of the
changing nature of work. While it is impossible to understand
or completely separate these concepts from a framework of
economic theory concerning the functioning of capitalism as
a system, it *is* possible to identify a number of tendencies in
capitalist production which in themselves constitute a distinct
body of labour process theory.[22]

The greatest advantage Marx held was that of refusing to
accept things as they appeared, accusing the political economists such as Adam Smith of taking 'the conditions of the
existing system of production for the necessary conditions
of production in general' (Weiss, 1976: 108). Consequently

the critique of fetishised attitudes to work relationships lies at the heart of the analysis. This enabled a clear distinction to be drawn between an inevitable differentiation of functions and a specifically capitalist division of labour.

This division of labour did not exist because of its technical superiority. As was indicated earlier, 'The social function of hierarchical work is not technical efficiency, but accumulation' (Marglin, 1976: 14). Furthermore, there is a number of potential ways in which the 'efficiency' of a production process can be achieved (Gordon, 1976). For capital, the labour process must be organised so as to ensure profitability and the reproduction of the class relations necessary for its domination.[23]

On this basis, Marxian analysis is able to make a critique of the social character of technology and science, emphasising the distinction and interaction between the forces and relations of production. In contrast to the conventional vision of a neutral technology determining the nature of production, its social construction is located inside class relations and their antagonisms.[24] The capitalist labour process is therefore subject to a number of identifiable tendencies, whose central features are deskilling, fragmentation of tasks, hierarchical organisation, the division between manual and mental work, and the struggle to establish the most effective means to control labour.

It must be stressed, however, that they are trends and not finished processes. Each aspect can take a variety of historically relative forms. For instance, a previous example was given of the erosion of craft skills in the nineteenth century. But this dilution was relative to the skills and mechanical means available. Four decades later, as the US sociologists Warner and Lowe (1947) were able to show, the shoe industry was once again subject to a cycle of deskilling as mass production took root in the industry.

Taking into consideration the points made in this reflection, it is clear that Marx's analysis of the capitalist labour process needs to be constantly reviewed and renewed in new conditions. This is the theme of Chapter 3 and the debates that follow it. But before this is examined it is necessary to trace briefly the trajectory of the Marxist understanding of work between the original formulations and recent additions. For as Braverman points out, such a renewal did not take place: 'Neither the changes in the productive processes throughout this century of capitalism and monopoly capitalism, nor the changes in the occupational and industrial structure have been subject to any comprehensive Marxist analysis since Marx's death' (1974: 9).

One Step Backwards: Explaining the Drift from the Labour Process

Marxist analysis inexorably drifted away from a concern with the labour process. A full explanation of these events would require a history of Marxism and working-class movements.[25] However, two major tendencies can be identified as having profoundly affected Marxist theory in relation to work.

Politics and the workplace

Although the labour process was central to Marx's theories, he was writing in an era when class struggle in industry was only beginning to take shape. Naturally, the early trade unions were focal points. Marx described them as organising centres, political movements and even as schools for socialism (Lozovsky, 1935). In the context of the whole Marxist tradition this was in the 'optimistic camp' regarding the limits and possibilities of trade union action (Hyman, 1971). More importantly, such optimism was not based on any viable theoretical and strategical framework. Marx failed to reconcile adequately his analysis of the transformation of work, and the form and content of workers' struggles. As Burawoy accurately comments, 'In his later study of the dynamics of the capitalist mode of production, politics only appeared as an external and unexplained given' (1981: 85).

The separation of the spheres of politics and economics, or factory and state, continued to bedevil the development of a proper politics of production. In its place the socialist movement established an institutional boundary between political activity and trade unionism. This division was partly a genuine reflection of the existing interrelations between capital, the state and the working class. The role of the state was largely to provide a political and legal basis for the socio-economic structure. Compared with today, there was little intervention in the economy, except in crises like the 1926 General Strike. Inevitably this encouraged the view that the workplace was a separate sphere whose struggles were restricted to relations between particular employers and workers.

Politics, for the reformist wing of socialism — like the British Labour Party and the German Socialist Party (SPD) — was regarded as the evolutionary conquest of parliamentary power. For the revolutionary wing led by Lenin and the Bolsheviks, the emphasis was on the necessity to challenge and overthrow the state itself. But while there were differences about the degree of support for militant mass action, both wings accepted trade unionism as a necessary and restricted 'politics' of the workplace. Lenin was insistent that only *trade union consciousness* could develop from within the labour process; socialist consciousness arose from the relations between all classes, the state and government.

Trade unionism comes in a variety of forms and ideologies, but its essence is the *bargain* between capital and labour over the terms of the sale of labour power. Historically it has tended to accept the existence of the division of labour, the nature of work and wage labour under capitalism in its practices, if not in its philosophies and constitutions. These questions have normally been the province of informal activity and unofficial shop-floor organisation. Friedman suggests that as a consequence of following Lenin's separation of categories, Marxism has failed to give due recognition to the importance of worker resistance as 'an extremely powerful and growing force in the development of the capitalist mode of production' (1977b: 44).

Goodrich's classic 1920 study of workshop politics (republished in 1975) showed how workers countered managerial power by extending their own 'frontiers of control' with respect to organisation of work, changes in technology, and methods of payment. Demands for workers' control were an extension of the degree of job control already exercised. But the official socialist movements showed little interest and sometimes active hostility, leaving such issues to syndicalists and others.[26]

As trade unionism and the working-class parties became more widely established, particularly after the Second World War, the failure to integrate a politics of production was consolidated. As Braverman notes, 'This labor movement formed the immediate environment of Marxism, and Marxists were in varying degrees compelled to adapt to it' (1974: 10), the critique of capitalism as a mode of production gradually giving way to one merely at the level of distribution. That adaptation led to an increased focus on intra-union preoccupations. If problems were seen in trade unionism, they were predominantly associated with the existence of conservative bureaucracies and the perennial 'betrayals' of leaderships, as noted by Lane (1974).

A number of Marxist writers did begin to chronicle the important changes in workplace organisation and consciousness. Particularly highlighted were the increased incorporation of unions and the growth and contradictions of the shop stewards movement and of unofficial organisation and activity (Beynon, 1973; Lane, 1974; Hyman, 1974, 1975; Clarke and Clements, 1977).[27] But until recently changes in the content of work and the interconnected changes in class composition and ideology were still relatively uncharted territory.

Already existing socialism

The experience of forms of 'socialism' has also had a major effect in determining the absence of an effective politics of production. This can most clearly be seen with respect to the Soviet Union. It has become a commonplace among sociologists and radical critics alike to note the Bolshevik admiration of Taylorism and use of capitalist technology. Lenin saw Taylorism as a 'great scientific achievement' in 'elaborating the correct methods of work', and as a necessary component of modernising the Soviet Union.

He was not wholly uncritical, however. Lenin acknowledged the role of Taylorism in increasing exploitation, but believed that by improving productivity of labour under socialism, workers would be freed to take a greater part in the running of society and state (Linhart, 1976). However, the exclusion of critical evaluation of social relations in the factory was to have major theoretical and practical consequences. Not only did it result in a failure to transform methods of work and relations between mental and manual labour; it also inevitably fed other trends such as the decline of factory committees, the erosion of workers' control and their replacement by one-man management (Goodey, 1974). Indeed, there was a link between the Leninist view of the working class as only capable of trade union consciousness, and a parallel conception of a labour process guided by experts (Claudin-Urondo, 1977). These ideas of the labour process were also linked to a particular and limited view of the transition to socialism.

It was basic to Marxism that a high level of productive forces was the essential basis for socialism. Ultimately socialism had to be based on abundance and freedom from want. But these productive forces had come to be seen as *neutral*, that is, reliant on production techniques developed under capitalism. In turn this was linked to a reproduction of existing models of industrialisation that were uncritical of the necessity and features of large-scale enterprise. These views were held not only by Lenin, but by Trotsky, Stalin and much of the international socialist movement (see Corrigan, Ramsay and Sayer, 1978).[28] Trotsky expressed the 'technicist' view perfectly when he said: 'Soviet forms of property on a basis of the most modern forms of American technique transplanted into all forms of economic life — that indeed would be the first stage of socialism' (quoted in Thompson and Lewis, 1977: 36).

Yet this limited view of socialism and the possibilities of transforming work were backed up by reference to Marx; notably to his thesis that the development of the forces of production stand in ever greater contradiction to the social relations of production in capitalist society. In a broad sense this is unexceptional. The technical and economic means and skills already exist as a *potential* basis for satisfying the needs of the mass of people. Yet their effective use is held back by the private character of their appropriation for profit. But as one set of critics noted, 'What is at issue is what the "productive forces" *are*, and what is involved in "developing" them' (Corrigan, Ramsay and Sayer, 1978: 30). The Bolsheviks and others took the concept of productive forces in *isolation* from Marx's critical analysis of social production (Colletti, 1972).[29] Yet if as Marx argues, the means of production indicate the social relations within which people work, the working class cannot merely appropriate them for itself. Workers will have to transform the technology and authority relations which embody their own subordination (Gorz, 1976a).

Inevitably this unfortunate legacy has shaped the 'official Marxism' of modern Eastern European societies.[30] Take this gem on the Soviet economy from a leading Russian theoretician: 'Machine technology does not divide people, on the contrary, it unites them in collective labour and teaches them to work together, teaches them discipline, collectivism . . . In that sense the technology of large scale machine production serves as the material basis for the establishment and development of socialist ownership' (Sukharevsky, 1974: 46). He goes on to say that the attitudes of workers in socialist factories are different because they are working for themselves, even when working the same type of machinery. No recognition is given to technology and work organisation embodying social relations, or to the fact that alienation concerns the separation of skill and knowledge from the worker, in addition to non-ownership. Contemporary accounts from *inside* Eastern Europe of actual work experience indicate that it differs little from the West with respect to hierarchy, division of labour and payment systems (Harastzi, 1977; Bahro, 1978).[31]

With existing socialism becoming identified solely with nationalised property relations and state planning, and measuring its progress by how much it can 'catch up with the capitalist world', it is easier to understand why many Western sociologists have come to regard Marxism in the technicist manner described at the end of the last chapter.[32] The course of events in Eastern Europe have appeared to confirm the prominent view that there is an inevitable *convergence* of industrial societies into a single type. Yet this ignores the real historical processes and ideas that shaped those societies. Furthermore, they are *not* of the same type, as the more detailed examination in Chapter 8 of the nature of work in Eastern Europe will show.

Conclusion

The result of our experiences of the dominant trade union and socialist practices has been that a critical perspective on the labour process was lost, other than generalities about class and alienation: 'Marxist theory between the wars almost entirely ignored the internal evolution of the world of work' (Mallet, 1975: 18). The trade union and labour movements were thus deprived of the theoretical resources to make sense of technological and other factors, as is illustrated by a statement made by a leading member of the technical section of the Associated Union of Engineering Workers at a conference on new technology:

> When you are on the shop floor in other countries, you cannot tell whether you are in this country, the States, the Soviet Union, Czechoslovakia, or Hungary, because the production lines all look the same. Basically they are working with the same kind of equipment. In some of the socialist countries the equipment is more advanced. But you come to the conclusion that our production is socialist. We do it together. We know how to do it. What we have not learned is how to socially distribute the profits that are made out of it.

> (TASS/NDC, 1979: 20)

It follows that any rediscovery of the labour process is also a *reaction* to existing Marxist theory. Not all theoretical developments followed the above path. But when orthodoxy was departed from in the post-war period, it was unfortunately often also away from a concern with work.[33] For example, in the early writings of Gorz (1965) and of Marcuse (1964), some of the assumptions of social science were implicitly shared, particularly the declining centrality of work and production-based classes. For Gorz, alienation was seen as being located increasingly in consumption, while Marcuse looked towards students and youth for the future source of social change. Nevertheless, events were soon to change many of these assumptions, returning us to the workplace.

PART TWO

The Contemporary Debates

3

Braverman and the Re-discovery of the Labour Process

After the long and largely barren period when work became a forgotten issue, studies of the labour process have blossomed to such an extent that they constitute a growth industry in themselves. The major research of Braverman (1974), Friedman (1977a), Edwards (1979) and Burawoy (1979) concerning the development of the capitalist labour process as a whole has stimulated, and coexists with, studies of particular issues or industries (Gorz, 1976a; Zimbalist, 1979; Berg, 1979; Nichols, 1980a; Levidow and Young, 1981; Wood, 1982).[1]

This research did not develop in a vacuum. Both theoretical and practical pressures developed to challenge the drift from the labour process. It became increasingly apparent that postwar capitalist development had created significantly new conditions for the nature of work and for class formation. This chapter begins by making clear some of the most important precursors to the emergence of labour process perspectives. The bulk of it, however, is an examination of what many regard as the seminal contribution, that of Braverman's *Labor and Monopoly Capital*. His analysis played such a pivotal role in later debates because he combined a renewal of Marx's categories with an explanation of the dominant trends in the world of work. In focusing on this and supportive contributions, we can set out the key issues, as well as omissions, for subsequent discussions.

New Beginnings: Theory and Practice

A central factor in the return to a workplace focus was the breakdown of the illusion of industrial consensus. Throughout the industrial world, recorded workplace conflict dramatically increased from the period of the middle of the 1960s. Even at this time the unofficial strike rate was so high in Britain as to justify a Royal Commission, which produced the Donovan Report (1968). In other countries a higher peak of industrial and social conflict was reached, as in the mass strike waves in France in 1968 and Italy in 1969. But as the impressive collection of evidence on European class conflict by Crouch and Pizzorno (1978) found, the significance lay in the nature as well as the scale of the action.

Pizzorno notes that they were 'chiefly struck by the new types of qualitative demands' (1978, vol. 1: xi). Activity and demands showed a marked shift towards issues beyond wages. Case studies from various countries, notably France, Belgium and Italy, gave a wide range of examples of struggles over the control of line speeds and piece work, authority relations in the plant, challenges to job hierarchies and classification schemes, over general upgradings, and so on. Although these are prominent examples, it is a long-term trend, as Kumar notes: 'The changing pattern of strikes, especially since 1945, gives further evidence of an increasing restlessness about the quality of working life and the nature of the job itself' (1978: 285).

As previously noted, academic commentators and official government and business circles began to take increased notice of these trends. In 1970 the US business magazine, *Fortune*, proclaimed that the 'blue-collar blues' were resulting in 'less efficiency, wasted manpower, higher costs, a need for more inspection and repairs, more warranty clauses and grievous damage to company reputations as unhappy customers rage over flaws' (quoted in Pignon and Querzola, 1976: 64). Work had once more become, in the words of Edwards, a visibly 'contested terrain'. *Fortune* has a particular explanation for this phenomenon, linking it to the increased number of younger, well educated workers. Similarly, other writers noted the role of newer groups in the workforce, particularly unskilled mass production workers (Dubois, 1978) and immigrant and female workers (Baudoin *et al.*, 1978).

This helps to shed some light on the subsequent theoretical development back towards the study of work from a Marxist viewpoint. For the debate started not so much about changes in the labour process, but about the extent of a new working class. Orthodox Marxism had followed the path of treating the working class as increasingly homogeneous and unified by the impact of capitalist production; only occasionally was it diverted into an examination of class differentiation by problems like 'labour aristocracies'.[2] Yet with massive changes in production and organisation of capitalist society, growing diversity needed explanation. Even Braverman's study of work started off as an examination of occupational shifts.

But well before that, major studies were taking place, particularly in France by writers like Mallet (1975, French original 1963) and Gorz (1967). In the early 1960s they argued that a new vanguard had come into being, consisting of highly skilled technical, white- and sometimes blue-collar workers, particularly in the high technology industries like chemicals, telecommunications and nuclear plant. It was said that workers in these strata were more interested in non-wage and control issues. The basis for this was the desire of such workers to maintain acquired skills and put them to creative use, in a situation where the workplace was still structured as an authoritarian and profit-orientated hierarchy.

The question of work changes *was* dealt with. Indeed, Mallet believed that the reshaping of technology and production relations formed the basis of any new type of class composition. But if the methodology is useful, the actual analysis is less so. Like many of his sociological contemporaries, Mallet accepted the inaccurate image of an emergent golden age of automation that would negate the trend towards the fragmentation and dequalification of jobs. Hence he drew the opposite political conclusions concerning class consciousness. Thus the material foundation for this new working class was partly unsound.

In the high technology industries there is still a strong reliance on semi-skilled workers, and many new skills are characterised by isolation and over-specialisation (Nichols and Beynon, 1977). In addition such industries are still a minority, and new working-class theory seriously underestimated changes in traditional manual jobs and their significance for patterns of organisation and conflict. The research carried out did not thoroughly examine changes in the labour process. Mallet himself relied on formal and general descriptions of technology and its relations to workers' attitudes, even in his case studies. Far from posing a 'fundamental questioning of capitalist production' (Mallet, 1975: 29), Mallet and Gorz saw the contradiction not as being *within* the labour process, but between work of an increasingly autonomous social character and the hierarchy of the workplace.[3]

Nevertheless, the events of May 1968 in France — in which educated young workers played a key role — appeared to confirm the notion of a new, vanguard working class. Furthermore, it led to an enthusiastic adoption of the ideas in many other countries, especially the USA (see Hodges, 1971; Welch, 1979). Enthusiasm was understandable. The theory provided a framework for understanding the important changes taking place in the jobs for which student radicals were largely destined. It offered the hope of a leading role in an enlarged and revitalised working-class movement.

Technical and professional workers were assigned the leading role by virtue of increased sources of antagonism to employers and the state, who would seek to limit and misuse their skills. But what of their privileged relations to the skills, knowledge and position of other workers? A close examination of their actual functions and relations in work would have revealed a far more contradictory process than new working-class theory allowed. As Gorz admitted in a later study (1976c), the theory extended the concept of a proletarianisation to insert a very 'mixed bag' inside the working class, let alone make it a leading component.

Nor was this the only attempt to rethink class by reference to work. In Italy there had been a substantial tradition of studying changes in the labour process, deriving from Panzieri (1976 and 1980).[4] This important school of Italian Marxism argued that developments in capitalist production were creating a deskilled labour force corresponding to Marx's collective labourer. As in France, practical struggles of these 'mass workers' on the assembly lines of Fiat and other factories in the 1960s boosted the ideas.[5] But in contrast, the Italian theory concentrated on a new manual working class, rather than new technical and professional strata, although such workers *were* held to be similarly proletarianised and part of an enlarged working class. Despite this welcome attention to changes in manual work, there were parallel weaknesses. Concepts were over-generalised and lacked an understanding of the complexities of the position and experiences of different strata in the labour process. Differences in conditions and consciousness within and outside the manual working class were covered over by a blanket application of the categories of deskilling and proletarianisation.

The early debates about new class composition were therefore inconclusive and often misleading. But taken together with other contributions like the Marxist industrial sociology of Nichols and Beynon, it constituted an important step forward. These trends did not represent a single theoretical or political tendency, but it was the beginning of a critical theorisation of work and the provision of a politics of production.

The Degradation of Work: the Braverman Thesis

In one of the first studies of the labour process, Gorz (1976a: vii) argued that the capitalist division of labour had been forgotten as a source of alienation until it found itself at the centre of many of the struggles just described. The subsequent awakening of sections of Marxist thought to the process of production led not only to a questioning of the 'tyranny of the factory', but also to the whole historical evolution of the world of work. To take the new beginnings further required a precise and detailed examination of the productive process. Braverman was the first to provide this, and in a manner which deliberately eschews any attempt to accompany it by an explicit theory of class consciousness and social change.

This preference for the 'objective' features of work and class has been the subject of much subsequent criticism. But the clarity of purpose, breadth of research and theoretical originality ensured its prominence, regardless of weaknesses. The latter point concerning originality is important, because Braverman's centrality arises also from the particular and distinct perspective advanced. One of the many writers using Braverman as a reference point for discussion of their own research sums up the basics of the perspective:

> A certain current in Marxism, seeking to elaborate the concept of the 'labour process' has been influential in representing changes in types and scale of new production technology, as effects of necessary and general 'tendencies' or 'laws' . . . proposed as primarily the subordination of the autonomy of manual production workers, through simultaneously decreasing the level of skill in production tasks and increasing managerial control over their execution.

> (Jones, 1982: 179)

In some senses Braverman and others in this 'certain current' have only advocated a return to Marx. Certainly Braverman begins (see his chs 1—3) by restating many of the essential features of Marx's theory of the labour process, with the addition of material from modern historians and critical comments on parallel sociological concepts. Indeed, all the major new studies of the labour process — Friedman, Edwards, Burawoy and Gorz — start with similar reminders of aspects of the original approach, although, as we shall see, modifications are proposed in some instances.

There are three aspects that Braverman chooses to emphasise. First, the necessity for capital to realise the potential of purchased labour power by transforming it into labour under its own control, thereby creating the basis for alienation.[6] Second, that the origins of management lay in the struggle to devise the most effective means of imposing employers' will within a new social relations of production different in kind and scope to what had existed before. Third, that a division of labour based on a systematic subdivision of work, rather than simple distribution of crafts, is generalised only within the capitalist mode of production. The separation of work into constituent elements reflects the necessary principle for capital of dividing the craft to cheapen the parts, providing the basis for the subsequent destruction of all-round skills.

Unlike others, Braverman does not seek to alter Marx, and the concepts of deskilling and managerial control are to be found in the original framework. In what sense, then, is Braverman distinctive? Essentially it derives from a successful attempt to *renew* Marx's theory of the labour process and apply it to subsequent historical development, taking a fresh look at skills, technology and work organisation. By doing so, he outlines the greater possibilities for widespread deskilling through the use of new forms of technology and science in the service of capital. In addition there is considerably more scope for tighter managerial control, a process that Braverman argues comes to be located round Taylorism.

Taylorism and control

In retracing the origins of management and hierarchy in work to the combined need for accumulation and control, rather than the imperatives of technology and efficiency, Braverman shares a similar perspective with two other studies often linked to his own (Stone, 1973; Marglin, 1976).[7] For aside from providing more detailed historical evidence on this score, particularly in Marglin, a further emphasis is added: that is, the centrality of the struggle to wrest control of the workplace from skilled craft workers. As we have seen, this degree of control was based on both the existence of craft skills and on methods of work organisation, notably the sub-contracting and 'putting-out' systems.

Whereas Marglin's evidence is largely contemporary to Marx, Stone provides a case study dealing with the steel industry at the turn of the century. She charts how the demands of competition forced employers to try to end the sub-contracting system. Under this arrangement craft workers organised production and even hired their own manual help out of the payments for the amount of tonnage made by employers. To break the 'equal partnership of capital and labour' and introduce labour-saving machinery, it was necessary for employers to make combined use of mechanisation, reorganisation of work that removed planning from the shop floor, and individualistic wage systems.[8] In this battle steel employers increasingly had access to Taylor's emergent theory and practice of scientific management, which was developed within the industry itself.

This is the emphasis taken up and made distinctive by Braverman. He was not the first to note the logical sequence of events that led to Taylorism, as Landes says: 'seen from the hindsight of the mid-twentieth century, scientific management was the natural sequel to the process of mechanisation that constituted the heart of the industrial revolution' (quoted in Kumar, 1978: 176). But Braverman showed that as a synthesis of disconnected ideas and experiments concerning the organisation of work, Taylorism was able to 'render conscious and systematic the formerly unconscious tendency of capitalist production' (1974: 121) with respect to the control and uses of skill and knowledge.

Hence it is not merely *one* managerial method, nor a *general* science of work, but an essential and defining feature of the capitalist labour process. Taylorism was an explicit recognition that the general managerial setting of tasks, order and discipline was insufficient, even within the factory despotism identified by Marx. Neither was machinery alone a reliable means of control of labour. Braverman argues that as long before this as Babbage's principle of dividing the craft to cheapen the parts, capital had been groping towards a theory and practice of management. By systematically combining together previous insights, Taylorism provided methods of control that could be applied at any given level of technology.

Scientific management was not just a framework of ideas. It was a set of tried and tested practices. As a gang boss in a steel mill, Taylor spent many years perfecting his methods of work organisation in a struggle against what he freely admitted to be perfectly rational means of collective workers' organisation for restriction of output and control of earnings. His battle against 'systematic soldiering' was written up in great detail and reproduced by Braverman, so as to give clear expression to the ideas. Out of his experiences, Taylor developed a series of principles, summed up by Braverman:

> Thus, if the first principle is the gathering together and
> development of knowledge of the labour process, and the

second is the concentration of this knowledge as the exclusive preserve of management — together with its converse, the absence of such knowledge among workers — then the third step is the use of this monopoly of knowledge to control each step of the labour process and its mode of execution.

(Braverman, 1974: 119)

This summary is not an unwarranted and excessive interpretation. Taylor was quite explicit that because the managers' and foremen's knowledge of the work 'falls far short of the combined knowledge of all the workmen under them' (quoted in Braverman, 1974: 101), maximum efficiency and profitability could never be achieved. Therefore management needed to gather together the knowledge possessed by workers and reduce it to their own rules and laws. Furthermore, 'all possible brain work should be removed from the shop and centred in the planning or lay-out department' (quoted in Braverman, 1974: 113). Once this had been done management could specify tasks in advance and determine *exactly* how and for how long they should be carried out.

The resultant deskilling could be as effective as through any mechanical means, although it is a by-product, not the purpose of the exercise. This rendering of the labour process independent of craft knowledge was previously noted by the German Marxist, Sohn-Rethel. He argued that Taylorism was a qualitative change in capitalist production, the distinctive feature of which 'is aimed at establishing a novel and clearcut division of mental and manual labour throughout the workshops' (1976: 35).[9] But Braverman characterises this more accurately as a separation of *conception* and *execution*, and he goes on to show that further to the separation of mental and manual labour, the tendency is for the former to be subdivided according to the same rule. Sohn-Rethel also raised the key role of payment structures in Taylor's system, a point recognised by Braverman, but perhaps not given enough weight. As part of work reorganisation, jobs were increasingly tied to individual incentive schemes. Taylor's dream of having a different rate for every worker, so as to eliminate any community of interest, was never a feasible possibility. But aside from emphasising the inseparability of payment systems and labour processes, it did point the way towards attempts to make higher wages compatible with high profits. This idea was taken up by Henry Ford with his 'five dollar day' and by other manufacturers and economists in the aftermath of Keynesianism.[10]

In presenting the above features of Taylorism as necessary components of the capitalist labour process, Braverman is partly accepting Taylor's own definition of his methods as opening up the solution to finding the 'one best way' of organising work.[11] He is thoroughly dismissive of the dominant strands of social science that believe Taylorism to have been superseded by humanistic forms of management, an issue already discussed in Chapter 1. His case does not rest merely on the grounds that these forms are the 'maintenance crew for the human machinery' (p. 87), leaving the Taylorist world of production untouched. The power of the analysis lies in the evidence provided that varied types of scientific management have been *extended* to wider areas of the occupational structure.

After proof that Taylorism could be extended from simple to complex production processes (Braverman, 1974: 110–12), the most notable example has been its use in the transformation of clerical labour. The concepts of control flowing from scientific management, allied to complexities of scale, required an expansion of administrative and office tasks. This 'paper replication of production' in the office was first based on the mental labour stripped from manual work through Taylorism. But the monopoly over conception and planning did not survive the pressures to transform office work into an administrative labour process in its own right. Taylor himself had no doubt that the costs of production could be lowered by sub-dividing mental labour and subjecting it to control and measurement (Braverman, 1974: 127).

Previously, clerical labour had been a relatively small part of production expenses, largely self-supervising and concerned with 'whole' tasks. But as early as 1917 the application of scientific management began to lead to the 'breakdown of the arrangement under which each clerk did his or her own work according to traditional methods' (Braverman, 1974:

307). Under the control of office managers, all clerical work began to be investigated for the most effective means of standardisation and rationalisation. In addition, piece work and incentive schemes began to be introduced.

A scientific management manual for the office (1960)	
Open and close	*Minutes*
File drawer, open and close, no selection	0.04
Folder, open or close flaps	0.04
Desk drawer, open side drawer of desk	0.014
Open center drawer	0.026
Close side	0.015
Close center	0.027
Chair activity	
Get up from chair	0.033
Sit down in chair	0.033
Turn in swivel chair	0.009
Move in chair to adjoining desk or file	0.050
Source: Braverman (1974: 321).	

It must be stressed, however, that these measures were effected *prior* to the extensive *mechanisation* of office work. However, Braverman argues that it signalled that 'manual work spreads to the office and soon becomes characteristic of the tasks of the mass of clerical workers' (1974: 316).

Deskilling: science and technology in the service of capital
Despite the extensive, if uneven and varied, spread of scientific management, Braverman recognises that Taylorism alone was not a sufficient basis for the further transformation of the labour process by capital. Both as a system of control, and as a means of deskilling, it was subject to a number of constraints. Braverman points out that 'Taylorism raised a storm of opposition among the trade unions' (1974: 136), because of the realisation that it was an effort to relieve workers of their job autonomy and craft knowledge. But, as is consistent with the methodology of the book in omitting reference to organisation and struggles, workers' resistance is only briefly mentioned,

and only then as an example of understanding the consequences of scientific management, rather than a substantial
limit to its development.

Such constraints are seen more in terms of the inadequate
scale of production for meeting the cost of 'rationalisation',
and in the limited degree of scientific-technological advance-
ment. It is to the latter that Braverman gives prominence,
arguing that Taylorism began to coincide with a new scientific
technical revolution. He restates Marx's view of science following labour into becoming an object of capital, thus restoring, along with other studies like Gorz (1976a), a critical
analysis of the forces of production. But both these writers
go further by giving considerable historical evidence of
twentieth-century research and technical innovation aimed at
reducing production costs.

New techniques and machinery are able to increase productivity rapidly through greater intensity of work, recalling
Marx's own account of the development of new forms of
surplus under the impact of large-scale industry (Palloix,
1976). Yet these elaborations of Marx's concepts are an
unacknowledged comment on the limits of the original
writings. For although Marx showed how science and technology aided mechanisation which strengthened the subordination of labour and deskilling, retrospectively it can be
seen to be a clearly incomplete process. In comparison large
companies, allied to state intervention, particularly in the
post-war period, were able to hasten the planned use of
research in technology and product design. These developments went beyond the former, largely spontaneous innovation evoked by the production processes.

The subsequently more intensive and sophisticated mechanisation brought about faster and more efficient machinery, which was incorporated 'within a management effort to
dissolve the labour process as a process conducted by the
worker and reconstitute as a process conducted by the management' (Braverman, 1974: 170). New forms of machinery
offer capital the opportunity to extend by mechanical means
what had previously been attempted by means of organisation
and discipline. Even in the sphere of scientific management,
Taylor's followers and successors were able to improve

methods of control through technical advance. Gilbreth, for example, added the concept of *motion* to time study, the chronocyclegraph providing a visual record of body movements. These elementary movements, named *therbligs*, became standardised data that could replace direct observation, thus constituting a more efficient means of measurement and control.

As Gorz has noted, 'Science, then, has helped to turn work into a strait jacket' (1976c: 172). But it has also deepened the trend towards deskilling and task fragmentation, which is most commonly associated with the emergence of the assembly line. Indeed, for some writers, notably those influenced by Italian labour process theory, assembly production is *the* characteristic form of mechanisation. Palloix asserts that this development, labelled *Fordism*, innovated and extended Taylorism, the flow line principle allowing for greater mechanical control by management, while high day-wage rates regulated the supply and conditions of labour.[12] The unskilled assembly worker is therefore seen as a central result of accelerated mechanisation.

Braverman recognises the innovative role of Fordism, but concentrates on the more general development and effects of mechanisation. One of his examples concerns machine tools and the introduction of numerical control systems. He shows how metal cutting has become virtually automatic. Numerical tapes control the movement of the tool, relieving the worker of the need to be in close control of the machine. Work tasks can be more easily fragmented between operators, who are required to know less; conceptual knowledge is placed in the hands of programmers. As computerised techniques become more complex, even the machine specifications for programming can be stored on the tapes, thus extending the deskilling process upwards.

Supportive evidence exists in the research of Noble (1979). Visits to twenty-four plants established that 'in nearly every case management had attempted to transfer skill from the shop floor to the programming office, to tighten up lines of authority, and to extend control over all aspects of production' (1979: 323). One of the interesting things he shows is that there were other ways of automating machine tools that retained operator skills and control, but he also shows that competitive pressures and deliberate managerial choice of the most effective means of control excluded this possibility. This strengthens Braverman's point that although conventional engineering approaches treat machinery as a technical given, different conceptions of machinery embody alternative designs and uses.

Once again Braverman establishes how mechanisation spreads to the office (see his pp. 326–48). Computer systems developing from simple card punching, through data processing to the latest microchip technology for handling information, have been the basis for the transformation of white-collar labour. Although initially it had some craft characteristics, data processing was quickly adapted to a new, highly specialised and hierarchical division of labour: 'the concentration of knowledge and control in a very small portion of the hierarchy became the key here, as with automatic machines in the factory, to control over the process' (Braverman, 1974: 329). Braverman approvingly refers to managerial sources that suggest that the computer will be to administrative workers, even at lower and middle-management level, what the assembly line was to manual employees. Although Braverman's research was published before some of the more recent office technology was introduced, his preliminary examination of machinery such as word processors indicated a strengthening of existing trends.

Regardless of which aspects of mechanisation are stressed by the different theorists mentioned, the theme of generalised deskilling as a necessary feature of the capitalist labour process is a common feature. Gorz refers to the historical tendency towards the 'dequalification of the direct producers' (1976b: 57), while Palloix argues that the tendency towards equalisation of work is part of a double movement of capital (1976: 57). The analysis of this strand of labour process theory is therefore directly supportive of Marx's homogenisation thesis, whereby the development of capitalist production erodes the differences between types and categories of work.

Variations of conditions and time-scale within the deskilling process *are* recognised. Each of the theorists referred to is concerned to point to vital contradictory processes involved. At the start of a cycle of technical change and work restructuring there is often a partial inversion of the general tendency. Widespread deskilling is often accompanied by an increased 'qualification' of a smaller layer of workers involved in planning, programming and similar tasks. But the general tendency immediately tends to reassert itself as the enhanced skills are subjected to similar sub-specialisation and the embodiment of skills in more complex machinery. Braverman's evidence of the progressive deskilling of computer programmers is a major example of this type of development.

It is therefore believed that the allied tendencies towards deskilling and increased managerial control will persist *through* changes in technology and work organisation. Braverman argues strongly that the dominant sociological view of automation as qualitatively different from mechanisation is profoundly mistaken. There is a continuum between the two precisely because technological developments are incorporated into the same underlying methods of organising the labour process. He draws extensively on the detailed study of automation by James R. Bright of the Harvard Business School who said: 'I was startled to find that the upgrading effect had not occurred to anywhere near the extent to which it is often assumed. On the contrary, there was evidence that automation had reduced the skill requirements of the operating workforce' (quoted in Braverman, 1974: 220).

Even in those industries where operators have been eliminated from the physical process of production — such as chemicals — the supervision of machinery in more congenial surroundings has often been confused with actual increases in the uses of skills and knowledge. These misleading perceptions of early process automation in the work of Blauner (1964), Cotgrove (1972), Goldthorpe, Lockwood *et al.* (1968) and others, has been convincingly refuted by the 'ChemCo' case studies of Nichols and Beynon (1977). The work in control rooms *was* less arduous, but it could also be stressful, lonely and meaningless. In addition to the 'scientific work', there was also 'donkey work': 'For every man who watched dials another maintained the plants, another was a lorry driver and another two humped bags or shovelled muck' (Nichols and Beynon, 1977: 12)

Braverman on chemical work

'Thus the chemical operator is singled out time and again, as the outstanding beneficiary of "automation", and the praises of this job are sung in countless variations. The work of the chemical operator is generally clean, and it has to do with "reading instruments" and "keeping charts". These characteristics already endear him to middle class observers, who readily confuse them with skill, technical knowledge, etc. Yet few have stopped to think whether it is harder to learn to read a dial than tell time.'

(Braverman, 1974: 224)

Process operators *do* have to be alert, knowledgeable and capable of reacting intelligently to the control machinery, and the group task nature of the work has traditionally made it resistant to scientific management techniques. But the practical utilisation of high skill levels was often a characteristic of the *early* stages of automated process plant. Research shows that the emphasis on problem-solving and teamwork referred to by Blauner has declined as the reliability and sophistication of the plant increased (see Hill, 1981: 97–8). In addition, the latest round of microprocessor technology is enabling management to expand the *self-acting* character of control systems, leading to deskilling of operatives and maintenance staff, although this results in a contradiction 'between excluding operators from the routine running of the plant and yet having to rely on them to deal with unusual events that go beyond the capability of the computer' (CSE Microelectronics Group, 1980: 79).

A related point about automation is made by Palloix (1976). He argues that the capitalist use of automation aimed at eliminating all manual intervention by the worker can carry dequalification of productive labour to some of its most extreme, machine-minding forms. He does, however, make the useful point that there are different forms of automation, describing them as continuous and discontinuous processes. The former are extensions of traditional mass production on Taylorist and Fordist lines, while the latter are based in high technology industries with a much higher proportion of investment in capital than labour. In the continuous-process industries there are small layers of highly skilled workers. This is in turn a recognition of the existence of a *dual labour market* for skilled and unskilled labour within the long-term trend towards dequalification.

Palloix also believes that recent attempts to modify work organisation do not change the basis of the capitalist labour process. Different schemes of job enrichment are seen as an adaptation of Taylorism and Fordism, reacting to new struggles and dissatisfactions in work and new conditions in the labour market, with the aim of preserving the profitability of capital. Braverman does not even grace job enrichment schemes with new theoretical categories like neo-Fordism and neo-Taylorism. His dismissal of them as mere *styles* of management is part of the general argument that Taylorism is the characteristic and necessary form of work organisation. Gorz, too, refers to attempts to reconcile workers to their work as appearing to be 'a new manipulation rather than a solution to basic contradictions' (1976b: 58). However, he correctly notes that alteration in the nature of jobs carries the useful recognition that there is no objective technical necessity for particular working arrangements. Evidence concerning new forms of technology and work organisation will be examined in Chapters 4 and 5.

From production to society
Unlike some labour process theorists, Braverman has been concerned to show the effects of changes in the sphere of production on the wider social structure. He begins by noting how the important developments in productive processes have dated from the same period as the rise of the *monopoly* form of capital. Scientific management and the scientific-technical revolution are prime aspects of this new stage of capitalist development, growing out of its framework and sustaining its existence.

Recognition of the monopoly stage of capitalism has become a common feature of the varieties of Marxist thought, but Braverman shows little interest in debates about its precise nature.[13] He follows certain lines of interest developed by his co-thinkers Baran and Sweezy (1968).[14] In the preface to Braverman's *Labor and Monopoly Capital*, Sweezy admits to neglecting the labour process in their major writings. In contrast Braverman looks at the convergence of trends in the modern corporation monopolies and effects on the occupational structure: for example, the growth of service occupations and the sub-divisions of managerial functions, each of which creates its own specific labour process.

But these processes have wider consequences in 'industrial shifts that change the entire social division of labour' (Braverman, 1974: 256). Following Baran and Sweezy, Braverman argues that one of the key problems of monopoly capitalist society is how to use and absorb the massive economic surplus that developed in the post-war period, while at the same time accommodating the masses of labour displaced by changes in the existing productive apparatus. The solution is that: 'The ample stream of capital meet the "freed" labor in the marketplace upon the ground of new products and industries' (p. 278). The consequent spread of a new range of commodities and locations for investment increasingly takes in spheres of social life previously unorganised through the market, for instance aspects of food and entertainment previously the province of family, farming or community.

The whole of society is now referred to as a gigantic market place. 'It is only in its era of monopoly that the capitalist mode of production takes over the totality of individual family and social needs and, in subordinating them to the market, also re-shapes them to serve the needs of capital' (Braverman, 1974: 271). This universal market governed by the quest for profit inevitably undermines community care and family functions. Social life in the new urban environment becomes increasingly atomised, and those excluded from participation in the market — sections of the old and young, and the poor — can be dealt with only by an expanded institutional network.

Combined with new economic functions designed to stabil-

The universal market

'new commodities are brought into being that match the conditions of life of the urban dweller, and are put into circulation in the forms dictated by the capitalist organisation of society. Thus a plentiful supply of printed matter becomes a vehicle for corporate marketing, as do scientific marvels of the twentieth century such as radio and television. The automobile is developed as an immensely profitable form of transportation which in the end destroys the more practical form of transportation in the interests of profit. Like machinery in a factory, the machinery of society becomes a pillory instead of a convenience, and a substitute for, instead of an aid to, competence.'

(Braverman, 1974: 278)

---

ise the system through planning and government spending, the social necessity for an agency to fill the gaps left by the market requires a vastly increased role for the state. A further consequence is the creation of a much larger service sector, which is of particular importance to the changed role of women in the labour force. As such opportunities develop, women are brought into the labour market, often to perform the kinds of caring and servicing tasks previously carried out within the home. Some commentators on Braverman regard the analysis of 'the penetration of the entire social structure by the commodification of social life' (Burawoy, 1978: 295) as a major aspect of the overall theory of the labour process.

The analysis of the universal market is, however, extremely schematic, and lacks most of the empirical detail of the material on changes in the productive process.[15] Nor is it the first Marxist study to examine the changed relations between production and social life. Gorz (1965) provided an important critique of the new patterns of consumption under monopoly capitalism, while the role of *social capital* was an essential component of Italian labour process theory.[16] Braverman's contribution can nevertheless be seen as furthering this area of analysis by situating it within a much more comprehensive theory of all the social relations of the new capitalist totality, and, in addition, by opening up important debates concerning under-recognised issues, notably the role of the sexual division of labour in new sectors of the economy.

The class structure

Marx did not explicitly link a theoretical model of the class structure to that of the capitalist labour process. In attempting to do this, Braverman therefore goes beyond Marx. The reason is not difficult to understand, given that *Labor and Monopoly Capital* started off as a study of occupational shifts and class composition. However, the different emphasis of the eventual study towards the labour process clearly enriched the discussion of the changing class structure. Furthermore, it has beneficially influenced more explicit studies of class (Wright, 1976; Ehrenreich and Ehrenreich, 1979).

The great advantage held by Braverman over much of orthodox sociological and Marxist theory concerning class is that the emphasis on work is brought in to produce a more complex picture of social relationships. This is particularly evident on the question of proletarianisation. Even in the best studies, such as Lockwood (1958), this phenomenon is primarily linked to deterioration of rewards and conditions, allied to the expanded scale and complexity of enterprises. Braverman draws on his analysis of the specific features of the development of the labour process in contemporary capitalism to explain how changes in the nature of work underly shifts in class location. He backs up the general analysis with richly detailed accounts of the labour of occupations such as clerks, secretaries and computer programmers. This enables him to pinpoint some of the contradictory features of white-collar labour that have been a source of confusion in sociology. A major example of this is the misleading increased demand for higher qualifications. These credentials are shown to be used for recruitment on the labour *market*, unrelated to the actual diminishing skill requirements in the labour *process*. To illustrate the point, Braverman (1974: 337) refers to reports showing that the practice of employers using well qualified girls as card punchers was a *screening device* related to their likely ability to be motivated, responsible and reliable.

These changes are sufficient for Braverman to place the expanded clerical and service sector workers unambiguously in a 'large proletariat in new form' (p. 355). While this is not presented as a simple homogenisation of work and conditions, particularly among the next grouping — the middle layers of employment — problems begin to arise in the analysis. Sensitive discussions of work and class do not necessarily translate into an accurate definition of class position. Braverman argues that the 'proletarian form' gradually asserts and impresses itself on the consciousness of white-collar employees, *without* indicating the basis for this development. Essentially, this limitation derives from the deliberate exclusion of any discussion of the subjective features of class and work experiences. Without this discussion, 'objective factors' of these phenomena, no matter how perceptively grasped, tend to be regarded as the dominant ones. The consequences of labour process theory for studies of class are therefore problematic, and form a distinct issue on its own to be examined in Chapter 8.

Conclusion

The framework of ideas developed by Braverman and other writers discussed in this chapter constitute only one strand of labour process theory. Subsequent research has either brought about alternative perspectives independently or through direct criticism, particularly of the central thesis of Braverman. These criticisms have largely been focused on questioning the extent and timing of, and variation in, the processes of deskilling and Taylorism. Alternatives have stressed far more complex and differentiated layers of skill, combined with the viability of other strategies for the exercise of managerial authority in the workplace.

Underlying these positions has been a further critique of the general methodology used by Braverman, and to a lesser extent other theorists. The root of the problem is seen as stemming from Braverman's deliberate exclusion of the dimension of class struggle and consciousness. While this is prioritised by him as a means of painting a picture of the working class *in work* 'as it really is', it is argued that this involves a neglect of the important effects of worker resistance and organisation on technology and labour processes. Capitalist control cannot be separated from and understood outside the supportive subjective components of work experience. This does not refer just to managerial strategy, but to the problems of ideology and the degree of consent given by workers to their exploitation and alienation.

By deliberately eschewing subjectivity, Braverman also accepts the traditional Marxist analysis that the trend towards homogenisation of work increasingly unifies the working class. This carries the danger of underplaying the way stratification affects the distribution and nature of work, particularly that which derives from the wider social division of labour concerning sex and race. In these points the location of criticism is shifted from Braverman's methods and treatment of consciousness to its *consequences* for an analysis of the labour process. Nevertheless, the role of Braverman and other earlier writers has provided a focal point of reference for a series of important debates, the examination of which will reveal the wider body of labour process theory.

4

Deskilling: The Degradation of Labour?

The Deskilling Debate

The issues of increased deskilling and managerial control have emerged as the two main areas of debate in labour process theory. Emphasis has been placed on the extent and nature of the trends, and their impact on the degradation of work. It is very difficult to separate the two questions. For example, Braverman has argued that the labour process has been affected by technical transformations and the reorganisation of work associated with scientific management. However, deskilling is not only a product of the incorporation of science and technology into capital, it is also interconnected with Taylorism.

As a strategy for managerial control, resting on the separation of conception and execution, skills are inevitably fragmented and routinised. Cooley comments: 'Seventy years of scientific management have seen the fragmentation of work grind through the spectrum of workshop activity engulfing even the most creative and satisfying jobs' (1981: 49). Nevertheless, the technical and control dimensions of Taylorism can be partially distinguished. Debates on the latter question have focused on Taylorism as one of the options for a capitalist *strategy* for organising workers and their work. This is distinct from the technical transformations affecting the use of skills and other aspects of the worker's capacity to labour. Retaining this distinction, this chapter will only discuss scientific management where it relates to the latter issue.

The focus of the chapter will be on the degree to which skills have been transformed and eroded through capitalist development, and the extent to which such changes can be described as a degradation of labour. An important weakness of the existing deskilling debate has been that research has centred on what has happened to craft work. Naturally this reflects the evidence deriving from our greater knowledge of the period from the turn of the century to the impact of mass production industries. Consequently the structure of the chapter starts with the question of craft skill. The substantive theoretical issues are discussed primarily in relation to such evidence, despite more recent vital changes in labour and product markets, workers' organisation, and other factors. Our knowledge of how contemporary changes in work and technology are affecting skills and experiences is inevitably limited. But the final part of the chapter attempts to bring the debate up to date, posing the theoretical questions in the new context.

It is not only Braverman who argues that deskilling is an inherent tendency of the capitalist labour process. A number of recent studies have reinforced the concept, either at the level of general theory (Brighton Labour Process Group, 1977) or in detailed case studies (Zimbalist, 1979). The Zimbalist collection is directly supportive of Braverman's central thesis that deskilling is a long-run tendency: 'in an absolute sense (they lose craft and traditional abilities) and in a relative one (scientific knowledge progressively accumulates in the production process)' (Zimbalist, 1979: xv). It is noted that the tendency is constrained only by the uneven development between and within industries, or what Braverman refers to as 'the nature of the various specific and determinate processes of production' (1974: 172).

The Brighton study is more critical, noting the necessity to take into account the specific effects of different phases of accumulation, as well as worker resistance, in that they are mediating factors to changes in the labour process. Nevertheless, deskilling is taken to be one of three 'immanent laws of the capitalist labour process' (Brighton Labour Process Group,

1977: 16).[1] Deskilling is said to be inherent in labour functions that are intended to achieve maximum possible speed, cheapness, replaceability, standardisation and calculability for the needs of capital. The authors are also quite clear about what deskilling involves, naming three aspects: the replacement of skilled workers by machines or machine operatives; the division and sub-division of jobs, with any remaining skill allocated to a few specialised workers; and the fragmentation of the remaining semi- or unskilled tasks. The latter is recognised as constituting only a tendency dependent on the particular division of labour and work organisation.

Yet the significance of the deskilling debate does not lie solely in the analysis of trends in the nature of work. Of equal importance are the potential consequences for class consciousness, action and organisation. Labour process theory is strongly connected to Marxism, and Marxism is ultimately a theory of social change, as well as of social structure. Although Marx did not systematically declare the relations between his analysis of changes in the labour process and class struggle, it was clearly implied that the trends towards homogenisation and degradation of labour were important aspects of class formation: objective preconditions for the transformation of society by the proletariat. Such themes have been taken up by contemporary Marxists: for example, Cooley (1981: 49) argues that technological proletarianisation will increase the likelihood of an alliance of scientific and technical workers with the working class and with progressive movements.

Taking these factors into account, critics have challenged the assumptions of leading writers such as Braverman both on the extent *and* the consequences of deskilling (see Wood, 1982, for the most comprehensive assessment and reference to other commentaries).[2] However, there are two major problems in embarking on an examination of this debate. First, the connection between changes in the labour process and their consequences for class formation and action are not always spelt out. We have already noted that Braverman deliberately excludes the component of working-class organisation and subjectivity.

The problem is further compounded by a lack of explicit theoretical consideration of concepts like homogenisation, although Braverman makes general reference to 'The giant mass of workers who are relatively homogeneous as to lack of developed skill, low pay, and interchangeability of person and function' (1974: 359). Ironically, the only direct comment on issues concerning the consequences of labour-process changes for class struggle is in a short commentary that Braverman made in relation to some of his early critics.[3] Here he recognises that the value of such analysis 'can only lie in precisely how well it helps us to answer questions about class consciousness' (1976: 122). Unfortunately, aside from a widely noted assertion of the revolutionary potential of the working class, the point is taken no further.

Second, it is not always clear what changes in skill are being measured against. Systematic definitions of skill are surprisingly hard to come by in the literature on deskilling. We have already seen how the Brighton study gave a detailed definition of the latter phenomenon, but nothing as exact on skill was forthcoming. Despite a chapter entitled, 'A Final Note on Skill', Braverman avoids a positive definition. As Putnam (1978) points out, skill tends to be defined negatively and by implication, as part of Braverman's case against the sociological 'upgrading thesis'. This critique centres upon an attack on misleading statistics, training times and a confusion between skill and *dexterity*.

However, the general picture built up in the assessment of changes in the labour process is that skill is largely based on knowledge, the unity of conception and execution, and the exercise of control by the workforce. This ties in with one of the few attempts to define skill closely, as 'knowledgeable practice' within 'elements of control' (Council for Science and Society, 1981: 23). But in most cases skill is measured less by a formal definition than by historical context and comparison. The central starting point of many studies has therefore been the nature and transformation of *craft* labour.

Craft: Destruction and Resistance

As Rubery (1980: 256) notes, 'The decline in skills in Braverman is essentially viewed from a craft perspective: before the advent of mechanisation and scientific management, craft workers could control the work process, for knowledge of it was stored in the craftsmen themselves.' This is not an idiosyncrasy of that author. A powerful set of writings has been developed which uses the craft experience to understand major changes in the capitalist labour process.

The perspective

The central theme is that general skills are reduced to job-specific ones, largely as a result of mechanisation. The skills and knowledge of craft workers were crucial to production, but over the first quarter of the twentieth century jobs were broken down, allowing companies frequently to dispense with skilled labour.

The example of the electrical equipment industry

'electrical employers transformed the work of making lamps. The jobs were simplified and divided into minute segments, with the former skills built into the specialised machines. This allowed the companies to cut costs, increase production, and eliminate skilled workers. The craftsmen, who had used their own specialist skill and knowledge to produce the lamps, were replaced by workers — predominantly women — who performed only one special operation and required little training to do the job.'

(Brecher, 1979: 208)

Historians such as Montgomery (1976, 1979), Hinton (1973) and Stone (1973) stress the essential role of *control* as the basis for the exercise of craft skill. According to Montgomery, industrial craftsmen such as iron and steel workers and miners were able to use this control to regulate the hours, pace and elements of the price of their labour. Much of this power and control was of course related to the sub-contracting arrangements discussed earlier, in sectors like mining and manufacturing (Dix, 1979).

Writers like Montgomery and Hinton go further than Braverman by emphasising the *political* importance of craftsmen's organisation in attempts to extend job control into wider movements for workers' control of production.[4] It was politically important, too, in another sense. The battle over craft skills was part of a general struggle by employers in this period to *rationalise* production throughout the USA and Europe. With the gradual destruction of the old labour system, mechanisation in the context of the emergence of the large factory became the framework for decisive changes in work organisation, technology and payment systems.

The stress on the craft period and the erosion of skills by mechanisation and later by scientific management implicitly identifies it with the transition from formal to real subordination of labour (Coombs, 1978). The trend is extended beyond the period described by Marx,[5] and the transition is theorised *as* deskilling by Braverman, Brighton LPG and others, as Cressey and MacInnes (1980) note in their critique of the concepts. Marx's stress on real subordination resulting in the creation of labour as 'living appendages' of machinery is filled out by reference to technical and organisational changes Marx could not have wholly forseen.

One such development was the assembly line. Gartman's (1979) study of the introduction of assembly work at Ford indicates that shortage of skilled labour and the indispensability of those skills gave a high degree of control to sections of the workforce. But assembly allowed the progressive dividing of labour, the all-round mechanic giving way to specialised operatives. The elimination of skilled workers was also made possible by the emergence of precisely machined and interchangeable parts. In a clear evocation of the idea of real subordination, Gartman comments that: 'Ford's mass production methods rendered workers largely powerless and hence gave capital a free hand to step up exploitation' (1979: 200).[6]

The other significant development was the fragmentation of even job-specific skills through work reorganisation on Taylorist lines. For example, in the jewellery industry in more recent times, semi-skilled workers who had traditionally done assembly and soldering tasks were confronted with the 'set-up' for the work based on an externally designed process on precut, heat-resistant boards, stamped with the design impressions of the jewellery style (Shapiro-Perl, 1979: 282−3).

It must be said, however, that many writers have been careful to stress the long and uneven process involved in deskilling. Crafts like carpentry and printing have undergone waves of deskilling in the past century, related largely to technical innovation. In the late nineteenth century, machine wood-working technology slowly developed into a strong challenge to the carpenters' craft position (Reckman, 1979). Not only could 'green labour' be introduced to perform task-specific jobs, but changes in the labour process allowed capital to launch an attack on the weakened craft unions. In many cases they were forced to sign working agreements which gave employers unrestricted use of tools, machinery and labour. Nevertheless, skills survived in modified form. Similarly in the printing industry, significant levels of operator skill were retained through a number of technical changes — including the teletypesetter — which allowed newspapers to receive news stories in the form of already perforated tape.

More recent changes in such industries have often provided a more profound challenge to traditional skills. Zimbalist notes that: 'When the computer made its debut in the news-paper composing room in 1962, the eventual extinction of all craft vestiges became a certainty (1979: 108). In carpentry, factory production of house parts (doors, windows, etc.) has been the main source of the challenge, rather than new tools and machinery used by carpenters themselves. Craft-designated work remains, but largely as a result of 'the evolution of a maze of archaic work rules specifying trade jurisdiction, responsibilities and prerogatives' (Reckman, 1979: 93).

The craft perspective does not only utilise industrial ex-amples. As in the case of Braverman, the notion of all-round skill and knowledge is often extended to white-collar work. Reid (1978) notes that older clerks working in local govern-ment experienced a 'loss of craft' associated with computer-related fragmentation; and similar observations are made by Crompton and Reid (1982) and Glenn and Feldberg (1979). Nevertheless, even allowing for modifications to the general craft perspective, it is still one that is rejected by other theor-ists as an inadequate means of understanding changes in skills and working patterns.

The critique
Even critics of the above perspectives agree that there *were*

varied modes of deskilling from the later period of the nine-teenth century. Littler (1978) shows how the decline of the internal sub-contract system led eventually to the introduction of supervisory labour, whereby 'feed and speed' inspectors, quality control and rate fixers fragmented craft control and the traditional foreman's role. However, Littler, like other commentators, argues that Braverman's analysis is permeated by idealised conceptions of the traditional craft workers.

This constitutes one of the two major strands of the critique of Braverman and the deskilling concept, and it has a number of different components. At its simplest level this involves a challenge to the significance given to skilled work of a craft nature. A large proportion of the industrial population was, and is, in non-factory, manual occupations like transport and mining. Although they had a specific type of skill and control of their own, it could not be compared with factory work concerned with discrete operations on separate machines (More, 1982). Even within the manufacturing sector the craft ideal obscures the fact that it was embodied in only a small minority of the working class (Putnam, 1978). This 'romance' is further challenged by Cutler (1978) on the grounds that it was an idealisation of the range of meaningful mental and manual capabilities exercised in the productive process.

This latter point has been consistently raised in more con-ventional empirical accounts of the period. More argues that it is possible to overestimate the actual degree of craft or skill, rather than dexterity, of such workers. Such arguments over-lap with sociological accounts of the social construction of skills as occupational strategies to control recruitment and rewards. The designation of craft work is seen as little more than a restrictive device (Flanders, 1964; Turner, 1962). Hence job control can be confused with genuine exercise of control over the labour process. This distinction allows Monds (1976) to make a very negative assessment of the craft tradi-tion, arguing that, even before Taylorism, craft control had been destroyed by new technologies and anti-union offen-sives.[7]

These views simply do not square with the substantial amount of evidence already examined indicating the genuine levels of skill, knowledge and control exercised by craft workers. Yet the criticisms do raise a very important point. By elevating craft workers to such importance, there is a danger that an analysis is constructed which unduly *separates* them from *non-craft* workers, many of whom were subject to similar pressures from capital concerning their skills, rewards and working conditions. For example, economic pressures built up in the late 1920s and early 1930s impelling employers to take a greater interest in neo-Taylorite and other rationalisation schemes. But by the time they were implemented, many of the industries had either already shifted to non-craft work, such as in metalworking, or, in the case of sectors like food, drink and tobacco, had been *set up* on the basis of semi- and unskilled labour (Littler, 1982a: 141).

Furthermore, outside the manufacturing sector work could not involve the same degree of specialisation, and 'involved a considerable degree of control over the process' (More, 1978: 4). Work traditionally defined as semi-skilled, such as dock-work, could embody high work satisfaction related to the variety of tasks and problems requiring use of experience and knowledge (Mills, 1979). Factories themselves still often depended on a variety of machines and operations, limiting the degree of specialisation for semi-skilled workers. The gradual development of new forms of work organisation and technology increasingly put non-craft workers under the threat of fragmentation and deskilling. Yet these trends are relatively unrecognised within a craft perspective. This threat did not always become actuality. Paradoxically, in idealising craft work, it is possible to overestimate its destruction.[8]

There were a number of mechanisms that counteracted deskilling, and these mechanisms have acted as the focus for the second strand of criticism of the perspectives associated with Braverman. The main theme of these criticisms is the effect of *worker resistance* on the deskilling process. It is not just a question of Braverman and others omitting reference to industrial struggles. It is wrong to study craft skills without examining the role of craft *organisation* in mediating the relations between technological development and skill in the labour process.

These are not just general points of criticism. Studies indicate a considerable amount of craft resistance to mechanisation in industries such as building, engineering and textiles (Friedman, 1977a; Penn, 1978; Lee, 1980). Such resistance could be quite successful in retaining levels of skill and rewards, with the key role being played by mechanisms of *social exclusion*. Penn shows how spinning and engineering workers were able to maintain structural support for their skills by retaining social control over the utilisation of machinery, and by a double means of exclusion: first, of management from complete control of the work process; and second of other non-craft workers who offered a threat to their position (Penn, 1978: 4–5).

Worker resistance can also have wider consequences. For example, attempts by skilled workers to control the supply of labour at the level of the firm and of society (and thus resist dilution by semi-skilled workers, women entering the labour force, etc.) can create *segmentation* in the *labour market*. This segmentation may help workers to retain skills, as it reduces employers' freedom to interchange the workforce. Furthermore, the question of the effects of the labour market is an independently important aspect of the study of skills and the labour process. The labour market often mediates the pace and extent of changes in work organisation and skill, and its fluctuating requirements can aid workers' tactics of exclusion. The result is the survival of a higher number of craft jobs than the deskilling thesis would appear to indicate. Such markets are themselves reflections of wider local and national economic contexts. A notable example was the situation in Coventry and the Midlands during and after the Second World War. Rearmament programmes and general economic expansion sustained a tight labour market in an area with one of the highest densities of skilled engineering workers in the world. This situation enabled workers to impose the Coventry Toolroom Agreement on the engineering employers, which was to guarantee high earnings and the protection of skilled status until the beginning of the 1970s.

A craft perspective is *not* incompatible with a recognition of worker resistance. Montgomery (1979) shows how workers used both technical knowledge and a code of moral collectivity often embodied in the work rules of unions to enable the continuation of resistance even through difficult periods of mechanisation. Yet the point remains that emphasis on skilled workers too often identifies them as the focal point of changes in the labour process. This takes us back to the theme of worker resistance, for such struggles were not the sole province of those workers. As Friedman (1978: 11) argues, it is an error to suggest that the material basis for worker resistance disappears following the spread of modern industry and its consequent partial erosion of skills. In fact the new situation can create the material conditions for successful and organised resistance by the semi- and even unskilled. As the increasing number of semi-skilled workers became proficient in the use of machinery, employers found it more difficult to replace them, and suffered heavy losses if equipment stood idle (Hinton, 1971). Moreover, as both Friedman (1977a) and Nichols and Beynon (1977) show, the distinguishing characteristic of class struggle in the twentieth century has been the use of the collective strength of non-craft workers to oppose capital. While this has been largely unconnected with 'skills', it has involved a more extensive use of tactics connected with machine utilisation.

Non-craft workers' struggle against machinery: an example

'A full documentation of the struggle against the Framing Bucks at Ford's Dagenham Body Plant would show a very high degree of workers' control of the process of production. This control was developed by co-operation among workers, who knew their machine better than Ford knew it, and who were able to use their knowledge in order to block Ford's "repression by the machine". Some people would call this sabotage. It is not. It is the workers' daily struggle against the machine. And in factories like Ford . . . the class battle tends to express itself in resistance to increased workloads, and in a battle in and around time and surplus labour time.'

(Red Notes, 1976)

The labour market could also be used advantageously by non-skilled workers. When there was still relatively full employment in the early 1970s, workers in the motor and other industries used their own mobility from job to job as a means of pushing general wage rates up. Labour turnover at plants like Ford's Dagenham was extremely high, although this situation has obviously changed in the new economic context.

What are some of the points of theoretical significance raised by the critique of craft deskilling? For some critics the inadequate understanding of the role of worker resistance in the labour process can be located in the nature or use of the underlying concept of real subordination of labour. Friedman (1978) argues that the successful retention of aspects of skills and control by workers throws into doubt the significance attached to the distinction between formal and real subordination. Cressey and MacInnes (1980), too, would rather discard this usage, and seek to avoid analysing the struggle between capital and labour within what they refer to as an ahistorical formalism that cannot deal with the complex relations of control and skill.

For others, the variation of trends within the workplace bring into question the concept of homogenisation of labour. *Before* the major deskilling offensives, skilled workers were not a homogeneous group, and their position afterwards with reference to the preservation of skills was often a function of relative strengths *prior* to the development of mechanised factory production (Penn, 1978: 27). But the argument that it is necessary to look at more *specific* situations doesn't satisfactorily resolve these and other major issues raised in the debate. That requires further examination of a number of key points in more general terms.

The Theoretical Issues

There were a number of apparently contradictory emphases in the previous discussion concerning the relationships between labour markets, workplace organisation and the construction and retention of skills. The aim of this section is to discuss whether it is possible to incorporate critical insights within a labour process perspective.

Labour markets and capitalist development

Labour market theories have developed as means of explaining the persistence of segmented and hierarchical structures of allocation and pricing of jobs in the economy as a whole and within particular firms. Some writers emphasise the impact of technological and industrial change in creating a *dual labour market* (Doeringer and Piore, 1971). The key element of this is the emergence of firm-specific skills that encourage employers to develop wage, employment and promotion policies that will develop a stable labour force. An *internal* labour market will thus be dominant over external market pressures. More radical versions emphasise the advantage to employers of the use of segmented labour markets as a means of dividing and controlling a labour force increasingly homogeneous in composition (Gordon, 1972). There is common ground in the assertion that segmentation creates a number of distinct sectors, usually distinguished by some variety of the terms primary and secondary. The former is the dynamic and technologically changing sector, where skills, crafts and professional work are concentrated. The latter is said to be largely stagnant technologically, flexible to demands outside the framework of the major markets, and requiring and using labour that is undifferentiated, low-skilled and irregular in commitment and access to work, for example immigrant and female labour (see Rubery, 1980, for a full discussion).

Such research therefore has direct relevance to the sphere of skills and work: as Lee puts it, 'the production process is overlain by the market process' (1980: 60). In practice, he argues, the labour market operates as a series of social filters between skill and the wider economy and class structure. An examination of the workings of labour markets can provide an important source for modifications of labour process theory. The most important point raised by both Lee and Rubery is the absence of a theory of wage and price determination in studies like Braverman's. The assumption of an immanent tendency towards deskilling relies heavily on the views held by Babbage and Marx that dividing the craft cheapens the parts. But this assumes too readily that 'the effect of price competition in employers will always be the same' (Lee, 1980: 74). In practice, market factors can alter the pace of technical innovation and affect the bargaining position of workers, and therefore their ability to retain skills.[9]

However, there is a difference between establishing the importance of these factors and mapping out the exact relationships between the labour market and the labour process. There are problems here that can be illustrated by looking at the analysis of Lee, who has made one of the most detailed attempts to explain the interrelationships. Priority is given to examining *systemic* (external) shifts in the size and nature of labour markets. There are said to be two forms of external shift, *industrial*, which pertains to factors like new products and processes, and *cyclical*, which refers to the overall fluctuations in economic activity. A third shift is internal to the workplace and is described as *occupational*. These correspond to the kinds of changes dealt with by Braverman. What is significant about Lee's argument is that external shifts are explicitly given more weight and counterposed to direct deskilling in the labour process itself.

Using official employment statistics and reference to a number of industrial studies, Lee asserts that the percentage of skilled operatives in traditional areas of craft work (engineering, shipbuilding, construction, printing) remains high. This is put down to the operation of industrial and cyclical shifts. While both processes have produced a certain amount of deskilling, this is said to have seldom been the product of change within an industry, but rather the result of new products in new industries that are based on an expanded use of semi-skilled labour. However, this trend is counterbalanced by the creation of new areas of skilled work, often using workers displaced from previous craft jobs, and by the survival of 'marginal' sectors using traditional methods.

While the distinction between deskilled *jobs* and deskilled *workers* is a useful one, Lee does not explain the *relationships* between the labour market and labour process, but merely asserts the domination of one over the other.[10] There is no attempt to examine changes in the nature of work in the occupations discussed, and the study is almost wholly reliant on quantitative and official statistics. The 'skills' represented in such sources inevitably tend to reflect existing *bargaining* frameworks rather than accurate assessments of the level of skill.[11] The growth of new industries, technologies and products does of course create new skills. But Lee does not ask whether the examples he gives — for instance electricians — are subject to the same long-term process of deskilling that have affected the older crafts. Evidence we shall examine later indicates that 'crafts' allied to the new electronic technologies *have* been deskilled, in the case of some electricians, by the incorporation of diagnostic skills within the means of testing and repairing machinery.

A serious attempt to link the labour and market processes must give greater emphasis to changes at the point of production. There is evidence that the structures of the labour market may be a partial reflection of what is happening to the nature of work. The erosion of skills has gradually weakened the bargaining position of many skilled workers. Thus workers will act to maintain their position against threats of substitution and competition, and in this battle 'their most effective tactic is to differentiate themselves from potential competitors' (Rubery, 1980: 260).[12] This necessitates attempts to control aspects of both the external and internal labour markets, including control of apprenticeships, promotions by seniority, restrictive practices and demarcation, with redundancy agreements working on the basis of 'last in, first out'. These practices are very likely to be harmful to the interests of sections with less of a stable foothold in the labour market, such as women workers.

Far from 'occupational shifts' having little relevance to deskilling, workers' attempts to control and shape labour markets are aimed to *compensate* for loss of skills and bargaining power, and this indicates 'workers' success in regaining some of the control lost through the destruction of the craft system' (Rubery, 1980: 259). This suggests that particular attention should be paid to *internal* markets. Such a focus does not leave the deskilling thesis unscathed, as it brings into question once more the concept of homogenisation.

Deskilling does not necessarily lead to undifferentiated work, as the labour process can be reconstituted as a new organisation of production dominated by internal labour markets. As Burawoy perceptively points out, *despite* the separation of conception and execution, the expropriation of skill and the narrowing of discretion, studies like Braverman's have 'missed the equally important parallel tendency toward the expansion of choices within narrower limits' (1979: 94). The growth of internal labour markets can therefore act as a counterweight to skill degradation, and this opens up the whole area of the subjective components of deskilling. This is an issue to which we shall return later.

The other area that the study of labour markets rather inadequately directs our attention to is the economic and class relations within which changes in the labour process need to be situated.[13] Too much emphasis in labour process theory has been placed on a generic impulse to deskill, without connecting it to specific economic circumstances. It is true that Braverman does refer to the crucial emergence of 'monopoly capitalism'. But, as mentioned in the previous chapter, this was a decidedly sketchy framework that was better at analysing the changes in the *structure* of monopoly forms and their labour processes than dealing with the problems and contradictions that capital faces in seeking to 'constantly revolutionise' the system of production. As Elger notes, 'Braverman tends to assume a general congruence between strategies of valorisation and accumulation and de-skilling, in which the former is directly lodged within the latter' (1979: 83). Yet this may not be the case. For example, mechanisation has to be financed, and this has to be situated within cycles of fixed capital renewal (Coombs, 1978).

But like other critics, Elger and Coombs do little more than indicate the *need* for an analysis of the labour process that would locate transformations in relation to phases of valorisation and accumulation and their contradictions. A more concrete analysis would have to explain the variety of national and international factors influencing workplace changes. We can return to the example used earlier of skilled engineering workers in the Coventry area. In 1971 the Coventry Employers' Association informed the unions that it was attempting unilaterally to abolish the district 'toolroom' rate, signalling a serious attack on pay, shopfloor practices and skilled status.

This was not just a matter of normal worker—employer conflicts; it reflected rapid changes in the ownership and control of the machine-tool industry in the mid-1960s. Several conglomerates moved in and bought up small and medium-sized companies, and the existing larger machine-tool firms attempted expansion and vertical integration with firms producing components and raw materials (see Coventry Machine Tool Workers' Committee, 1979). The state played a significant role through the Department of Trade and Industry and the Industrial Reorganisation Corporation in encouraging rationalisation in order to strengthen the competitive position of British manufacturers in the face of sharp international pressures. In the 1970s international competition further tightened the screw and gave companies a choice: automate or decline further. Subsequent restructuring inevitably had important effects on skills and the labour process in the industry.

This example highlights the role played by *product markets*. In this context, Kelly (1982a) shows how the massive growth of the consumer goods sector in the post-war period inevitably put a strain on their assembly-line methods geared to long runs on single products. Firms responded in a variety of ways, through built-in obsolescence, factory or section specialisation, and, most significantly for our purposes, attempts to reorganise the labour process itself: hence the experiments undertaken in job enrichment and enlargement such as at Volvo in an effort to create production flexibility.

Pressure from product and labour markets, plus exhaustion of the possibilities contained in the 'Fordist' model of work intensification, therefore *lead* in a number of directions. Aside from the programmes of work humanisation, other important trends include the moves to decentralise production to smaller units and even to outwork in Italy, and the 'export' of Fordism and other methods of advanced capitalist production to parts of the Second and Third Worlds. This search for cheap and docile labour zones has taken place in Eastern Europe, as well as in countries such as Brazil, South Korea and Turkey (Lipietz, 1982). International developments of this kind have acted to strengthen previous trends towards *runaway shops*, where multinationals transfer production to 'underdeveloped' regions. We therefore have to recognise that labour processes are shaped by the contradictory, rather than unilinear, development of capitalist production.

Worker resistance, skill and job control

There is no doubt that there are *cycles* of deskilling and resistance, and that Lee is right in saying that 'the skilled trades have been declared dead at the hands of mechanisation and deskilling many times, but the defence of craft identity and difference lives on' (1978: 3). One manifestation is the consistent practice of 'clawing back' concessions to management on questions of skill and control. Craft control can be re-established at plant level, as engineers did in the early part of this century, using tactics like demarcation disputes (Penn, 1978: 12). Recognition of these processes does cast doubt on the viability of Braverman's objectivist methods. The result is that Braverman is surprisingly deterministic concerning the shaping of work by technological change (Mackenzie, 1977), and overreliant on managerially derived evidence concerning skills and control (Elger, 1979: 64). This creates the paradoxical situation that while the book clearly recognises the role of class struggle in creating workplace antagonism connected to the degradation of labour (Zimbalist, 1979: xii), it ignores its role in the consequent evolution of the labour process.[14]

It is interesting to note that defenders of Braverman, e.g. Zimbalist, rather than make an extensive defence of his methods, tend to argue the long-term ineffectiveness of worker resistance as it has existed. Zimbalist uses his own case study of the printing industry and the inability of craft unionism to reshape or even halt technological development as proof of this point (1979: 125). It is important to make a distinction between resistance that is often informal and unorganised, and a conscious and collective struggle. However, either dimension can modify the course of development of the labour process. But the more important question is, does worker resistance actually retain skills? We have already seen the considerable evidence concerning the social construction of skills for bargaining purposes. Lee dismisses this argument. Union power to enforce skills would not work unless it was based on what he calls 'real technical use-values' of skills. Mechanisms of exclusion and construction so as to control entry and regulate the supply of craft labour are independent phenomena in themselves, rather than a means of compensating for deskilling. Unfortunately, talk of 'real skills' was once again largely unsupported by qualitative evidence on the occupations concerned.[15]

An example of socially created skills

'In Coventry . . . you've got two categories of skilled worker. There are the traditional skilled workers — the toolmaker, the machine tool setter, the engineering maintenance worker — as well as certain other craft skills that are still necessary. These are usually people who've served their time, though in some cases they might be upgraded from the lines. Then there are also a lot of jobs in the motor industry, like fitting on the car track, which in other parts of the country have been allowed to become semi-skilled, whereas here in Coventry we've managed to maintain them as skilled jobs. In fact there's a large number of workers in Coventry who are classed as skilled workers, and who get the skilled rate, even though their "skills" would only take a few days for anyone to pick up.'

(car worker quoted in *Factfolder*, 1972)

The essential confusion is between the ability of workers to retain skills and *job control*. There is considerable evidence that workers can exercise the power to determine elements of working conditions and rewards, *after* deskilling has taken place (Elger, 1979: 74—7; Rubery, 1980: 262, 264). In his case study of electrical workers, Brecher shows how, in the wake of mechanisation and subdivision, the establishment of industrial unionism in the 1930s involved the creation of a substantial amount of direct control over the work process through the grievance procedure, steward system and regulation of production (1979: 213). In fact deskilling can sometimes *confer* bargaining power in circumstances where mechanisation replaces craft labour with semi-skilled workers who have been previously unskilled. This enabled such workers to exercise some control over output and in general to extend workplace organisation (Rubery, 1980: 256—63). Once established, it is possible for machine operatives to use that strength, leading Nichols and Beynon to note correctly that: 'Skill is not essential to control' (1977: 108).

What *are* often retained are specific dexterities, which still involve levels of training, if for no other reason than they are the 'tricks of the trade'. Forms of expertise may be narrower than traditional skills, but they can still 'constitute effective obstacles to capitalist initiative' (Elger, 1979: 76). Once again, therefore, the struggle in the labour process persists through craft deskilling, and it is unnecessary to deny the importance of the erosion to acknowledge that worker resistance reconstitutes the struggle at a different level. Where does this leave the concept of real subordination of labour?

The lesson is that no amount of deskilling or mechanisation can lead to the *complete* domination of capital over labour. There is always a danger of conceiving of real subordination as a finished and self-contained process. This is particularly the case when allied to major changes in the organisation of production such as the assembly line. Real subordination is best thought of as a *tendency*, and as a *precondition* for a more direct control of labour given by the use of developments in the productive forces (Friedman, 1978: 13).[16] As the concept primarily pertains to issues of control rather than skill, we shall return to it in Chapter 5.

The Contemporary Restructuring of Work

Compared to the amount of material that exists on the mechanisation of craft work, evidence is patchy about contemporary changes in the labour process allied to newer forms of technology. The critique by Braverman, and Nichols and Beynon and others of the naive optimism of industrial sociology's 'golden future of automation' was necessary, but insufficient. To go further requires a close look at what is happening to the nature of work under the most 'advanced' conditions of capitalist production. This is particularly important in that

much of the craft discussion simply did not update the analysis
to the more recent period.

Motive forces for change

As well as trying to show how automation is a logical extension of previous forms of organisation of production, it is
important to examine what is different about the contemporary situation. New technologies and work organisations have
always provided the opportunities to impose greater control
over the workforce and to lower costs through dividing and
reducing skills. Current developments, centred upon computer technology, radically increase those possibilities. One
study of automation in the factory quotes a worker as saying,
'They have wanted to slam us for a long time. Now they have
the bat to do it with' (quoted in Shaiken, 1979: 26). One
example of a direct hit was the attack on the key trade group
of pipeline welders through automated 'robot' welding machines. The organisation of flying pickets was understandable
when management intentions were revealed: 'With these
machines we can have less qualified people and pay them
considerably less' (Project Director on Norwest Socea Site,
quoted in *The Sunday Times Business News*).

The advantages of automation over conventional mechanisation for capital have been recognised for a long time. As
Palloix points out, the co-ordination and utilisation of mechanised production could never provide the conditions for
maximum productivity. A considerable amount of discretion
was left in workers' hands (1976: 54—6). But extensive automation has always been limited by technical and economic
factors. Two major developments have altered this. First,
'The microprocessor offers the possibility of copying intel-
ligent human responses and incorporating them into machinery
at a minimal cost' (CIS, 1980: 4). Second, the recession has
accelerated the tendency towards the restructuring of capital
on a national and international scale.

Declining rates of profit not only lead to pressure for the
competitive rationalisation of resources, but impels a search
for new forms of technology that can be used to restructure
work relations. But it would be misleading to say that the

major force of change was an *intention* to deskill. New technologies and products have led to frantic reorganisation within
and between companies on a national and international scale.
On the whole, therefore, effects on skills have been consequences of the exigencies of the market. For example, most
micro-electronic companies were originally located in what
was dubbed 'Silicon Valley' in California. However, using
cheap, largely female and immigrant labour, the production
of chips was still capital-intensive. But related assembly
and testing is more labour-intensive. This provided the basis
for an expansion into countries like Malaysia, the Philippines
and Indonesia, which had the potential for greater subordination of a labour force that had no experience of factory work
and was susceptible to the manipulation of patriarchal cultural
traditions (Duncan, 1981).

But even in the metropolitan countries new forms of technology can make worker resistance more difficult, and this
constitutes another distinctive feature of the contemporary
situation. Some of the difficulty is related mainly to market
pressures, when, at a time of technical innovation, employers
can threaten to shift production unless new machines and
practices are accepted. But much of it is related directly to
the use of the technology to modify the labour process itself.
A dramatic example occurred when General Motors smashed
a die-makers' strike by taking away the computer tapes and
resumed production at another plant (CSE Microelectronics
Group, 1980: 85). Past practices of extracting rewards and
maintaining job controls, even when the structure of the
labour force has been bypassed technologically, is much less
likely to be successful. Indeed, traditional defences against
deskilling are now being more seriously challenged. Computer-
based machinery can allow employers to cross demarcation
lines by alternative programming, or change the speed of work
without entry on the shop floor (TUC, 1981).

At present most trade union efforts have been understand-
ably directed towards delaying new technology until job
protection and attractive buy-out clauses have been worked
out. Whether in bastions of craft unionism like printing (Zimbalist, 1979) or centres of traditional job control like the
docks (Mills, 1979), it has proved extraordinarily hard to

resist the combined effects of adverse market conditions and technological change on skills and control. This is particularly the case when new technology can be projected as highly sophisticated and requiring a stable and skilled workforce. This has happened in dockwork related to containerisation, and only after implementation did workers come to realise that 'the range of skills and experience which routinely come into play is dramatically narrowed' (Mills, 1979: 139). It all adds to a general feeling that 'you can't fight the machine'. The possibilities of alternative strategies for dealing with new technology will be considered in Chapter 8. To take this discussion further it is necessary to examine some case-study evidence in major sectors of the economy.

The application of new technology

It seems apposite to start at the heart of new technology — computer work itself. As Kraft (1979) shows in his study of the *industrialisation* of computer programming, there has been a long history of sub-division of the previous 'whole tasks' involved. But the three major sub-divisions — systems analysis, programming and coding — still had substantially overlapping boundaries and dependence on the software skills of programmers. Research by Kraft and other writers shows that subsequent developments in the electronic data-processing (EDP) industry have strongly modified that position in a number of ways, as managers have come under pressure to exert greater control over the workforce in the face of greater competitive pressures (Greenbaum, 1976).

A key facet of the changes has been the development of specialised high-level computer languages which require less trained operatives both to write complex programmes and retrieve data (Reid, 1978: 12). These standardised programs known as 'packages' or 'turnkey', require fewer technical skills and less knowledge of how the computers actually work. 'Structured' programming emphasises management-set patterns of work that allow tighter methods of control. One article in *Data Processing* argued that the programmer must be 'separated from both hardware and software programming so he can produce an independently measurable amount of work ... It is imperative that the specific task of the programmer be made as small as possible' (quoted in Harman, 1979: 11). The last point indicates that the freeing of management from dependence on highly skilled software workers made possible widespread task fragmentation (Kraft, 1979: 11) and the separation of conception and execution, as the former is now built in to the automatic process (Crompton, 1978: 4).

Furthermore, the new content of work made it possible to establish a clearer hierarchy of authority as responsibility and skills were pushed upwards. This more specialised and segmented division of labour can involve geographical and technical separation of the work of computer operators, programmers and systems analysts (Reid, 1978: 10), even to the point where in some workplaces programmers are prohibited from entering the computer room (Greenbaum, 1976: 47). One result is that employers are able to recruit new staff with fewer qualifications. Rapid routinisation and deskilling restrict career opportunities within companies, and splits develop between routine programmers — often women — and male, highly skilled sub-occupations in specialist areas (Kraft, 1979: 17).

This is one example of the way in which technological change is developing for the first time in the office and white-collar sectors, jobs that have often previously been immune from the deskilling process. We have already referred to the use of new office technology such as the word processor as a means of accelerating the routinisation of office work. A recent study by Glenn and Feldberg found no evidence of increased autonomy or integration of tasks. Instead, computerised machinery requires that information be treated in a standardised and fragmented form. Although clerical workers may be less directly supervised, the requirements of the machine replace the directness of an immediate supervision (1979: 57). Furthermore, although some routine jobs such as tabulating are eliminated, others like keying data into terminals come into being. Once more the creative tasks are located further up the occupational hierarchy.

Obviously such developments also create a new division of labour, with a greater 'polarisation between top secretarial, administrative jobs on the one hand, and routine, machine minding jobs on the other' (CSE Microelectronics Group,

1980: 49). The resultant depersonalisation of the relations between managers and secretarial staff is intensified by the reorganisation of work on the basis of clerical pooling arrangements. Recognition of the consequences of these types of changes is given in the sales pitch of companies dealing in office automation. One reproduced a testimonial from a grateful customer that: 'a less experienced typist is able to produce the same quality of work as a really skilled girl and almost as quickly' (quoted in CIS Report, 1980, 11). Another source has stated that careful staff selection of the new 'correspondence secretaries' related to the word processor should be designed to ensure that they 'have an aptitude for thoroughness and application, but are not perhaps particularly extrovert personalities' (quoted in ASTMS, 1980: 43).

As far as new technology in the factory is concerned, great publicity has been given to the introduction of robots. But this is partly misleading, as high purchasing and installation costs are limiting their use at the present time.[17] The jobs that robots *are* doing, such as paint-spraying and welding, are indicative of the low-skill tasks which existing devices are capable of replacing, although additions such as sensors will expand this range. It is more important at the moment to look at extensions of the trends associated with intensive mechanisation, for example in numerical control machinery. The introduction of numerical control (NC) reduced the amount of operator skill and control, but left a reasonable degree of discretion in the worker's hands through mechanisms such as the use of the 'override' switch for cutting out tape control (CSE, 1980: 58). The new generation of direct numerical control (DNC) and similar systems can further erode this discretion. Because the machine tool is linked to a central computer that guides and monitors the machine operation, it allows greater control of the machinist's activity.

There is no inevitability in this. The systems embody the possibility of greater creative input from the operator through powerful mini-computers that allow the part program to be altered at the machine. Indeed, recent research at Manchester University has shown that programming at the machine by skilled workers can be *more* efficient. However, this course of action can be blocked by a key on the control panel that locks it against unauthorised operator use. As Shaiken shows, this

is the most likely course of events. He quotes the chairman of
an industrial development division as noting that it would be
'very undesirable to have the operator do any programming.
This would take away control of the production environment'
(1979: 33). Detailed evidence of the progressive loss of skill
and job control is also provided by engineering workers themselves, although future developments are still problematical
(Coventry Machine Tool Workers' Committee, 1979).[18]

Numerical control is also being applied to other areas such
as the clothing industry, where the sewing machine can be
automatically programmed for a variety of different tasks
(GMWU, 1980: 10), and the stitcher becomes a machine
loader and fabric positioner able to tend more than one
machine at a time, and requiring less training (Lamphere,
1979: 263). But this kind of automation is also affecting
technical factory jobs such as the work of draughtsmen. The
techniques of computer-aided design (CAD), first developed
in the 1960s, mean that the designer no longer works on a
drawing board, but in front of a cathode-ray tube. The computer can follow the 'pen' of the designer, greatly increasing
the speed of the drawings, and can automatically show the
design from various angles and dimensions. It can also delete
lines, hold all information in a 'data file' and produce drawings automatically if needed.

The CAD machine

'This is likely to be accompanied by the subordination
of the operator (designer) to the machine (computer),
with the narrow specialisation of Taylorism leading to
the fragmentation of design skills and a loss of panoramic
view of the design activity itself. In consequence, standard routines and optimisation techniques may seriously
limit the creativity of the designer, because the subjective
value judgements would be dominated by the "objective"
decision of the system . . . There is already evidence to
show that the CAD when introduced on the basis of so-
called efficiency, gives rise to a de-skilling of the design
function and a loss of job security.'

(Cooley, 1980: 29—30)

One of the most interesting applications of new technology is the MINOS system in the mining industry. Following a massive investment programme, collieries will be operated from a central control room, using a system of minicomputers installed in coal-face machines (Feickert, 1979). Miners were one of the groups that actually gained in *power* following the mechanisation of face-work after the Second World War. Access to a higher level of technology gave groups of workers considerable job control and arguably increased aspects of skills (Yarrow, 1979).[19] However, the precise effects on skills of the new situation remain unclear: 'The MINOS system will subordinate labour to machinery and shift control of production above the surface to management' (Duncan, 1981: 198). Under existing arrangements there is little other than the financial 'supervision' of piece-work schemes, deputies being primarily responsible for safety. This will be replaced by computer control, although the operators themselves will be unskilled. As Feickert shows, they will be using a simple push-button command system, whose ultimate planning and control will rest with a secondary *management* computer with restricted terminals located only in managers' offices. If, therefore, control can be an important dimension of skill, then a reduction in such discretionary powers must be included as part of the deskilling process.

The persistence of limits to deskilling
New technology does add to the power of capital to restructure the labour process, but it would be wrong to present it as if there were no important constraints. As is normal in any period of major technological change, new skills are still being created. In fact there appears to be a consensus among trade union commentators that the general trend is towards a *polarisation* between a minority of highly trained and rewarded workers, and the majority of the low skilled and less well rewarded (GMWU, 1980; TGWU, 1979).

This is particularly the case in the computer industry itself. Whereas hardware production is machine-dictated and management-controlled, the software design process is still often at a *craft* stage of development with a high level of worker discretion and skill. An indication of this is the way that programmers refer to working on *their* program (Duncan,

1981). However, this is under attack through the standardisation of programming, and the creative input is at its peak in the design and development stage. This is confirmed in my own research on the development of the new System X automatic telephone exchanges. Technical workers were highly involved in complex testing of the machinery, but were aware that it will get to a stage 'where it's very elaborate, just pushing a button and quite literally getting told where the fault is and fixing it, but they're not there yet' (quoted in Thompson, 1981: 220).

Nevertheless, such examples indicate that the application of new technology is taking a highly varied form. Moreover it cannot have universal application. For example, in wholesale distribution full automation is normally only possible with homogeneous stock. Partial automation is more likely, with overhead cranes controlled by microprocessors substituting for fork-lift drivers, and the additional 'hidden' jobs involving unskilled labouring and machine overseers. In small-batch production such variation is inevitable, given the number of potential products and components. Indeed, microelectronics will extend the range of machines that small-batch production managements can choose from, and these conditions 'still require, to the annoyance of capital, a considerable degree of worker involvement, initiative and control' (CSE Microelectronics Group, 1980: 60).

The introduction of new technology will not only depend on costs and existing industrial situations, but on factors already identified, such as the state of workers' organisation and labour markets. In a study of the use of numerical control in engineering, Jones (1982) argues that these factors are independent influences on the *divisibility* of skills. The uncritical attitude taken by most unions towards the effects of new technology on the *content* of work, rather than on the amount of jobs, makes it unlikely that serious resistance will be put upon this level, at least in the short term. However, management cannot fully control the conditions under which labour is utilised, and this allows workers to 'claw back' skills.[20] In addition, management does not always utilise the full potential of micro-electronics. For example, in office work a small number of word processors not linked to a larger computer system will have a very different effect on skills — both positive and negative — than a fully integrated system in a larger concern. The research of Reid (1978) also gives useful evidence of the constraints related to the operation of the labour market for computer work. Employers may be unable to afford to routinise the labour process beyond a certain point owing to the negative impact this would have on the ability to recruit high competence staff and avoid excessive labour turnover. In addition an employer may not benefit from complete homogenisation of the workforce. A uniform mass of low grade workers may bring problems of control that are more costly than the cheapening of labour through deskilling.

This raises the question of whether the trend towards deskilling is actually *reversible*. Friedman (1977b, 1978) argues forcefully that deskilling is not an inherent tendency and that there is no single technological direction under capitalism. This is said to result primarily from managerial accommodation to worker resistance. That such accommodation takes place is undeniable. Numerous studies have shown that in the face of 'labour problems', a variety of types of job enrichment and enlargement have been introduced by capital (Pignon and Querzola, 1976: Bosquet, 1980).[21] But this does not necessarily indicate an alternative general direction for skills and the labour process, for as the Brighton Labour Process Group points out, the re-combination of fragmented tasks through job enlargement *presupposes* deskilling (1977: 20). More importantly, the purpose for capital is to ensure the retention of *control* in a context where more qualified workers are often faced with less skilled and demanding work (Reid, 1978: Coriot, 1980).

It is possible to identify technical aspects of job enrichment whereby work satisfaction and commitment may be increased by modifying marginal aspects of work organisation. But the key focus remains control. Friedman confirms this with his presentation of alternative strategies open to capital of *direct control* and *responsible autonomy*. In the latter instance, groups of workers or an individual operative are given a wider measure of discretion over the direction of work, with a minimum of supervision as a means of maintaining overall managerial authority (1977b: 48). While discretion *is* a dimension of skill, the full discussion of job enrichment is best located within an analysis of strategies and forms of control. We will therefore return to this question in Chapter 5.

Conclusion: the Unsubstantiated Connections

Friedman is right to say that there may be times when capital prefers not to deskill in its own economic interest, but to assert further that 'capital has nothing against skilled workers' (1978: 16) is stretching the case beyond credibility. Evidence does now show that factors such as labour markets and worker resistance operate as constraints on the divisibility of skills. It is also the case that there are cycles of deskilling, related to the conditions of capital accumulation, that manifest contradictory tendencies between and within industries. These constraints and variations are important, and question the rather one-dimensional and unilinear approach of writers like Braverman. Workers' skills, however, *are* normally an obstacle to the full utilisation of the means of production by capital. *How* that obstacle is modified or removed depends on the specific circumstances. But the fact that variation of circumstances between and within sectors negates a crude deskilling thesis has unfortunately been used to construct an overly 'agnostic' perspective, as in Wood's introduction to his (1982) collection of articles. Deskilling remains the major *tendential* presence within the development of the capitalist labour process.[22]

The real problem with the debate, particularly concerning criticisms of Braverman, is that far too much emphasis has been placed on the *extent* of deskilling and not enough on the assumed *consequences* for the nature and experience of work. This particularly affects the concepts of homogenisation and degradation of labour. In the case of homogenisation, it has already been noted that it is a concept generally used unevenly and by implication, rather than in an explicit sense. Nevertheless, it underlies important aspects of the work of Marx, Braverman and modern writing on manual work (CSE Microelectronics Group, 1980: 82) and white-collar workers with reference to the parallel concept of proletarianisation (Cooley, 1981; Glenn and Feldberg, 1979). Homogenisation is a weak link in the chain of argument on skills and the labour process. There is a great difference between all work being subject tendentially to the same *trends* with respect to skills, and saying that all work is the *same*. As the starting points of occupations are different, experiences and consequences will vary correspondingly.

This can be illustrated if we take the process of proletarianisation. It can be misleading to say that clerical workers have suffered a loss of skill and control. Many jobs were created *after* changes in the general conditions and nature of work, thus making meaningful comparisons with the past problematic (Gagliani, 1981: 281).[23] Even where proletarianisation is experienced, the different conditions of clerical labour render the idea of homogenisation inadequate as a means of comparison with the deskilling of factory jobs. As Jones (1978) points out, Braverman is either imprecise or objectivist in concluding that the 'proletarian form' impresses itself on the middle layers of employment. The crucial question is what aspect of the work is concerned. Middle-layer occupations have been affected by routinisation and fragmentation, but they still carry out important functions on behalf of capital in relation to other workers (Crompton, 1978; T. J. Johnson, 1980). Shifts in types of consciousness and activity should therefore be looked at from both angles and not assumed to be part of a single tendency covering all workers. Similar points can be made about manual work. Not everyone experiences deskilling directly. My own research into the telecommunications industry has shown that new technology that has largely eliminated craft work and further eroded other assembly skills is located in a completely separate plant, using largely different labour that had little conception of the previous work (Thompson, 1981). Hence there is a distinction between whether deskilling is technically taking place and its effects on workplace consciousness. This understanding has to be added to the more traditional criticisms that homogenisation is limited by worker fear of competition from the external labour market (Rubery, 1980: 260), and because of the strength of resistance from different groups of workers in general (Friedman, 1977b: 47). A more realistic picture of skills and differentiation in the working class is indicated by Elger in his comment that deepening subordination and mechanisation have not created a simple homogeneous mass of deskilled labour, but 'a complex, internally differentiated apparatus of collective labour which contained an uneven variety of narrow skills and specific dexterities' (1979: 82).

This highlights a further unsubstantiated connection in the deskilling argument: that of the degradation of work. There is no doubt that for many the experience of work has become more alienating, with respect to loss of skills, discretion, or other factors such as the decline of an occupational culture in jobs such as dockwork (Mills, 1979). But once again, degradation is a matter of *experience*, and this is affected by phenomena wider than the conventional 'objective' features of work. In her study of women clerical workers, Tepperman shows that many are taking an increasing 'pride' in their work. This is partly because of the realisation of its economic importance, partly because of the retention of problem-solving skills, but it is also in *reaction* to the labelling of female, clerical labour as mindless and unimportant (1976: 7—9). It is also possible that the 'gadgetry' aspect of advanced machinery in offices and other areas creates a positive identification with the new skills, even if they are located in the machine and not in the operator! Similarly, semi-skilled manual workers can feel some positive identification with their specific dexterities, again comparing their own detailed knowledge of production conditions with that of foremen and management (Mulcahy and Faulkner, 1979: 238). For craft and technical workers, their extensive theoretical knowledge can counteract degradation, even if there is a disjuncture with its actual usage in the work situation.

These factors also emphasise a previous point, that participation in workplace labour markets and structures can 'allow the degradation of work to pursue its course without continuing crises' (Burawoy, 1979: 94). Even when acknowledging a more limited connection between deskilling and degradation, the consequences may not always be positive in terms of working-class action. The same processes that deskill labour can also partly atomise workers (Ehrenreich and Ehrenreich,

1976), and encourage 'horizontal' forms of conflict directed more at other workers than management (Burawoy, 1979). These themes will be taken up again in the final chapter. But what can be said for the moment is that while the deskilling debate has added considerably to our understanding of the nature of work, it has not, in Braverman's words, painted a picture of the working class 'as it really is'.

5

Forms of Control and Resistance

Under all systems of social production, management of physical and human resources is necessary. Within capitalism, the managing of resources has become *management*, a specialised function with two dimensions. *Co-ordination* is necessary to avoid the haphazard and wasteful use of the instruments of labour, and to meet the requirements of purchasing, finance, marketing and other factors. *Exercise of authority* over the labour of others is, however, a means of obtaining 'the desired work behaviour from others' (Edwards, 1979: 17). Edwards goes on to clarify the components of any *system of control*.[1] These consist of the mechanisms by which employers direct work tasks; the procedures whereby they supervise and evaluate performance in production; and the apparatus of discipline and reward (1979: 18). Of course, such means of coercive workplace power are not limited to capitalism, but are characteristics of any class-divided society.

This chapter examines the key issues connected with forms of management and control, and the responses of workers. Of particular importance are the specific origins of control within the capitalist mode of production, for in the development of the factory system loose forms of control became *systematic* management. A critical evaluation of that transformation is a necessary precursor to a proper assessment of Taylorism, taking the discussion of Chapters 1 and 3 to a more detailed conclusion. One of the problems of dealing with the labour process debates on control is that the major alternatives to the tradition deriving from Marx, Braverman and others are so self-contained in their particular conceptual and historical structures that direct comparison between them is difficult. The common theme is a rejection of the view that the capitalist development of the labour process is accompanied by the growth of the authority of management and employers. Therefore the chapter assesses in different sections the major alternatives associated with Friedman and Edwards by setting out their major ideas and linking them to related and more general issues such as the significance of job enrichment and the interrelations between modern control structures. The adequacy of concepts of control and management can then be examined in the light of the overlapping ideas.

The Origins of Capitalist Control

All of the major writers on the labour process and systems of control — Friedman, Edwards, Braverman and Burawoy — retain Marx's framework, discussed in Chapter 2, which states that when the capitalist purchases labour power, he is only acquiring potential. As Friedman points out, 'Marx emphasised this managerial problem by calling labour power "variable capital" ' (1977a: 78). That variability, based on independent worker activity, means that to turn labour power into labour for profitable production requires systematic control by capital of the labour process. When Marx wrote about the shift from manufacture to large-scale industry, the methods of capital were related to the high degree of control exercised by the immediate producers in that period. But even now, with greater sophistication in managerial methods and technology, the same problem is reproduced in different and modified forms.

This much, then, is common ground. Complications arise when attempts are made to specify *how* control is acquired and maintained. Although no specific schema is spelt out in great detail by Marx, we have seen that he relies on concepts like factory despotism and the transition to real subordination of labour. For despotism to exist requires neither the personal dictatorship of employers, nor methods that are overtly repressive. But it does require a hierarchical chain of command. That command is given a material framework when capital can use science and machinery to control labour through the production process itself. Hence Marx's usage of the notion of real subordination.

We have already discussed some of the problems attached to that concept. Yet it is an important one, for it establishes the necessity for capital constantly to *revolutionise* the labour process in order to secure increased productivity and profits. The relation of ownership itself is insufficient, a point not grasped by Monds in his argument against the view that employers had to *win* control over working conditions and rewards from craft workers:

> After all, the employers had negotiated the wage scales in the first place. They also bought the raw materials, decided on the level of output (by deciding on the level of employment) and, ultimately, realised the surplus value produced by selling the final product. 'That is all', as Montgomery might say, but surely that is everything.

> (Monds, 1976: 90)

If it *was* everything, the struggle for control would be irrelevant, and the assumption that employment levels wholly determine output is utterly naive. A similar point is made in a more practical way by Friedman. He points out that there is a confusion in the use of the word *control* between 'an absolute sense, to identify those "in control", and in a relative sense, to signify the degree of power people have to direct work' (1977a: 45). Real subordination may indicate a new stage in capital's command over work, but it is still a *relative* process, given that it is possible to develop further the technical means of control in production. We shall return to this issue in the remaining sections of the chapter. If the period of the establishment of large-scale industry is examined, it is clear that capital was developing means of control based on the personal and mechanical discipline of the factory. Yet despite the increase in the authority of capital, there was still little evidence of a conscious strategy of *management* of labour: why? Edwards suggests that under the conditions of *competitive capitalism*, employers were able to exercise authority directly. This is described as *simple control*.

This structure was based on the small size and lack of sophistication of manufacturing activity. As a result it is argued that the entrepreneur directly supervised the work, foremen and pay arrangements. In an environment where the employer saw, knew and decided everything, his personal control rendered workers equal in their powerlessness (Edwards, 1979: 25—6). Only when the size of the workforce grew beyond the personal ties to the employer was there a basis for successful worker resistance. The dominance of simple control is held to be further undermined by the growing concentration of economic resources, with the increased social and complex character of production re-quiring planning and delegation of authority. Out of the consequent contradictions of controlling the workplace and coping with shopfloor action, capital is said to be forced into experimentation with systematic forms of management.

This is a persuasive image of the transition from control to management. But it is inaccurate and misleading. Evidence on the small size and capitalisation of the firm is not matched by any parallel accounts of the actual operation of firms. Although workshops and early factories were often set up to maximise the potential of direct supervision of labour, this was still relative to the skills and job control exercised by many workers, particularly in the craft category. Even if the evidence of Braverman, Stone, Montgomery and others is taken as partly romanticising the craft tradition, the idea that employers knew and decided everything belies the real struggle over control that raged as the factory system matured. In addition it ignores the sub-contracting arrangements which gave workers and foremen degrees of control over output and rewards (Littler, 1978) and the efforts by capital to utilise science and machinery to subordinate labour.

In practice the degree of direct authority varied from one industry to the next, the differing forms of control and organisation of work making it futile to talk of *the* labour process (Burawoy, 1981: 96—7). Circumstances varied among established crafts, sub-contracting and internal labour markets, emergent mass production, and remnants of domestic industry. In some of these industries, for example cotton, control was already beginning to be exercised as much through technical as personal means (Burawoy, 1981: 96). Furthermore, it was often not just variation by industry that mattered. Forms of control could alter in relation to economic changes and the degree of pressure on firms. As Friedman shows, there are periods when combinations of high product demand, scarce labour and strong worker organisation pushed some employers into trying forms of control which left considerable autonomy in workers' hands (1977a: 173).

The Development of Systematic Management

The origins of systematic forms of management cannot be adequately understood in terms of the decay of a single structure of control, whether 'simple' or otherwise. Variations in the nature of the labour process already contained the seeds of experimentation in new managerial practices. Indeed, such experimentation was impelled by a combination of falling profit rates and the weakening of traditional forms of control such as sub-contracting. Littler indicates that, in the 1880s, the possibilities for new structures of control were open, indeed a small minority actually experimented with profit-sharing and participation schemes (1978: 11). Much more prominent, however, were the strengthening of forms of direct authority over labour through foremen and new supervisory, white-collar layers who could wield considerable power, as well as piece-work and bonus systems which began the system of recording job times and rate-fixing (Littler, 1978: 12–15; Friedman, 1977a: 91).[2] When added to the greater use of science and technology in production, these trends constituted significant shifts towards control systems associated with subsequent management methods.

As competitive capitalism slowly developed into monopoly forms, Taylorism came to be seen as the most publicly important of these methods. Yet Littler argues that 'There was literally no shop floor Taylorism in Britain before 1914'

(1978: 18), given that time study was not systematic and piece-work was still largely based on the knowledge of foremen and craft workers. It is commonly acknowledged that, compared to the uneven and hesitant pace of change in Britain, management methods such as Taylorism developed much more quickly in the USA. But this is not necessarily incompatible with the argument of Braverman and others concerning the importance of Taylor's methods. They are regarded as the most conscious and systematic expression of existing trends in the organisation of work, rather than as the single source of experimentation. Nevertheless, given the extension of the argument that Taylorism *became* the core component of control structures, it is necessary to evaluate it more closely than has been attempted so far.

Taylorism reassessed

While it is generally agreed that scientific management was a vital component of experimentation towards new control systems, its lasting success and significance has remained open to doubt. Many labour process writers are as critical as those within industrial sociology concerning the viability of Taylorism as a managerial strategy. Burawoy believes that, 'As a practical tool of increasing capitalist control, Taylorism was a failure' (1978: 278). Some prefer to view it as important in particular conditions, but insufficient and inapplicable in others:

> Braverman too must be criticised for confusing one *particular strategy* for exercising managerial authority in the capitalist labour process with *managerial authority* itself . . . Taylorian scientific management is not the only strategy available for exercising managerial authority, and given the reality of worker resistance, often it is not the most appropriate.

> (Friedman, 1977a: 80)

We have already examined the weaknesses of the sociological treatment of Taylorism. But what of the debate within labour process theory? In evaluating the discussion, the main problems arise from the scope attributed to Taylorism.

Because theorists such as Braverman present it as the summation and focus of trends in capitalist production, it can easily become a 'catch-all' concept that hides differences in circumstances of origin, context and impact of new control structures. Braverman *does* indicate that scientific management and monopoly capitalism coincide, the latter creating the scale of production necessary to sustain the resources for effective control structures. But there is little attempt to show how the objectives of scientific management can be located in specific crises within the accumulation process, and the uneven development of monopoly capitalism in different sectors (Elger, 1979: 78—9; Elger and Schwarz, 1980: 399).

This is particularly important if consideration is given to variations on an international level. Fridenson (1978) shows that there were 'remarkable similarities' between the USA and France concerning the speed and nature of the introduction of Taylorism. In Germany and Britain, however, particular national factors pertaining to both employers' preferences and to organised labour meant a slower and more variable introduction of such schemes. Even in France, modifications from the US experience were apparent in the particular role played by war-time rationalisation, the interventionist efforts of the state, and parallel movements towards regularisation of production. The latter comprised *Fayolism*, which tackled the administrative organisation of the enterprise as a whole, and the *Bedaux* system, which refined and extended methods of work measurement.

Nor is there recognition that Taylor's methods constituted only one, albeit an important one, of a number of experiments influenced by the increasing number of engineers taking a closer interest in the problems of production (Palmer, 1975; Edwards, 1979). Such initiatives concerned technical innovations such as the standardisation of tools and tasks; the restructuring of systems of wage payment; and personnel and welfare schemes that were characteristic of this period of transistion from old to new forms of control.[3] The result is that the 'Taylor movement has been confused with a broader re-orientation of management' (Edwards, 1979: 98). Even when defined within a narrower framework, Taylorist experiments ran up against substantial limits and constraints. These are said to be mainly of two kinds. Firstly, there is well documented worker opposition, although it refers mainly to the USA. Even prior to the First World War, resistance to time study, job analysis and incentive wage schemes was strong (Nadworny, 1955). In the most famous case, unions in the government arsenals succeeded in getting the stop-watch and bonus system banned from 1916 to 1949! The obvious attack on the power and conditions of craft workers led to them rejecting Taylor's system on practical and ethical grounds (Montgomery, 1979: 11). Even among the rank-and-file semi- and unskilled workers, strike waves such as those in the East during 1909—15 were located in sectors being rationalised by scientific management. This 'sowed class conflict on an epic scale', influenced by the Industrial Workers of the World (Davis, 1975: 77).[4]

Naturally enough, this made employers wary of persisting with this type of managerial scheme. But there is a second source of constraint. The results of the initiatives did not always convince employers of their usefulness. Piece-rate schemes may have carried the tempting promise of payment for actual work done, but they also allowed scope for deception by workers, thereby restricting output (Edwards, 1979: 99). Even aside from workforce resistance, employers may suffer from the 'ultimate vision' of Taylorism that workers are economically calculating creatures whose labour can be tightly controlled and rewarded. This vision ignores what Friedman calls the 'positive aspects of labour power which are forgone when people are treated as machines' (1977a: 95). Introducing new machinery or working practices often relies on workers' goodwill to overcome difficulties. This may be lost unless managerial methods leave a greater amount of discretion in the hands of the workforce than envisaged with Taylorism.

From the viewpoint of these critics, Taylorism always had limited usefulness. Edwards went so far as to claim that only 1 per cent of companies had tried such schemes (1979: 104). This leads to a final recurrent theme of criticisms, namely the necessity to distinguish between Taylorism as *ideology* and *practice*. As the most prominent of new management theories — with its own Taylor Society — it was inevitable that Taylorism was at the forefront of an employers' offensive counterposing the efficiency and rationality of management to the dangerous conceptions of craft and workers' control (Palmer, 1975). It can therefore be seen as important more as a mode of ideological legitimation of the emergent forms of systematic management than as a means for reorganising the labour process (Burawoy, 1978: 276–81).[5]

These points make clear the need for a much more careful examination of the role of Taylorism in the establishment of systematic management. However, that critique is severely flawed by its misapprehension of the nature and scope of Taylorism. Because writers like Braverman define Taylorism so broadly, it is easy for others to describe it as a failure by defining it narrowly as a series of initiatives specific to *Taylor*, rather than as the movement towards 'scientific' management *generally*. Yet all the grounds put forward for this supposed failure are problematic. As a 'lifelong crusade against the autonomous and inefficient worker' (Davis, 1975: 66), it is hardly surprising that Taylorism created a sustained opposition. But is it really the case that workers 'fought it to a standstill', as Edwards claims? Montgomery admits that the initial wave of overt opposition had been crushed in most of the basic industries in the USA by 1922 (1979: 14). Furthermore, unions like the American Federation of Labor increasingly reached an accommodation with scientific management, particularly with the less beligerent *followers* of Taylor, who saw a role for union involvement and recognition (Nadworny: 1955).[6]

While this obviously did *not* eliminate shopfloor resistance, the important point is that it highlights the tendency for unions to try to incorporate phenomena such as scientific management within a collective bargaining framework. This has certainly been the trend at shopfloor level after the Second World War in Britain. Resistance to work study and other managerial methods continued, but largely as a means of extracting the highest rewards through controlling the conditions under which scientific management is *utilised*. The existence of the methods themselves are reluctantly accepted as a basic fact of industrial life. This mixture of conflict and accommodation will be illustrated later in the chapter with reference to the British motor and engineering industries.

The claim that only a tiny minority of firms ever implemented the methods is therefore absurd, and based on an extremely narrow definition of Taylorist experiments. Firms such as the Bedaux company of consultants specialised in guiding hundreds of firms in introducing incentive payment schemes and time and motion studies on both sides of the Atlantic (Friedman, 1977a: 98). According to Branson and Heinemann, 240 firms were listed by Bedaux as operating the system as mass production grew in Britain in the 1930s (1971: 96). Littler shows how the diffusion of Bedaux's neo-Taylorite methods in Britain was helped by refinements such as the incorporation of fatigue and rest into a universal system of measurement (1982a: 139–42). Once again, the undoubted worker opposition did no more than delay that diffusion. By the end of the 1930s most of the major European countries had some form of scientific management, regardless of the national variations (Fridenson, 1978).

Those who call Taylorism a failure normally provide considerable evidence to the contrary in their examination of the subsequent development of trends in the workplace. Edwards admits that, 'One important element that did endure was the aggressive attempt to gain management control over the special knowledge of production . . . Another element . . . was the notion that each worker's job should be carefully defined, including standards of "adequate performance" ' (1979: 104). Contemporary studies of the workplace are full of details of the operation of basic features of scientific management. Burawoy — another of those who talk of the failure of Taylorism — shows how a modern engineering factory depends on the industrial engineer rather than the stop-watch. But, 'Time study has been professionalised and made more "scientific" ', while the struggle against it 'remains a profound feature of shop floor culture' (1979: 167). In Britain the same story is told, for example in studies of women workers in the tobacco and motor components industries (Pollert, 1981; Cavendish, 1982). Even the classic studies of industrial sociology concerning the restriction of output are saturated with the language of practices — rate-cutting, speed-up, stretch-out — which only make sense in the context of the daily operation of scientific management in its varied forms (Roy, 1973; Lupton, 1963).

To suggest that the relevance of Taylorism has been that of a mode of legitimation is to reverse the real long-term processes. In its inception and early stages it is true that Taylorism played such a role. But once incorporated along-side technical means of control, as a basic feature of pro-duction methods, scientific management itself is rendered insufficient as the main source of legitimation of capitalist social relations in the workplace. It was argued earlier, in Chapter 1, that it is wrong to suggest a strict division between a Taylorist work design and 'habituation' and 'adjustment' of the worker through humanistic management techniques. This is a point also made by Friedman (1977a: 82). But he is mis-taken in believing that management cannot be a 'two-tier process'. Precisely because scientific management is often insufficient as a means of securing effective control, consent and legitimation have shifted to a different terrain. In his study of computer workers, Reid grasps this point: 'Although the use of pseudo-scientific job evaluation, time and motion studies and other Taylorist techniques have remained vital parts of the managerial armoury used to rationalise and control the labour process, they have been complemented by notions of staff participation, improved organisational communication and the "humanisation" or "personalising" of the work environment' (1978: 16).

In the light of this debate, those who argue that Taylorism has been the dominant management practice are in *general* terms correct. Their failure, nevertheless, has been to obscure the pattern of its varied implementation, the variety of poten-tial forms and, more seriously, the number of alternative and additional methods of control available and sometimes necessary to capital. As stated earlier, there are distinctly dif-ferent conceptions of the nature and historical development of those alternatives and variations, and it is to the first of these — associated with Friedman — that we now turn.

The Frontier of Control

For a number of theorists, notably Edwards, Burawoy and Friedman, the main constraint on scientific management is its rigidity. The attempt to create a managerial 'monopoly of conception' runs against a parallel requirement for some level of creative participation of shopfloor workers to keep production going. The latter tendency is described by Friedman as *'responsible autonomy'*, and defined in terms of 'the maintenance of managerial authority by getting workers to identify with the competitive aims of the enterprise so that they will act "responsibly" with a minimum of supervision' (1977b: 48). He argues that responsible autonomy constitutes the major strategic alternative form of management in exercising overall control of the labour process.[7] Friedman perceives the one-sided emphasis on forms of *direct authority*, such as Taylorism, as a legacy of the neglect of the effects of worker resistance originating in Marx and reproduced in Braverman and other contemporary Marxists (1977b: 43; 1977a: 48—50). In particular, Marxist orthodoxy has failed to examine the means by which capital has to deal with contradictions within the labour process to sustain the mode of production.

The forms of authority and control are therefore held to be a product of confrontation and accommodation, an example being the retention of craft workers after the 'technical' necessity for their skills has been eroded. From this point of view, a further important qualification to Marxist orthodoxy is made. The emphasis on the inevitable drive by capital to cheapen labour costs through increasing subordination and deskilling is recognised to be an uneven and complex trend. Valorisation cannot be encapsulated in any single form, while the price of labour may include concessions in the interest of a longer-term view of profitability. The result is support for what has previously been called a *frontier of control* (Friedman, 1978: 13). A range of possible tactics by capital are allowed for, the degree of discretion being conditioned by the pressure of worker resistance and competitive market pressures. While these tactics may be adopted as a result of a forced reaction to workers' power, or though deliberate strategical intent, the emphasis is placed on the latter. These are important concepts, but how useful are they in explaining the historical development of the capitalist labour process?

Direct control and responsible autonomy

In some ways Friedman does not present a historical analysis, in that a schema of stages of development in forms of control is absent. Direct control and responsible autonomy are seen as strategies that can be adopted in any period to deal with a specific managerial problem of capital. Two qualifications, however, can be made to this. First, responsible autonomy is said to be more applicable to dealing with relatively privileged skilled workers, who already have elements of job control and discretion. In contrast, direct control is most suited to large firms with stable product markets and poorly organised workforces. Second, Friedman believes there is a long-run tendency towards using responsible autonomy strategies. New forms of control and managerial methods are, as with other writers, associated with the emergence of monopoly capitalism. A measure of monopoly power gives firms the means to experiment consciously in more favourable economic conditions.

It is admitted that such experiments encompassed scientific management complemented by flow-line methods as an additional direct control. But the inflexibility of managerial operation and the degree of adverse reaction is held to limit its usefulness. Given that top managers in monopoly conditions have to deal with greater potential worker resistance, this accentuates the use of responsible autonomy to co-opt the workforce. Greater size and stability of firms also encourages the parallel use of internal labour markets, which are themselves a means of integration into company operations and hierarchies. Along with Burawoy and Edwards, Friedman agrees that this once again pushes managers to grant or concede certain levels of discretion to the shop floor, rather than use direct and coercive measures.

In the post-1945 situation, the previous mix of direct and discretionary methods is seen as inadequate. A further shift is noted towards managerial strategies to counteract rigidity and resistance. This search, plus the specific conditions of economic expansion and shop-floor power in a sellers' market, leads to the prioritisation of forms of responsible autonomy. To help problems of inflexibility, management can apply different stategies to sections of the workforce. Friedman distinguishes between *central* and *peripheral* workers according to how essential their skills and capacities are to the securing of high, long-run profits. Central workers are likely to be dealt with in terms of responsible autonomy, while the expendability of peripheral sectors makes them vulnerable to direct control. This distinction bears a marked resemblance to that between the characteristics of primary and secondary labour markets, although, as will be shown later, Friedman makes a critique of aspects of those theories.

The major case study illustrating Friedman's general thesis is the car industry in Coventry. Historically the battle to assert rival forms of control had always been a major feature of the industry. Although numerous attempts were made in the inter-war years to impose direct means of management, the shop floor had centred its fight on the principle of *mutuality*; that is, the price paid for piece rates and the introduction of new methods were both fixed by mutual arrangement between the employer and workers' representatives. A significant level of shopfloor discretion and involvement was strengthened by co-operation in production during the war, and by the growth of the shop stewards' movement in the boom conditions that followed. The combination of a 'gang system'[8] and piece-work payment not only consolidated workers' control over aspects of productive activity, but it also had benefits in terms of flexibility in the workshop necessary for introducing changes allied to new machinery and methods. As a consequence, 'Within car firms during the 1940s and early 1950s the vast majority of workers were treated as central workers with Responsible Autonomy strategies' (Friedman, 1977a: 221).

Managerial strategies of this type came to be eroded by the changing conditions of intensified competition, which brought to the fore the disadvantages involved: rigidity of manning and shopfloor practices, and the high costs of changes in production. The result was a shift back to attempted direct control, manifested by speed-up, threats of movement of plant and withdrawal of investment, and the abandonment of piece work and agreements which guaranteed high earnings for Coventry car and engineering workers.[9] Particularly important within this shift was the move towards measured daywork. This not only introduces a payment system which negotiates rates on a factory-wide basis, thus helping to eliminate sectional wage-drift, but it also provides a framework for a new work study offensive as tasks are measured for the new rates. These trends have continued with the deepening recession, but they have been tempered by attempts to incorporate union and steward structures into partial managerial responsibility (Hyman, 1979).

Within Friedman's historical framework and case studies there is valuable material which adds to labour process theory and our understanding of the variety of means of control. But whether the interrelations and relative weight between control methods are accurate is another matter. The recognition given to internal labour markets corresponds with other contemporary evidence (Burawoy, 1979; Edwards, 1979; Rubery, 1980). But the basic argument of a gradual shift to strategies of responsible autonomy under monopoly capitalism is not sustainable. This can be shown by reference to the motor industry case study.

It is true that car workers had considerable job autonomy in the post-1945 period. Counter-controls, operated through shop stewards in companies like Ford, enabled influence to be extended over job allocation, overtime and other aspects of working arrangements (Beynon, 1973). However, this was always *within* a high level of technical control by capital through the assembly line, backed up in many cases by equally high levels of supervision. Indeed, extensive mechanisation provided a basis for intensification of production in many industries in this period. Job autonomy must also be situated within considerable use of scientific management techniques that were an integral accompaniment to such organisation of work. If mutuality is closely examined, shop stewards were trying to sustain the means of monitoring, modifying and materially benefitting from the large array of measurement techniques that were a necessary part of payment and production methods (Turner, Clack and Roberts, 1967). The efficacy of counter-controls therefore depended on the context of workers' organisation and the wider economic and class relations, rather than any straightforward managerial 'strategy'. What Friedman calls responsible autonomy was more often accommodation in different ways to shopfloor job controls.

Managerial accommodation: an example from Chrysler

'On the Door-Hanging section last year, the Superintendent instructed the men to work to their man assignments (i.e. job specifications). Their written instructions were that they were to do 14 two-door cars, 14 Estates, and 21 four-door saloon cars. The men accepted — but management couldn't get the cars into correct rotation. The result was chaos, as the workers did just what they had been told to do. Two-door cars were coming down the line with doors for four-door cars — 7 inches too short . . . Estate car doors were being smashed into position on whatever car turned up next! The Superintendent begged the men to return to their own patterns of working. But the men insisted on working strictly to their instructions for the rest of the shift. The result of this was that management allowed us to work to our own work patterns. They left it to us. The situation is the same today.'

(shop steward, quoted in Red Notes, 1976: 2(a): 4)

When the space for that accommodation was later eroded, capital did not change to a wholly different strategy of direct control. It merely sought to alter the balance of the frontier of control by intensifying the techniques of 'scientifically' controlling work that were already present despite job discretion and internal labour markets. In these conditions mutuality therefore became a more defensive device for countervailing increased managerial control associated with these and other trends such as productivity deals (Nightingale, 1980: 328). While mutality and other tactics could limit the

progress towards enhanced control, its limited use throws
further doubt on conceiving the frontier of control primarily
in terms of rival alternative strategies. Before moving to an
examination of alternative concepts, it is necessary to consider
the effect of an evaluation of Friedman's ideas on wider
theoretical questions. The concept of responsible autonomy
has clear and acknowledged links to job enrichment programmes (Friedman, 1977b: 51–3). Direct control and
responsible autonomy actually have parallel dichotomies in
sociological theory, such as Fox's low and high discretion,
and the mechanistic and organic systems of management of
Burns and Stalker (Crompton, 1978: 7). What assessment
can therefore be made in the light of the previous discussion?

The significance of job enrichment

In previous chapters, the question of job enrichment has been
briefly examined in a critical manner, reflecting the rejection
of labour process theorists of the claim that such schemes
fundamentally alter the nature and experience of work. But
part of the problem in evaluating job enrichment is to avoid
simply reacting to the grandiose claims of those like Dickson
(1977) who talk in terms of a 'work revolution'. Evidence
does show that 'These techniques . . . have had some success
in improving the quality of working life, in reducing absenteeism and labour turnover, and in increasing productivity
and quality of work' (Council for Science and Society, 1981:
38). But to concentrate on the *limits* to these developments
is perhaps to deflect attention away from a more fruitful
emphasis on job enrichment in terms of *control*. As Friedman
points out, industrial social science has been searching since
the 1920s for a way of articulating alternative managerial
strategies to direct control (1977b: 51). Regardless of the
inadequacies of the theoretical basis involved, the British
management writer, Flanders, unwittingly highlighted the
key orientation when he commented that management must
'regain control by sharing it'. In this context, capital hands
over control of small areas of production, hoping that greater
participation to labour will result in improved efficiency
(Cressey and MacInnes, 1980: 21). What is the extent and
significance of this trend?

For some theorists, modern management is being forced by the reality of labour problems and revolt against work to question whether factory 'despotism', fragmentation and hierarchy are really indispensable (Bosquet, 1980: 370). The language of the new capitalism talks of the end of the assembly line, participation in and enrichment of work, and a career structure for all workers (Pignon and Querzola, 1976). Even those who believe that job enrichment represents a genuinely new departure for the capitalist organisation of work recognise that it is a minority trend in a world of work still dominated by mass production and Taylorism. Nevertheless, there are more examples than the famous ones such as the Volvo car plant in Sweden. Bosquet reports that work humanisation schemes were being applied in 200—300 factories in Europe and the USA by the early 1970s. More detailed evidence of the efforts of the 'progressive' wing of capital is given in the case studies of Donnelly Mirrors and American Telegraph and Telephone (AT&T) by Pignon and Querzola.

In addition, there has been a growing interest in 'Japanese-style' management techniques. More than eighty UK firms have been experimenting on an 'after Japan' basis, setting up discussion groups involving various skill sectors of the workforce with the aim of breaking down the 'I'm not paid to think' attitude. The resultant tapping of the creative impulses of workers is directed towards making work processes more productive (*CAITS Quarterly*, September 1981). Meanwhile, by 1975 at least fifty companies had a new 'group technology' system used in the batch manufacture of metal-worked products. By combining workers and machinery together in a 'cell' system in which they can express greater discretion in the allocation of tasks and directing work methods, its proponents argue that it 'can promote substantial gains in terms of job satisfaction and social conditions on the shop floor' (quoted in Green and Bornat, 1978: 1).

These diverse examples illustrate the problem of evaluating the significance of the trend, particularly because they are only part of the variety of new or revamped measures manifested by the abolition of the time-clock, salaried status, the elimination of direct supervision, the replacement of assembly lines by job-enlarged 'roundabouts', elaborate staff participation schemes, and a host of other new working arrangements. Examples of the more far-reaching schemes are given by Pignon and Querzola (1976), Bosquet (1980) and Coriot (1980). At Donnelly's, AT&T, Philips and other companies work has been reorganised around 'autonomous' teams who carry out job-enlarged tasks based on the combination of previously fragmented operations. The new teams are responsible for work co-ordination, speed and the monitoring of errors. As a consequence much of the repressive function of supervision is cut out (Pignon and Querzola, 1976: 78). In some instances the new arrangements are reproduced at the individual level. For example, clerks are made responsible for their own sections of town and clients, and therefore their own accounts and working practices. In parts of the French motor industry, a 'new assembly line' is segmented into distinct work spaces which are the province of small groups of workers with their own stores of tools and components. Compared to the one person, one job, one position line, this allows for partial determination of work speed (Coriot, 1980: 35). The results on both group and individual bases have often been spectacular increases in productivity, at least in the short term.

There seems little doubt that some of these initiatives constitute a form of 'responsible autonomy', as they are based on high trust strategies and low levels of supervision. What is more, they do have genuinely new features compared to the traditional human relations approach. Most far-reaching job enrichment schemes involve the mobilisation of applied social science to the management of human resources within production. Many of those concerned — Lickert, Argyris, McGregor, Herzberg — perceive previous attempts as not reaching far enough into the contradictions of work. Bosquet draws a useful distinction between the new talk of 'adapting the task to the man', and the traditional human relations approach of adapting workers to the existing technology and organisation of work, describing the latter as a gigantic brainwashing enterprise (1980: 371). This suggests that Braverman may have been mistaken in confusing the older patterns of 'habituation' with new strategies of control which recognise that winning consent means altering work practices. Furthermore, it provides evidence for Friedman's assertion that at least some employers are thinking in terms of alternative strategies.

But there are limits in the supportive evidence. There is no single trend towards responsible autonomy. Many schemes of participation and enrichment offer little or nothing that is new, and are often disguised forms of intensified control and rationalisation of the labour process. Some measures are not much more than new types of paternalism. For example, relaxation of supervision can have a variety of causes, including that of being a 'sweetener' for employer resistance to unionisation (Roy, 1980; Zimbalist, 1979: xxi).[10] On a wider level, Ramsay's historical account of the significance of participation measures shows that they have 'attracted management attention on a large scale at particular periods of time, particularly when they have experienced a challenge to their authority from below, this usually coinciding with a crisis in the need for motivation of labour effort' (1980: 390). It is also the case, as stated in a different context earlier, that new managerial methods are far from incompatible with the old. Nightingale indicates that the new managerial ideology of participation and joint regulation associated with the movement for productivity deals went hand in hand with the expansion of 'Taylorism' in its widest sense of more sophisticated means of control and measurement over pay and work (1980: 320).

Nor does the application of more developed social science techniques mark a break from scientific management. These techniques extend the technological rationality directed at making control a 'science', and its practitioners sometimes acknowledge the links to Taylor (Pignon and Querzola, 1976: 78). Actual environment and enlargement techniques in practice often involve little real autonomy. The management of ChemCo described their new working arrangements as a programme of change without parallel in British industry. Yet according to Nichols and Beynon, for workers 'it meant no fundamental change at all in their power of decision making or conditions or work' (1977: 70). Trade unions and 'involvement' were a means of integration and formalisation of workforce responses, while techniques of enrichment, such as job rotation, appeared to do little for genuine involvement or work satisfaction. Green and Bornat argue a similar case concerning group technology. The scope for worker discretion in tasks, speeds and methods is severely restricted by the standardisation of components and processes, which means that management 'sets the production norms and seeks by appropriate procedures and systems of organisation to ensure more certainly than before that the norms are achieved in the time allowed' (1978: 20).

Modern management is dominated by 'the problem of motivation', even where, as Nichols and Beynon point out, the workforce is not conventionally militant.[11] Job enrichment, or what Coriot calls *controlled autonomy*, must be situated in terms of a response to that situation. Furthermore, even in cases where substantial changes have been made in the organisation of work, the technical content of *work itself* often remains unchanged. Pignon and Querzola talk of the division of labour and working conditions remaining unaltered in their case studies. They are clear that the new methods of limited autonomy do not lessen capital's grip, but merely change its form: 'To activate this source of mass initiative in the interests of capital, while maintaining complete control of the production process, this is in a nutshell the aim of the re-organisation we have been studying' (1976: 78). The idea that what matters is not literal 'management' or direct supervision, but *overall* control of the labour process, is common to many of the writers concerned with these developments. Of particular importance is the use of autonomy as a means of self-discipline. By making workers responsible for clients, or defects in the product that are traceable to source, control is ensured through the greater immediacy of the market; in some cases it is enforced by wage penalties (Coriot, 1980: 40). A clerk interviewed in one study summed it up nicely: 'When they set up the Administrative Services Centre, they said it was more democratic. We wouldn't have "bosses" anymore, just clients. But they were just trying to save money. A clerk gets 150 dollars a week while a secretary gets 185 dollars, just for serving one person (Glenn and Feldberg, 1979: 67).

A new frontier?

Despite these qualifications, Coombs is right to suggest that the dismissal of job enrichment — by Braverman and others — underestimates the room for manoeuvre inside the control methods exercised by capital (1978: 84). To take the critique of orthodoxy further, the changing form of the command structure requires a re-examination of the nature of relations between authority in the workplace and the coercive pressures of the market. In some instances analysis shows that particular patterns of work organisation are not primarily the result of control experiments or methods at all, despite managerial presentation of such changes. As Kelly (1982b) shows, management often mystifies initiatives in job design by describing them in terms of enrichment, autonomous groups and so on, when reorganisations of the labour process were essentially technical responses to cost pressures and product market competition, rather than attempts to deal with human motivations and needs.

Forms of authority are combined in a more complex manner than when Marx wrote that factory despotism was in an inverse ratio to the anarchy of production (Pignon and Querzola, 1976: 80). None of the changes actually dispenses with hierarchical command altogether, and they are quite compatible with the idea of an extension of real subordination. We must be careful to keep the changes in proportion. Pignon and Querzola say that 'the division of labour and forms of authority that constitute the present day capitalist organisation of production now appear obsolete in terms of the logic of capitalist rationality' (1976: 88). But this implies a spurious single thread of development impervious to conditions, struggle and context for which there is no evidence.

Even Friedman's rigid distinction between the rival strategies of direct control and responsible autonomy carries the danger of 'collapsing management's potentially wide-ranging repertoire of practices at this level into essentially two' (Nichols, 1980a: 276). Direct control and responsible autonomy are best seen as opposite ends of a *continuum of practices* rather than as all-encompassing strategies. When control is seen in the latter sense, it tends to overemphasise the degree of long-term conscious planning by management. Burawoy argues that while 'concessions in advance' by enlightened management do happen, much more frequent have been accommodations as a consequence of shop-floor struggle, or as a result of changes in the competitive position of the company (1979: 180—3). He also points out that to make sense of control policies, it is necessary to understand the interrelationships between factions of management.

Compared to quality control and industrial engineering, those concerned with personnel have a high stake in the preservation of the idea of a shift to a more democratic ethos in the workplace, as it often legitimises a philosophy and practice central to their own professional self-definition. They are, in Nichols and Beynon's words, 'dealers in ideology', necessarily juggling with the balance between 'the value of the empty phrase, the nod and the wink, the pat on the back, and the occasional kick in the balls' (1977: 120). Which emphasis, tactic or strategy depends heavily on the context inside and outside the workplace.[12] This recognition requires a more complex setting out of the varieties of control inside the historical development of the capitalist labour process.[13]

Contested Terrain: the Edwards Thesis

The most comprehensive attempt to provide such an explanation has been undertaken by Edwards (1979). It therefore stands as the final major alternative theorisation of control and the capitalist labour process. This section will seek to evaluate Edwards's contribution and related evidence as a means of focusing on the relationships between modern structures of control. Aspects of Edwards's analysis concerning the concept of simple control and his interpretation of Taylorism have already been discussed. These aspects exist within a clear historical framework whereby the evolution of forms of control is governed by workplace conflict and economic contradictions in the firm's operations. Hence the 'contested terrain'.

Managerial experiments
Simple control under competitive capitalism is said to have

given way, under the impact of intensified class struggle and centralisation of capital, to a period of experimentation parallel to the emergence of monopoly. This experimentation included not only scientific management, but also welfare schemes and company unionism. As none of these experiments was successful, Edwards argues that there was a shift to *structural* forms of control. They are embedded in the physical or social structure of the workplace, rather than dependent on the personal power of the employer or his functionaries. The first of these was of a *technical* nature, corresponding broadly to the assembly line and other types of mechanisation. Following further contradictions of technical control came the development of institutionalised, hierarchical command based on systematic administrative structures. This *bureaucratic* control routinises the functions and procedures of management, stratifies work and job titles, and governs appointments and promotion by impersonal rules.

As capitalist production has developed unevenly, modern industry is characterised by the existence of all three structures of control in different sectors, for example simple control in small businesses. Nevertheless, Edwards clearly states that these forms of control represent 'both the pattern of historical evolution and the array of contemporary methods of organising work . . . each form of control corresponds to a definite stage in the development of the most important or representative firms' (1979: 21). Edwards's method does not simply draw from historical example, but is based on a historically *successive* understanding of structures of control, evidence being drawn from a 'panel' of notable US companies.[14] Earlier in the chapter there was sharp criticism of both Edwards's notion of simple control and of the account of control structures in the transition to monopoly capitalism. In the former instance criticism focused on the reduction of the variety of structures to a single type. Regarding the latter, the problem is a very narrow definition of Taylorism, leading to underestimating its importance. However, Edwards's presentation of a period of transition and experimentation between competitive and monopoly periods contains much useful material.

Like other writers, Edward uses a distinction between *core* and *periphery* sectors of the economy to explain the ability of large companies to dictate aspects of market behaviour, thus creating the room for discretion in trying out new methods. Such methods were needed in the face of accumulating problems for companies. Existing hierarchical control was unable to cope with worker resistance to close supervision and the consequent control struggles of the early part of the century against the most oppressive features of capitalist relations in the workplace.[15] Although the First World War and the subsequent repression of radicals blunted the cutting edge of aggressive trade unionism, the problems still persisted, particularly as employers had to contend with their dependency on the growing numbers of non-production workers.

Beginning in the 1920s, emphasis began to be put on initiatives like selected non-job benefits, which Edwards calls *welfare capitalism*, for example the 'Betterment Program' of US Steel. This reflected an awareness of the need for positive incentives to integrate the workforce. In some cases there were virtual bribes to accept the patterns of authority. In other cases *company unions* or works councils aimed at similar results through formal grievance procedures. Neither was successful, in that they spread a veil over the underlying causes of discontent, allowing no substantial mechanisms for workers to press their collective interests. Hence they lapsed into disuse or caricature, at best delaying the onset of industrial unionism. Edwards usefully points to the lessons learned, notably the superiority of rules, procedures and rewards to management by whim and command. The problem with the analysis is its insistence that each experiment, including scientific management, was equally significant, was a failure and was separate from other experiments.[16] The rigidity of control categories and their elaboration in sequential terms unfortunately carries on into the contemporary discussion.

Interrelations between modern control structures
Of the subsequent modern forms, technical control is defined as that which 'involves designing machinery and planning the work flow to minimise the problem of transforming labour

power into labour as well as to maximise the purely physically based possibilities for achieving efficiencies' (Edwards, 1979: 112). This is seen as a qualitative advance on work that has undergone mechanisation, or machine pacing, in that such developments are said to increase the productivity of labour without altering structures of control. Technical control only emerges when the entire production process or large segments of it are based on a technology that paces and directs the labour process. The assembly line contained the fullest potential for its time, creating the key condition for relieving the foreman of the responsibility for setting tasks, allowing foremen to enforce the requirements of the technical structure: 'The work quota is no longer laid down, negotiated and imposed by a human authority which remains open to argument; it is ordered by the machine itself, imposed by the inexorable programmed advance of the assembly line' (Bosquet, 1980: 374—5).

Computer-based technology enables a further advance of technical control, but a distinction is maintained between mechanisation and machine direction of the whole labour process. For example, direct numerical control — discussed in Chapter 4 — is held to provide a total feedback system for the evaluation of work, whereas numerical control represents 'simply an advance in machine pacing of individual workers' (Edwards, 1979: 123). Other recent developments such as the MINOS system — also discussed in Chapter 4 — could certainly be seen as a more sophisticated form of technical control. Edwards regards the weakness of this form of control as the way it creates a homogeneous workforce by producing common pace and patterns of work. So while the control problems of the individual section and foremen are solved, conflict is displaced and raised to a plant-wide level.

This stimulates companies to find ways of simultaneously *re-dividing* the workforce, integrating it into company structures, and winning its loyalty. Introduced in a gradual manner in companies like IBM and Polaroid, bureaucratic control establishes the impersonal force of company rules as the basis for the regulation of work. The situation at Polaroid is used to good effect as an example of this 'divide and conquer' strategy.

The Polaroid job classification scheme

'With eighteen different job families, three hundred job titles, and fourteen different pay grades, not to mention the dichotomy between the salaried and hourly workers, it might appear that Polaroid had gone far enough in dividing and re-dividing its workers. Not so: each job is now further positioned on the pay scale so that for any given job, seven distinct pay steps are possible . . . Polaroid has created roughly 2,100 individual slots for its 6,397 hourly workers. And that leaves out a number of ancillary means of subdividing workers — the seniority bonus, 'special pay' status, the incentive bonus, and so on.'

(Edwards, 1979: 134)

Each job has an approved description setting forth in considerable detail the tasks workers must perform, once having been rated. This drastically alters the role and power of supervision, in that they are subject also to supposedly objective rules and procedures. For Edwards, bureaucratic control constitutes 'the most important change wrought by the modern corporation in the labour process' (1979: 132). While this may seem exaggerated, it does correspond with the considerable evidence already examined concerning the growth of *internal labour markets* (Burawoy, 1979; Rubery, 1980; Friedman, 1977a). Bureaucratic control is said to allow for mobility within the firm, more rights, and job security and rewards for positive behaviour by workers.

The identification of this trend away from control by *coercion* towards control by *consent* and integration is strongly backed by Burawoy (1979: 106—8; 1981: 99—100). There is a common acknowledgement of collective struggle being stifled and a long-term partial identification with company practices, leading to an indirect intensification of work. This argument concerning consent will be examined fully in Chapter 6. But can the trend be described as a system of bureaucratic control? Burawoy argues that Edwards ignores that such markets are partly in workers' interests, in that they expand the amount of discretion within given limits, as well as providing protection from unfettered managerial authority.[17] The same point is made from a different angle by Friedman and Rubery. They both attack the notion that internal labour markets are primarily the result of divide and conquer strategies, preferring the view that such arrangements are the result of accommodations to the kind of workers' struggles to retain job control and security that were examined in Chapter 4.[18] Referring to Edwards and his co-thinkers, Rubery comments: 'Thus the radicals have overstressed the control offered by the bureaucratic division of the labour force, and at the same time underestimated or ignored the benefits for the working class of a sheltered, secure, albeit stratified, labour market' (1980: 266). Furthermore it is quite wrong to suggest that stratification of the labour force is a recent phenomenon compared to its previous homogenisation. While the trend towards bureaucratisation of structures and procedures is an important development, the 'overemphasis of stratification as a direct result of conscious managerial strategies' ignores the systematic 'divisions on the basis of sex, race, skill or other educational attributes that not only predate Monopoly Capitalism, but also capitalism' (Friedman, 1977a: 114).

Even *if* bureaucratic control is taken as a distinct category, there are further problems contained in the attempt to treat it as a separate structure. Edwards quotes with approval the statement that the training for new job procedures means 'The system is to bureaucracy what Taylor was to the factory' (1979: 137). But surely this misses the point. The trend to bureaucratisation cannot take place without the use of established scientific management procedures *to produce* the job evaluation, grading and rating of tasks. Similarly the whole emphasis on the objectivity of procedure is an extension of patterns already established in work study. It is also not clear why bureaucratic control is separate from technical control. After all, industries supposedly characterised by the latter, such as cars, clearly combine a high level of overall machine direction with complex grading and stratification systems. Furthermore, payment systems are vital additional means of control to the technology.

The attempt to make technical control into a self-contained system is ill-considered. This is not merely shown by the necessity for supplementary measures already mentioned, but by the exaggerated difference between overall machine control and machine pacing. Significant points of mechanisation, e.g. numerical control in engineering, clearly reduced workers' job control; and the computer-linked direct numerical control system extends its principles of operation. Similarly the major wave of mechanisation associated with the development of large-scale industry was advocated by people like Ure precisely *because* it altered the elements of control in the social structure of the firm, therefore providing a basis for increased productivity. Nor is it the case that technical control eliminated sectional and supervisory conflict, displacing it to plant-wide level. Once again, the British motor industry in the post-war period provides contrary evidence. Small-scale conflict of a sectional nature, frequently involving questions of supervisory power, line speed and pay rates, was the chief characteristic of the period.

Edwards has raised two crucial considerations for labour process theory, namely the variety of control structures and the contested nature of the workplace terrain as a major influence governing changes. But neither question has been dealt with satisfactorily. The example of the treatment of bureaucratic stratification in terms of divide and rule at the expense of the effects of worker resistance indicates a failure to integrate the concrete results of contestation. The main problem, however, lies in the failure to discuss control structures in their *combined* forms. For instance, the assembly line can never be reduced to a technical dimension. It may have altered the role and pattern of supervision, but its successful operation always depended on a *human* agency. What do these problems indicate for the general adequacy of control categories?

Conclusion: the Dimension of Control

The main debate in this chapter has been the question of how capitalist control of the labour process is obtained. Control implies hierarchy. Even in those circumstances of 'responsible autonomy', where the immediacy of the market replaces direct supervision, the links in the chain of command have simply been rearranged or obscured. The degree of worker discretion is subject to the dictates of the purpose of the enterprise. Hierarchy exists because that purpose under capitalism is profitability, not because it is the only way of organising production, nor because it is technologically required.[19] A number of writers therefore seek to draw a distinction between profitability and efficiency. Hierarchical control is necessary to the former, but not identical with the latter (Edwards, 1979; Gorz, 1976a; Pignon and Querzola, 1976; Marglin, 1976; Stone, 1973).

They are attacked strongly by more orthodox Marxists for implying that capital has a choice between accumulation and efficiency (Palloix, 1976: 62; Brighton Labour Process Group, 1977: 8). It is true that it would be wrong to imply that the motivation to impose structures of control could be based on domination by capital for its own sake. But surely this is not the essence of the point being argued.[20] The fact that the dictates of accumulation *require* control of the labour process by capital does not tell us what *form* of control will be applicable in different circumstances. Nor does it distinguish between management choices based on considerations of short- and long-term profitability. No one has convincingly demonstrated that a particular form of control is necessary or inevitable for capitalism to function successfully. Neither has the real subordination of labour been identified with an increase in direct authority.

In contrast, the debate has revealed that within the *overall* control of the labour process by capital there are a variety of techniques and structures available. The most consistent weakness of existing theory has been the tendency to counterpose one form of control to another. But the existence of varying types of control is a reflection of what Crompton refers to as the fundamental tension of management: 'that of attaining maximum control over activities, at the same time as achieving a measure of voluntary compliance. "Direct control" and "responsible autonomy" therefore may not be so much *alternative* strategies of managing the workforce, as a reflection of this persisting managerial dilemma' (1978: 8).

It is better, therefore, to consider differences in terms of *dimensions* of control. The task of labour process theory becomes that of understanding the *combinations* of control structures in the context of the specific economic location of the company or industry. Pollert expresses this well in her case study of a Bristol factory:

> Churchmans, like any other factory, imposed discipline at several levels. There was the tight hold over the labour process, as described in job evaluation, grading and work study. Then there was personal supervision in the presence of chargehands, foremen and supervisors. And there were rules — the written rules of the rule book, and visual reminders stuck up on notices.
>
> (Pollert, 1981: 129)

Another important question is raised in the study, as it is in many other analyses of women workers: that is, the use of an ideology of femininity as a means of securing compliance. In social relations on the shop floor, even something as simple as sexual banter could become the language of discipline, so that 'class control was mediated by partriarchal control' (Pollert, 1981: 141). Nor is this the only social relation which generates the conditions for control. It is the central argument of Burawoy that the labour process itself creates a framework of informal rules and relations which workers adapt and transform as a means of coming to terms with the nature of their working life.

Some theorists, like Braverman, pass over entirely the relational components of work. Others have more rounded conceptions of control, but deal with the phenomenon primarily as conscious top—down strategies. Existing categories of control therefore do not reach deep enough into what some would call the 'subjective' facets of people's experiences of work. Even those policies of employers that seek to control through the devolution of responsibility require a further step. As Burawoy puts it, 'It then becomes a matter of eliciting support for managerial goals from workers' (1981: 92). The objective fact of control ultimately depends on the existence of subjective consent. It is to the processes by which this consent is generated that we now turn.

6
Legitimation and Consent in Work

Workers do not always need to be overtly controlled. They may effectively 'control' themselves, particularly if they are in white-collar or professional jobs. Hales, in his case study of design workers, refers to the puzzle about why they work so *hard* for ICI (1980: 52). One answer may be that, despite the myth of independence implied in the 'managerial revolution' thesis, the trend towards tighter and more bureaucratic control subjects them to an ever greater degree of accountability to the dictates of capital accumulation. As another study of the chemical industry said of foremen, 'These men are under no illusions that they are, or ever will be, "employers". But they know that if they are to succeed at ChemCo they must act as if they were' (Nichols and Beynon, 1977: 49). The level of consent or compliance of such strata of the workforce thus rests largely on their place in the productive apparatus.

But what of those who are merely wage labourers? How do we account for the widespread, if varying, acceptance of the capitalist labour process? There has been persistent, and correct, criticism of Braverman for ignoring the importance of worker resistance; but resistance is not the whole story. As Burawoy points out, there is a further factor: 'He makes no reference to the psychological and other processes through which subordination to capital is secured, the processes through which workers come to comply with and otherwise advance their own dehumanisation' (1981: 90). Nor is

Braverman alone. The objective and subjective factors which legitimise social relations in the workplace have been neglected in the main body of labour process theory, either because of the stress laid on changes in the structural features of work, or because traditions of resistance have been emphasised at the expense of the day-to-day reproduction of consent.

Conceptual tools exist in Marx's writings, particularly where he was concerned with relations between ideology and commodity fetishism that result in capitalism appearing to be an unalterable order of things (1976: 163—75). As he said, 'The advance of capitalist production develops a working class which by education, tradition and habit looks upon the conditions of that mode of production as self-evident laws of nature' (quoted in Nichols and Armstrong, 1976: 58). We are not primarily referring here to the well known concept concerning the *general* dominance of the ideas of the ruling class in any epoch.[1] While there are important consequences of ideological reproduction at the societal level, an emphasis on this dimension has too often meant a failure to be specific about ideological processes in the workplace. At the heart of the notion of commodity fetishism is an understanding that, 'As men and women engage in production, they generate a world of appearances' (Burawoy, 1979: 16). It is not just 'things' that are produced, but social relations between people. As these relations concern the functioning and distribution of ownership, control, skill, power and knowledge, we are also talking about the production of ideas about those relations. Ideology therefore constitutes a lived experience, not just an imposed set of ideas.[2]

These concepts can be concretely applied to the production of consent at work, as we shall see later. Yet Marx did not seek to connect the concepts in this way. The conditions for securing profitable production were seen mainly in terms of changing methods to increase exploitation, by prolonging the working day or increasing its intensity, by the use of machinery, and by the introduction of new structures of payment and control. Burawoy's argument that Marx dealt with the expenditure of effort solely in terms of coercion underestimates the importance of the more general writings on ideology and work. But he is surely right in saying that

'Marx had no place in his theory of the labour process for the organisation of consent' (1979: 27).[3] Friedman puts it another way when he says that Marx did not closely examine the means by which capital accommodates contradictions through reorganising production to sustain its dominance (1977a: 49). In the absence of such guidelines, how has the problem of consent been approached in subsequent theories of work and class relations?

Work and Consciousness: Alternative Problematics

Insights into the labour processes of advanced capitalism, particularly on the question of consent, could provide vital means of connecting the spheres of work and class. But to do so would require moving outside existing problematics within both sociology and Marxism governing the relations between those spheres. In the past discussion has tended to take place within the framework of links between objective and subjective dimensions of class, or what Marxism refers to as class-in-itself and class-for-itself.[4] While the relations between work, ideology and behaviour *are* examined, it is largely confined to the question of the conditions under which class consciousness exists and how it is advanced.[5] Even when *constraints* to the development of class consciousness have been considered, the issue of the organisation of consent in work has not been given a great deal of attention.

Traditional Marxism

As a theory of social change, Marxism has been concerned with the conditions under which the working class could develop sufficient unity and consciousness to challenge, and then replace capitalism. When considering the potential contribution of the circumstances and struggles at work, the original assumption of Marx and Engels was that developments such as the homogenisation of labour and the concentration of workers under large-scale production would create the basis for a class-in-itself. As we noted earlier, Marx did not really develop a politics of production to extend this basic analysis. This was to be provided by Lenin, who argued that the 'leap' to a consciously socialist class-for-itself required struggle *outside* the workplace led by the external agency of a revolutionary party. Without this intervention, the spontaneous struggle of the working class at the point of production would be dominated by bourgeois ideology, a far stronger system of ideas, with much greater means for dissemination at its disposal (Lenin, 1963: 35).

In the subsequent evolution of Marxist theory these formulations have been subjected to various critiques. Some have suggested that the divisions between categories are too rigid (Hyman, 1971). Consciousness is said to exist in a continuum rather than a simple division between socialist and bourgeois, while trade unionism is too complex to be regarded as just a manifestation of the latter. This theme has been picked up in other studies, which argue that it is more accurate to talk in terms of factory or micro-level trade union consciousness that can go further than orthodox unionism, despite the narrow confines of the workplace (Lane, 1974: Beynon, 1973; Clements, 1977). Others believe description of workplace struggles to be too pessimistic, referring to the tradition of informal action challenging the capitalist organisation of work, and the exemplary occasions of mass strikes that have reached upwards to shake the power structure (Glaberman, 1976; Brecher, 1972).

Such critiques are more perceptive about the range of workplace action. But they do not get to the heart of the problem of the traditional analysis. This is the assumption that it is necessary to analyse the work situation only in terms of the *limits* on class consciousness and struggle, and how they may be overcome, rather than the positive *constraints*. In fact, alternative theories can reproduce the problem in more virulent form by stressing the *extraordinary*, as in Glaberman's misleading comment that: 'it is in the best classical Marxist tradition to base theory on the peak that the working class has reached in any stage of society. . . we are living for the peak, and not the valley' (1976: 39). While such events are important, our starting point has to be the contradictory features of everyday normality at work. Friedman notes that 'it is more important to examine how the capitalist mode of production has accommodated itself to

worker resistance, rather than simply how the capitalist mode
of production might be overthrown through worker resistance' (1977a: 48). It is not enough to discuss problems
solely in terms of fragmentation and division among workers.
Emphasis must be put on the forces operating to sustain
and reproduce capitalist social relations through the labour
process.

Burawoy is therefore correct that Lenin is unhelpful primarily because 'there is no attempt to come to terms with
the production of a specific type of consciousness or ideology
at the point of production that has as its effect the obscuring
of surplus value and of relations of production' (1978: 264).
A 'reverse problematic', which starts with consent, challenges
the notion that the development of the capitalist labour
process automatically produces the basis for a class-in-itself.
Few major Marxist theorists have gone in that direction,
although Gramsci is often identified as providing some point-
ers for a useful framework. He stressed that the control of a
ruling class is based on the permeation of a whole system
of beliefs, morals and values through the cultural and ideological apparatuses of society and state. Because this *hegemony*
is contrasted with control by domination and coercion —
although these methods are also used — a number of labour
process writers have drawn on Gramscian concepts as sugges-
tive beginnings for an analysis of workplace consent. But
even if those concepts are an important alternative to more
mechanistic theories of capitalism and consciousness (Boggs,
1976), the concern with the organisation of consent is located
almost wholly on the wider political terrain, and not on work
(Burawoy, 1979: xi).[6]

Sociology

Mainstream sociology has not generally been any more help-
ful on the question of consent, even if the worst survey
research with its dry and inaccurate descriptions of class
consciousness is set aside. Important debates *have* taken place
on the nature and causes of variations in class consciousness,
particularly in response to post-1945 economic expansion
and changes in rewards and occupations (see Bulmer, 1975;
Westergaard, 1970, for articles and commentary respectively).

Part of the research indicated that the organisation of work played an important part in the development of conceptions of class. Like Marxism, it was not really concerned with the issue of consent, but with the relations between work situation and class imagery. As Westergaard points out, although the formulation of the problem was not explicitly why there has been no revolution, the preoccupations of research have been remarkably similar in nature (1970: 113).

Even the more radical writers who were willing to allow for occasional 'explosions of consciousness' at times of intense industrial conflict (Mann, 1973) tended to take the normal functioning of the workplace for granted as based on aggressive economism and defensive job control. Once again the 'leap' from normality to advanced class consciousness left aside the question of consent. Only in the material on the operation of informal work groups has the problem even been partially approached (Roy, 1973; Whyte, 1955; Crozier, 1964). Practices engaged in by workers to create relief and space from the tedium of work have been correctly seen as possible ways of absorbing hostility and diffusing conflict (Burawoy, 1978: 270). Within this framework, the most important insights came from Baldamus (1961). He saw workers as seeking compensations for unpleasant work realities through 'relative satisfactions' based on forms of play and creative escape from routine. Even hard work can become acceptable if the worker loses himself in the rhythm and pull of activity, which Baldamus described as traction.[7] The problem with analyses of the informal work group has been that such insights have been outweighed by the dominant problematic of 'restriction of output'. Workers' activity thus becomes judged from the viewpoint of whether the effects are negative on production and industrial relations in the plant. More relevant have been writings from the *interactionist* tradition dealing with how employees *negotiate* work realities (see Salaman and Thompson, 1973: chapter 10); but, once again, it is not explicitly within a consent theme.

There *is* useful material in traditional Marxism and sociology relating to the themes of this chapter. Issues have certainly been raised concerning the processes whereby subordinate classes tolerate and consent to capitalist society as a whole. But that is not the same as consent to capitalist *work* relations, and the two cannot be investigated within the same terms of reference. Marx's prognosis, that the unfolding of capitalist production would increasingly make the exploitative and oppressive nature of that society become apparent, remains unfulfilled. It may be fruitful to return to the sphere of the labour process as part of the path back to asking adequate questions about the broader potential for class formation, struggle and a new society. Such a view is a central part of the thesis advanced by Burawoy, the major labour process theorist concerned with consent at work. The next section will seek to explain Burawoy's analysis and the related and supportive evidence, before moving to a more critical examination.

The Manufacture of Consent

Burawoy argues that twentieth-century Marxism has been wrong to attribute the failures of class struggle and consciousness primarily to factors dependent on new theories of the state, the family, the mass media, psychology, and so on. It is to the labour process itself that mechanisms exist of 'constituting workers as individuals rather than as members of a class, of coordinating the interests of labour and capital as well as that of workers and managers, and of redistributing conflict and competition' (1979: 30). On a general level Burawoy puts emphasis on the way that the particular relations of capitalist production are *concealed* from the worker, a process enhanced by the separation of visible ownership and control in industry. The origins of profit in unpaid labour is obscured by its ostensible dependence on the workings of the market, patterns of investment, or the personal efforts of the entrepreneur.

Of course, this is not a new point. Marxists have traditionally pointed out that the surplus-producing process is masked by the wage form, whereby workers cannot directly identify the distinction between labouring to produce the equivalent of wages, and working additionally to create surplus value.

Connections between wage struggles and the overall system of production are correspondingly difficult to sustain, as Nichols and Armstrong illustrate in their ChemCo case study: 'the idea that there is a relation between squabbling over 1p or 2p an hour and the fact that the firm is owned by share-holders and run for them by managers, who are well paid, is not thought significant' (1976: 55). But contemporary writers are also referring to specific ways in which work has come to be organised and restructured through systems of grading, control and measurement. These developments not only have implications for factors such as skill and control, but also for concealment of, and consent to, class relations. The whole design of work 'behind people's backs' acts to obscure the origins of relations like hierarchies of skill, knowledge and power:

> although many of the most fundamental conditions of the society they live and work in have been consciously worked into the apparatus of the working day. . . .these designed relations are far from obvious. Because they have been thought out at such a concrete level and then material-ised in the apparatus of production, the generality of these relations has been made effectively invisible.

> (Hales, 1980: 58)

To these general points Burawoy adds and highlights the part workers themselves play in creating the conditions for consent through their means of adapting to work.[8]

Games and practices

For Burawoy such adaptation is often in the form of 'games'.[9] In his own participant observation study of a piece-work machine shop, games are constituted as informal rules and practices aimed at creating space and time, controlling earnings, and making work more interesting. Around the piece-work targets there developed shopfloor culture and be-haviour in the idiom of what industrial sociologists have called 'making out'.

Making out

'In other words, making out cannot be understood simply in terms of the externally derived goal of achieving greater earnings. Rather, its dominance in the shop floor culture emerges out of and is embodied in a specific set of relations in production that in turn reflect management's interest in generating profit. The rewards of making out are defined in terms of factors immediately related to the labour process — reduction of fatigue, passing time, relieving boredom, and so on — and factors that emerge from the labour process — the social and psychological rewards of making out on a tough job.'

(Burawoy, 1979: 85)

Burawoy draws consciously on the observational tradition of writers like Lupton (1963) and Gouldner (1954), particularly in explaining the way that games take place within the indulgency patterns of management. Even extensive fiddling can be accepted by management if the relaxation of rules brings the conpensatory benefit of enhanced control and worker integration, as in Ditton's study of bakery salesmen (1976). For these reasons Burawoy argues that: 'One cannot play a game and question the rules at the same time; consent to rules becomes consent to capitalist production' (1981: 92). For example, even workers' experience of 'being screwed' was deflected from the relations of exploitation by blame being attached to the company's failure to provide the proper conditions for making out.

This connects to a wider point made in the analysis, that the pattern of games and practices shapes a distinctive pattern of conflict. Tensions in the assertion of worker discretion over time and money may be a consequence of managerial control and allocation of resources, but it is often *experienced* as obstructions on the part of other workers. This, in turn, 'accentuates a lateral conflict that is endemic to the organisation of work' (Burawoy, 1979: 66), transforming and redistributing management—worker conflicts into intra-employee competition. Piece-work machine shops cannot be said to be characteristic of most industrial situations, yet there is support for Burawoy's thesis in other labour process literature. The ChemCo case studies of Beynon and Nichols and Armstrong put considerable emphasis on the dominant orientation of workers in terms of similar informal adaptations. These are said to flow from the experience of the technology, division of labour and managerial ideology in terms of there being no other way to do the work. Survival in alienating surroundings means that individuals 'have devised their own particular means of "getting by" ' (Nichols and Armstrong, 1976: 73).

While these means of getting by included the making-out games described by Burawoy, it is dangerous to conceive of consensual practices in too narrow a way. This is illustrated in Hales's study of design workers at ICI. Having worked in the plant himself, Hales referred to the persistence of workers policing their own behaviour. But this has to be situated in the culture of workplace social relations, and not just the work-group. The practices of design workers are determined by capital, whose skills 'lie in thinking through capitalist relations of production in concrete terms' (1980: 56). Inevitably this leads beyond policing their own behaviour to a commitment to shaping and rationalising the functions of others, notably manual workers. Although subject to a labour process under which their labour is increasingly proletarianised, they remain, in Braverman's terms, beneficiaries of the deskilling of work. Within the built-in division of mental and manual labour, such 'thinkworkers' are part of the apparatus of what Hales calls *pre-conceptualisation*. Their privileged access to knowledge has to be situated inside a constellation of practices which help reproduce managerial hegemony and enhance the capacity of management to determine workers' activity through the instruments of labour. As Hales correctly points out, hegemony is not just the spinning of ideas, but part of a material culture at work. It is the totality of these conditions that produces the basis for consent for this strata of the workforce, rather than simply adaptive games.[10]

There is also evidence to back up the concept of the functioning of the labour process as a means of redistributing conflict into lateral struggles. In a study of mill workers, with distinct echoes of Burawoy's approach, Mulcahy and Faulkner outline the effects of the separation of workers in the labour process. What they call *work individuation* is encouraged by management in the physical arrangement of production. Difficulties in achieving targets are likely to be manifested as conflicts among the various types of operator, who blame each other for problems, a trend also noted in Cavendish's case study of women engineering workers (1982). While conflict between operators and management is not uncommon, 'The thrust of ABC's shop floor ethos is individual independence' (Mulcahy and Faulkner, 1979: 239). Once again we are back to relative satisfactions, or what is called here the correlation between the private, situationally induced desires of the operator for technical competence and self-interest, and the requirements of the factory.

In addition, my own joint examination of conflict in a Merseyside telecommunications plant (Thompson and Bannon, forthcoming) produced similar trends towards lateral or horizontal conflict. This resulted directly from a combination of piece work and sectional divisions of skill and power embedded in the particular labour process. The effect of the latter on the ability to manipulate the payment system produced a situation where some groups became 'high fliers' in terms of earnings. Disparities became so great that it provoked continual friction and sectional action among the lower paid, pushing the company into introducing a 'Robin Hood' scheme in which the 'high fliers' would subsidise other workers through a portion of their bonuses. In turn this spilled over into continual conflict between work-groups, which resulted in the collapse of the scheme. How much lateral conflict increased consent is, however, open to doubt, as will be argued later.

From coercion to consent?

Where Burawoy goes further than the above studies is in advancing a distinctive argument that these are not just partial trends, but expressions of a shift from coercion to consensual hegemony in the organisation of the labour process. From this position those theorists who have stressed the *necessity* for capital to tighten its grip through new control methods are regarded as failing to note the counter-developments based on limited discretion and organised consent. These arguments highlight connections with the control issues of Chapter 5. As was noted then, Burawoy supports the contention of writers such as Edwards that there has been a move towards methods of bureaucratic control dependent more on rules and procedure than coercion. Like Friedman, Burawoy prefers to talk in terms of the rise of *internal labour markets*. This is the idea that by internalising the features of the external market, they foster competitive individualism at the point of production, which results in greater commitment to the enterprise.

Dislocation within the functioning of such systems is handled by the parallel rise of an *internal state*; political processes confined to the jurisdiction of the factory extend collective bargaining and grievance machinery. It is recognised that structures for incorporating worker resistance and trade unionism are not new. But Burawoy argues that the *forms* taken are new, and more significantly are located inside the supportive framework of hegemonic management, as it evolved from despotism. Collective bargaining beomes the site of a further institutionalisation of conflict that increasingly sets out common interests. Burawoy goes on to argue that the worker is constituted as an 'industrial citizen' with contractually defined rights and benefits, consolidated by a state legal framework that creates parallel forms of protection and obligation for capital and labour. By protecting management from itself in terms of curbing excessive use of authority, the overall power of capital is secured. He refers to the use of legal guidelines for affirmative action programmes aimed at expanding the employment rights of minorities or women. Examples relevant to the British experience could include legislation such as the Sex Discrimination Act and the Employment Protection Act.

For Edwards, bureaucratic control, like an internal labour market, also has the effect of weakening even the most elementary forms of class consciousness based on 'them and us'. Workplace culture is said to express less of the worker and more of the firm, for instance in notions of the company as a family developed by firms such as IBM. As in the small firm or early office, this results in workers becoming enmeshed in a network of enterprise relationships, though bureaucratically rather than personally based. Although the workplace remains a contested terrain, capital is said to have reorganised the labour process 'in such a way as to minimise workers' opportunities for resistance and even alter workers' perceptions of the desirability of opposition' (1979: 16). Friedman also speaks of internal labour markets as expressing the modern requirement for an elaborate ideological structure to co-opt workers' organisation, as well as providing relative employment security (1977a: 106). Although both writers make clear that these trends cannot eliminate contradictions in managerial strategy or worker resistance, their evidence is generally supportive of the argument that there has been a broad shift to consensual methods of organising workers in the labour processes of monopoly capitalism.

The Limits to Workplace Consent

The emphasis on consent is a welcome and necessary corrective to a labour process theory that has been primarily concerned with the extent and nature of changes in objective features of the work situation. The most important and coherent explanation, associated with Burawoy, rests strongly on an interpretation of consent which locates it firmly in the workplace. The next section will examine the contending claims of non-workplace factors. Meanwhile, although the stress on everyday relations and practices in the labour process contains important insights, whether the consequences of games and other forms of adaptation to work are so consensual in nature, needs to be examined critically. Burawoy's statement that in the course of thirty years conflict between management and workers has diminished, while that between workers has increased (1979: 70) is carefully qualified by acknowledging that the machine shop at 'Allied' is in a specific US and corporate context. Nevertheless, that qualification appears to be overridden by generalisations that the prospects for 'local crises' at the point of production are bleak because of 'the ability of the factory to contain struggles and produce consent' (1979: 202). Socialism is therefore held to be on the agenda only in the Third World. This admitted pessimistic perspective carries the danger of obscuring and even obliterating the existing and potential basis for class struggle concerning the nature and organisation of work.

This is indeed the consequence of the position reached by some commentators such as the Ehrenreichs (1976). In an analysis of Braverman's *Labor and Monopoly Capital* they share Burawoy's view that it is wrong to blame 'external' factors for the lack of genuine class consciousness. Braverman's analysis of the degradation of work is used to argue that 'certain objective features of the productive process in monopoly capitalism may militate against the development of proletarian class consciousness' (1976: 11). Accepting without qualification the erroneous thesis that all elements of skill and knowledge have been stripped from workers, the Ehrenreichs assert that the result is a decollectivisation of labour based on the parcellisation of tasks and atomisation of class. As Braverman notes in a rejoinder (1976), this is not his interpretation of that thesis, but given his omission of worker resistance, it is hardly suprising that others would reach those conclusions.[11] Moveover Burawoy takes up the same theme: Braverman is not wrong to exclude worker resistance, he just doesn't explain why he is right to do so! (1981:106).

Yet the above picture is curiously one-sided in its rejection of the collectivising potential of the large socialised workplace. After all, we have already seen that there is a considerable body of research which indicates that such industries provide extensive problems for capital in the management of its enterprises. This can be illustrated by the previously described trend towards more flexible forms of control to deal with 'labour problems'; and even more so by the previously noted phenomenon of 'runaway shops' relocated in the Third World, and the significant moves to *decentralise* production in Italy and elsewhere as a means of circumventing the power of workers' organisation (Mattera, 1980; 1981).

A similar one-sidedness exists when Burawoy and others talk of the repercussions of internal labour markets and more bureaucratic methods of organising work. Evidence presented in Chapter 5 has already shown that such developments were not incompatible with other methods of direct technical and human control. Nor do they necessarily diminish workers' job control and autonomy where shopfloor organisation is sufficiently strong, and the economic-political context favourable. Referring to the growth of methods of bureaucratic incorporation inside and outside the factory, Nichols and Beynon comment that, 'The trend in our society is a *corporatist* trend and Riverside in the early 1970s is just one example of this. But it *is* only a tendency, and has its contradictions' (1977: 163).[12] Some of the contradictions relate to the ability of workers to use the existence of elements of job discretion and procedure to enhance their power on the job.

The perpetuation of conflict

Burawoy argues that 'only rarely did we observe struggles over production goals . . . or on whether to participate in making out or some other games' (1979: 177), but this negative view is not shared by other writers concerned with conflict and consent at work. For example, Nichols and Beynon state that in spite of all the barriers erected by the company, and although it is often individualistic and reactive, workers at ChemCo 'act — and to a degree informally organise — against work, and the management which directs it' (1977: 107). It is also worth remembering that it was the degree that workgroups exercised control over manning, overtime allocation and levels of output that provided the major impetus for the Donovan Commission to investigate industrial relations in Britain (Clements, 1977: 320).[13] However imperfectly expressed, issues of job control reflect some level of attempted imposition of an alternative rationality over the production process.

Also, can it be so certain that it is always the case that 'where games do take place, they are usually neither independent of, nor in opposition to, management' (Burawoy, 1979: 79–80)? The explicit denial of any radical content to 'making out' is contradicted by the research referred to earlier on telecommunications workers. The working area of the 'high fliers' was known throughout the plant as the 'games room'. To encourage the men to stay in the plant, management allowed them to play games which included chess, poker, dominoes and even table football! One senior steward from another section observed that: 'What they were doing was working rotas and, whilst they were working the "welt", they were allowed to play games. . .While my people were pulling their guts out, these people who were playing games were still hitting top bonus targets. It sounds incredible, but it was true' (Thompson and Bannon, forthcoming).

It may be objected that these were different sorts of games from those referred to by Burawoy. Yet they arose from precisely the same sort of attempt by workers to create space for themselves by using the piece-work system and their relations with the technology to their own advantage. Management may have 'allowed' the situation, but that was an acknowledgement of the existing power relations and the lack of consent built into the normal functioning of the labour process. Neither did the games reduce conflict. The high fliers remained the most militant section in the plant. Further examples of 'alternative games' are provided by Nichols and Beynon: 'The "technical imperatives" cannot prevent the operators having their games with the foreman. Anonymous notes are written in the log books, the foreman's boots are filled with water — "just to cool him down" — and any additional work is resisted' (1977: 138). The politics of the effort bargain may be limited, but as they say, it still provides a 'muffled challenge to capital'.

Counter-evidence of this kind shows that, although there are powerful forces producing consent, it is unwise to present the course of events in terms of a whole transformation of the conditions for conflict and coercion. The ability of capital to organise consent depends in reality on the *context* of productive activity. It is not just a question of the context of a particular labour process — machine shop, assembly line, or chemical plant — but of a broader framework. A sensitive reading is necessary of the differing conditions over periods of time, between industries, and even between countries. For example, the circumstances favourable to consent reproduced through internal labour markets and the institutionalisation of bargaining, underpinned by state leglisation, are largely dependent on the political and economic climate. Events in Britain in the early 1980s — such as the anti-union Employment Bills, and the encouragement of management to *break* procedures, tear up agreements and appeal directly to the workforce over the heads of management — indicate a clear rolling back of the 'industrial citizen'.[14]

The ability of procedure to set common interests assumes the resources to sustain them. Take the example of British Leyland (BL). It was brought into state ownership, and through the Ryder Report 'participation committees' were established with the aim of integrating the apparatus of shop-floor representation. Clearly it was a case of trying to turn geniune job autonomy into an emasculated co-operation. This can be seen in the *Financial Times'* description of this 'participate or else' scheme: 'The Company's proposed plans include renunciation of unofficial strikes, maximum commitments to its new participation schemes, and an end to sectional claims from different unions and groups of workers' (quoted in Red Notes, 1976: 3(a) 5). Having failed to achieve its objectives, BL turned to a harder line which exposed the hollow nature of managerial participation plans.

The view of a Leyland shop steward

'when the shop stewards showed no sign of being easily integrated or of becoming watchdogs for the management, the carrot was replaced by the stick. At the end of 1977 Michael Edwardes was appointed Chairman with a carte blanche to restructure the company and to break the power of the shop stewards. In the first few months he ordered 25,000 redundancies, abolished the Participation Committees, and cleared the decks for an open confrontation with the shop stewards movement.'

(Ahsan, 1981: 67)

Nor was this the only case of leading UK employers using the discipline of the market and mass unemployment to alter the terms of employment, to restructure production, and to increase productivity. Unfortunately, Burawoy fails to account properly for national and sectoral differences, or for changing contexts. Some explanation and qualification on occasion *is* made. It is admitted that the hegemonic organisation of work does not pervade the whole of monopoly capitalism due to differences in market conditions (1979: 199–200). But it is a relatively token comment that fails to do justice to the full variations in forms of organisation of work or workers. Similarly, it is recognised that the forms of internal labour market or internal state differ in countries such as Britain and Japan. Management hegemony is less in Britain, it is argued, primarily because of the relative timing of unionisation and mechanisation (1979: 189). Because British unions established themselves prior to the twentieth-century surge of mechanisation, they were able to create and sustain elements of job control. This meant that managerial reorganisation of the labour process had to accommodate that reality, whereas in the USA unions had to take the reverse situation as a *fait accompli*.

While this may have been a significant factor, it cannot constitute the basis for an analysis of national differences. Burawoy continues to bend those different experiences within one distorting, theoretical construct. In an elaboration of this question, he asserts that: 'In short, despotism under competitive capitalism gives way to hegemony under monopoly capitalism, whether it be the bureaucratic pattern of the United States, the anarchic pattern of Britain, or the corporatist pattern of Japan' (1981: 100).[15] In this article Burawoy begins to talk in terms of the effect of state intervention and class struggles on a society-wide level as factors shaping national variations in the labour process. Going beyond the factory gate signifies a necessary shift in the focus of analysis. The question of context is important not only in illustrating the limits of consent, but also its origin and sources.

The Relevance of External Factors

The idea that workers' attachments and behaviour in work could be strongly influenced by external factors has long been raised by some sociological schools of thought. Theorists such as Goldthorpe and Lockwood have stressed the concept of 'prior orientations to work'. However, the problem with the central features of this approach has been a tendency to counterpose intra- and extra-work factors, and to deny the continuing importance of work experience. Because there is no attempt to provide data on what workers actually *do*, it is easy for Burawoy and others to make the kind of criticisms of weakness in theory and method identified in Chapter 1. Unfortunately these weaknesses merely reinforce Burawoy's belief that external factors have very limited relevance.[16]

Burawoy argues that variations in imported consciousness do not give rise to anything other than minor differences in production relations among workers and between the workforce and management. In normal times the effects of the family, education system and mass media do not greatly affect the nature of subordination of workers to the labour process (1979: 156—7). Evidence for the perspective — admitted to be tentative and based on 'flimsy data' — is thin. Take the question of race and work, the major example that is used in the analysis. After minor reference to other studies, Burawoy relies on his observation of racial interaction at Allied. Off-the-job association was based heavily on racial cliques, and prejudice persistently punctuated the idioms of shopfloor life. But *attitudes* were said to have no effect on *activities*, a dislocation mediated by joking relationships based on the exchange of friendly racial insults.

Such a conclusion could only be reached through an extraordinary notion of what constitutes activities and the means of their measurement. The apparent proof of the lack of importance of outside racial divisions is based on a statistical analysis of the relation between group membership and variations in output! No correlation of any significance was found. This is extending the orientation towards games and output to the point where the genuinely significant questions about race and production are lost from sight, regardless of their specific manifestation at Allied. To say that external racial stratification has no relevance is to deny the persistent segmentation in the labour process concerning the distribution of skills, authority and rewards (see the evidence in Chapter 7); and the reproduction of those divisions in the course of industrial conflict itself. An example of both was the Imperial Typewriters strike in 1974. Angry at low pay and poor conditions, the differential treatment of black and white workers, and racism in the election of stewards, Asians at the Leicester plant struck for thirteen weeks. During the course of the eventually successful dispute, the Asian workers found themselves up against, not just the management, but most white workers and their own union, the Transport and General Workers' Union. Not surprisingly this kind of circumstance has provided the impetus for the formation of independent workplace organisation and union caucuses by black workers in the USA and Britain over the last decade or more.

Burawoy and other writers have made a vital contribution in linking the production of consent to a set of material conditions and social relations at work, but consent cannot be confined within these boundaries. As an aspect of real subordination, consent *must* be reproduced within the labour process: 'But this does not mean that the relation can be generated and sustained wholly within the workplace: rather it is reproduced within the social formation as a whole' (Brighton Labour Process Group, 1977: 24). Two major examples illustrate this point.

Class, culture and trade unionism

Social differentiation affecting the production of consent is not just a matter of differences between categories of class, race or sex, Class itself is an important factor: not so much the 'fractioning' caused by different relations to production, but attitudes brought to work that are rooted in class as a social and cultural phenomenon. This can be seen in the case studies of ChemCo. Behaviour and attitudes of the workforce are shaped by its location in 'an area of England remarkably free from confrontation and industrial strife during this century' (Nichols and Beynon, 1977: 109). If experience is the material out of which people construct their ideas, then regional variations are an important source of indirect shaping of those ideas affecting immediate work experience. The most socialist-inclined group of workers at the plant were a group of foremen from the North of England, who regularly bemoaned the lack of solidarity and militancy among the workforce. Yet they were also quick to condemn strikers and assert that the dole was too high. This could only be explained by the disjuncture between their formative experience of hard times, hard work, and a sense of community and struggle in the North, and their insertion as foremen in a relatively affluent sector of industry and society. Their distorted class consciousness is not just a function of the ambiguities of their supervisory position, but is also 'a nostalgic celebration of a common cultural heritage in the Northern working class' (Nichols and Armstrong, 1976: 142).

An orientation to class as a totality also helps to explain the greater consent by clerical and professional workers. Once again there are obviously factors to do with their immediate experience of work. Clerical workers have their own version of labour process games of adaptation based on the culture of the office, like the autonomy of having own desk and telephone, and the ability to devise individual arrangements or work with the boss (Tepperman, 1976: 12). In one study, clerks using an office vacated by social workers went in for parties, presents and the decoration of desks, all conspicuously absent among the former occupiers (Valmeras, 1971). But such practices only develop because they are connected to wider conceptions of class, conceptions in which white-collar workers are encouraged to accept the cultural compensations of status for the limits of their position in the hierarchy of rewards. This is a phenomenon identified in all the major studies of clerical workers dating back to Lockwood (1958) and Mills (1956).

Similarly the professional strata, such as the design workers studied by Hales, are affected by more than their functions on behalf of capital. Beyond their considerable job autonomy and access to knowledge, clusters of ideas, partly external to production, bind them to accepted work practices. Hales gives the example of 'scientism', i.e. the belief that scientific knowledge — applied in this case to the design and operation of production — is neutral and technical in content. Ideas of this kind can only be understood at the level of ruling-class hegemony in society as a whole, rather than just in work. They are part of the self-definition of professional groups, and as Clements comments, 'At the level of ideology "professionalism" is only effective when its claims coincide with the dominant ideology' (1977: 315—6).

In contrast, manual work-groups are seldom able to develop a counter-ideology to legitimate their own oppositional activities, ensuring that they remain 'hidden' even to themselves. Even on the conventional terrain of wage struggles, workers have difficulty in articulating their needs in a way that can protect them from the effects of the dominant 'national interest' ideology. Hence the tendency for trade unions to present their claims in the framework of 'special cases', thus limiting their class-wide impact. This brings into focus a final point — that external factors interlock strongly with trade unionism. Unionism is more than a reflection of sectional trade divisions. As Nichols and Beynon point out, there are different conceptions of trade unionism and they correspond to different ideological traditions and experiences within the working class (1977: 107). If Goldthorpe and Lockwood had studied Vauxhall workers on Merseyside instead of Luton, they would have found a different picture of militancy. It is normally one of the predictable events of the industrial relations calendar for Merseyside workers to travel in coaches to Luton to lobby their colleagues against accepting the latest pay offer. They invariably fail.

If consent to work is affected by the nature of trade unionism within and between industries, then the same goes for countries. It was misleading for Burawoy to attempt to compare Britain with the USA, and even with Japan, without reference to either the broader cultural context or the specific experience of trade unionism. The prevalence of centralised, non-ideological and highly integrated 'business unionism' cannot have failed to influence the tendency towards cynicism and acquiescence among the workers at Allied. Gallie's (1978) comparative study of French and British chemical workers, referred to in Chapter 1, is useful here. He shows that the more critical attitudes to work prevalent among the French were heavily influenced by the existence of a control tradition and policies for self-management in the trade unions, a factor related to the socio-structural patterns in French society as a whole.

The social preparation for work

Most studies of women workers, whether in the office or factory, have noted a greater passivity and compliance with the conditions of work. Once again, this *may* be specific to intra-work factors. As Barker and Downing (1980) show, the loyalty of female clerical workers is enhanced by the position they occupy in the hierarchy of mental and manual labour. For example, the status of the secretary is often dependent on that of her boss. Such 'attractions' do not exist on the shop floor, and this motivates employers to shape work experience in a way that consolidates their control: 'For management, the point is to preclude any desire by workers to organise themselves to challenge the management-imposed factory consensus' (Grossman, 1979: 32). Thus in Malaysian microelectronics plants initiatives such as beauty contests and production competitions, which appear to be fairly successful in their aims, are organised among the workforce.

This is not just a product of coercive control. It works also because it connects to spontaneous consent derived from the experience of women in the wider society. Socially constructed femininity can also invade the culture of the office. As one of the earlier studies of secretarial work put it:

> Confined in their ghetto, such women make a virtue of necessity in the manner of all ghetto inhabitants. An elaborate ritual of skiving and sharing builds up in the pool; friendships are intense and solacing. Gossip and daydreams are shared. Anniversaries of joining, birthdays, leavings, engagements are ardently celebrated, with noisy all-girl parties at flashy but inexpensive restaurants.
>
> (Benet, 1972: 152)

Burawoy argues that external experience is relevant, but that they are only small variations in the common consciousness that capitalism inculcates in all its subjects (1979: 156). But this is clearly wrong, for we are not all socialised in the same way.

This is particularly important for understanding workplace behaviour and how it is determined by what Pollert calls the ideological preparation for selling different types of labour power (1981: 95). She uses Willis's (1977) study of the processes by which working-class boys slot themselves into manual work as a point of comparison to the socialisation of girls. Boys come to consent to their future as labourers, because such work is associated with the cultural apprenticeship they receive which stresses the masculinity of hard work and 'really doing things'. This does not preclude resistance, as the masculine ethos also resents authority and control. In contrast, girls — particularly working-class — are groomed for marriage. In Pollert's case study they were aware of the futility of their work, but as it was not the primary interest, the resulting low commitment could easily be translated into a stoical acceptance of the organisation of production. Furthermore, the feminine culture of escape and romance, with its stress on individualism and competitiveness, acted to defuse conflict, even allowing for its parallel function as a shared set of meanings impenetrable to the work of management and men. We will return to these themes in much more detail in Chapter 7.

Conclusion: Integrating Consent

It will not be easy to integrate an analysis of consent fully into a theory of the capitalist labour process. Difficulties arise from ambiguities in the concept of consent itself. The beginning of the chapter referred to the consent *or* compliance of workers, and the differences between these terms have not always been clear in the resulting discussion. Abstractedly, they *are* different. Consent implies some level of *agreement*, in this sense to a set of work relations. Compliance indicates that workers *give way* to the structure of power and control inherent in capital's domination of the labour process. Burawoy's definition of consent, as the organisation of activities which involve workers in making choices, partly avoids the problem. That consent is not just a subjective state of mind is a useful point. But by defining all co-operation in production as consent, then workers' adaptations to work can only appear as consent to its rules. Acceptance, however, can arise from concessions to the shifting balance of power. Practically, consent and compliance are therefore linked in that consent is the other side of the coin to control: it refers to the *self*-control determined through participation in practices reproducing the capitalist labour process.

The theoretical task is to develop an analysis that can distinguish between structures of control and consent, and therefore provide a framework for understanding what determines the boundaries between them. Along this boundary, both structures can break down, producing varied types of workplace conflict. It is therefore necessary to sort out what circumstances are favourable to the evolution of counter-hegemony to capital. Hales's example of design workers is illuminating here. Participation in the *general* labour process through which their knowledges are used to shape and control production and other workers is increasingly outweighed by their own *specific* labour process under which they are frequently subject to aspects of proletarianisation, e.g. tighter control, worsening working conditions and potential job loss. Ironically it is precisely because their skills are so integral to capital's organisation of production that they are vulnerable in a recession to dequalification and even redundancy in the search for the cheapening of costs. For instance, chemical engineers have been affected by the sub-contracting of part of their work to outside specialist companies, or to less qualified contract workers employed in-house (Hales, 1980: 104). This kind of situation can provide pressures for such workers to become more critical of their functions and begin to consider, with other workers, alternative uses for their labour power. This is exactly what technical and scientific workers have done in the Lucas Combine in their plan for alternative production, an example to which I shall return in Chapter 8.

A further problem in integrating a rounded picture of these 'subjective' features of work experience is the inadequacies of analytical tools. Not only are theoretical concepts just beginning to be extended, but practical investigative methods are still underdeveloped. The sphere of ideology and consent cannot be studied in a wholly external way. It is no accident that the best studies, like those of Hales, Burawoy and Pollert, have included close observational methods, or in the case of Nichols and Beynon, the very sensitive use of informal interviewing techniques. The tension of inadequate analytical tools surfaces in the frequent comments on the need for a more sophisticated means of understanding the way values and practices are internalised *beneath* the surface consciousness of workers. Hales refers to the need for a materialist psychology that can be integrated with the analysis of production (1980: 86). Burawoy goes further in arguing that a Marxist psychology will have to depart fundamentally from Marx's own writing, which conveys the impression that the social relations in which people are involved are, in the famous phrase, 'indispensable and independent of their will'.[17] This reduces the space for an examination of people's psychic make-up and how that may influence their reactions to those relations.

A Marxist psychology *has* slowly developed. But its lack of firm foundations and application to the workplace is indicated by Burawoy's rather dangerous plea for a theory of the 'invariant characteristics of human nature' that could explain the apparently universal 'instincts' to construct games and assert control.[18] At this stage we can only, as Hales says, 'register an absence, and a theoretical challenge yet to be adequately taken up' (1980: 86). Part of the related challenge is to make clearer the interrelations between the objective and subjective features of work. In fact the discussion of consent and the labour process shows that it is impossible to separate the two mechanically, as if the former were solid economic reality and the latter mere ephemeral ideas (Hales, 1980: 102). Once conceived of as material practices, subjective conditions affecting consent must be considered within objective structures. This raises questions concerning how best to analyse the forces shaping the formation of *classes*, as well as more general issues of Marxist theory of social structure, both of which will be considered at a further stage.

A final point concerning the problems of integrating the consent theme is how to understand the way external factors are reproduced inside work. Of particular importance is how *divisions* outside affect internal differentiation. As has been made clear, workers are not just divided from each other and their potential for remaking society by management, grading or payment, but also by geography, culture and other forms of stratification such as ethnicity and gender. To grasp the functioning of social relations in work, these 'external' divisions need to be examined in terms of their own independent dynamic. It is to that task that we now turn.

7

The Other Division of Labour

> A worker needs more than a vague sense of contentment.
> He needs, let it be repeated, to feel that he is participating
> responsibly, whether alone or in a group, in an enter-
> prise the overall objects of which he can understand . . .
> The one exception here may be women workers who,
> their minds usually being full of subjects out and beyond
> their chore, are conceivably happier doing repetitive work.

(Falk, 1970: 164)

This not untypical quote emphasises that all labour power is
not regarded or treated equally. So there is 'another' division
of labour, in this case a system of allocating particular tasks
to men and others to women. Marx used the distinction between a *social* and *technical* division of labour to differentiate
between the process, in any system of production, whereby
groups of workers are allocated to different branches of
production, under capitalism through the market, and the
division of tasks between workers producing the same commodity. That double division has enormous significance for
a study of the labour process, for as Philips and Taylor
indicate, 'the technical division of labour is almost invariably
hierarchised along sexual lines; women sew what men design
and cut out; women serve what men cook; women run
machines that men service; and so on and so on' (1978: 1).

It is therefore impossible to understand the distribution of skills, methods of control and organisation of work, different rates of exploitation, or any other factor connected to the labour process, without seeking to explain the relations between those social and technical dimensions.

Sex is, of course, not the only aspect of the social division of labour. For example, racial or ethnic differences in many instances play an equally important role in the productive process. The sexual dimension will provide the focus for this chapter for two reasons. First, because a substantial literature has emerged on women and work. More specifically a number of feminist writers have engaged directly in debates about the labour process itself, and this therefore directly ties in with the central themes of the book. In comparison, relatively little has been written from the angle of race and the labour process. Second, however, even if there were sufficient material, given the differences between ethnic and gender stratification, justice could not be done to either by assuming that the contours of debate are identical.[1] Examples drawing on ethnic divisions will be used as a point of comparison where relevant.

What is the scope, therefore, of an analysis of women and the labour process? An immediate problem arises in that there has been a tremendously rich debate concerning the origins and nature of gender differences in modern industrial societies. Yet it would be impossible and undesirable to attempt to encompass the wider issue of the sexual division of labour in society as a whole, and the general origins of women's oppression. Our concern must be the expressions of that division in waged work, and the relative determinations of those processes by factors inside and outside the relations of production.

Women: Labour Market and Labour Process

When Mexicans who can no longer live off the land come to the border region they meet US companies in search of cheap labour for their assembly plants. Yet they are not willing to accept all those who sell themselves at a low cost.

One advertisement specified: 'we need female workers; older then 17, younger than 30; single and without children; maximum education secondary school; minimum education primary school; available for all shifts' (quoted in Hilsum, 1982). There is something clearly *special* about the characteristics associated with female wage labour. Like Silicon Valley in California, with its largely female and immigrant workforce, 'A sexual division of labour, with women doing the production jobs and men the design and management, is one of the foundations of this industry' (CSE Microelectronics Group, 1980: 17). Such examples highlight the problems of an emphasis on the quantitative expansion of women's employment, yet until recently this was the predominant conceptual framework.

Opportunity and inequality

The early post-war period saw a remarkably optimistic picture painted of women, work and family life, for example by the influential analysis of Myrdal and Klein: 'The technical and social developments of the last few decades have given women the opportunity to integrate their two interests in home and work. No longer do women need to forgo the pleasures of one sphere in order to enjoy the other' (quoted in Blackburn and Stewart, 1977). The main concern was to minimise the disruption to the general social fabric by reconciling the 'two roles' (Wajcman, 1981). The problematic was one of economic opportunity and the related social problems. *Explanation* — beyond the surface familiarities of earlier age of marriage, smaller size of family, and increased demand for labour in the expanding economies — barely came into it. Even if the fact that the 'problems' in such literature concerned mainly the minority of professional middle-class women is set aside, the analysis failed to investigate and account for the differentiation built into women's participation in the labour force, right from the beginning of the 'expansion of opportunity'.

The facts of these inequalities have been presented in different forms many times in recent years. Nevertheless, some repetition of the relevant aspects is necessary to provide an adequate context for the subsequent theoretical discussion.

The increased proportion of the labour force that is female, 30 per cent to 40 per cent from 1911 to 1974, is mainly accounted for by married women, and about a quarter are part-time workers. This expansion has had little effect on either the restricted categories of women's employment, or its status or rewards. For example, in the above period the female share of the lower professional, technical and skilled manual sector actually declined by 10 per cent (Reid: 1978). In 1971, 61 per cent of all women were employed in just ten occupations where they generally comprised the overwhelming majority of the total. In 1966, 93 per cent of all professional women were located in minor professions, 72 per cent of all non-manual women were in the routine, low-status grades, and 78 per cent of all manual women were in semi- or unskilled jobs. Once again these proportions were either static or worse than in the early part of this century (Siltanen, 1981: 24).

The best collection of data, particularly in giving a sectoral breakdown, is contained in Huws (1982). Not only are women manual workers concentrated in relatively few industries, reflecting traditional stereotypes of women's work or skills — such as clothing, electrical engineering, textiles, printing and publishing — but all of them have a clear separation of male and female work. As Huws points out, this detailed information about key components of the labour process, such as the distribution of skills, is hard to come by as the official statistics classify work according to industry, without indicating precisely what sort of jobs women are doing. Such information is best obtained from the kind of case studies discussed in this chapter. Cavendish gives a graphic illustration of one such instance based on a participant observation study in a plant supplying components for car assembly. Except for one woman training officer, one chargehand, and a few in quality control, all the women were in the same grade as semi-skilled assemblers. The men did not form a single group, but apart from labourers, all had a recognised skill, training and career structure.

I knew the sexual division of labour would be like that but it still shook me every day. You could see the difference on the shop floor: everyone who was working was a woman, and the men in their white coats were standing about chatting, humping skips or walking about to check the number of components. It was obvious that the only qualification you needed for a better job was to be a man.

(Cavendish, 1982: 79)

The position, of course, does not stand still. One of the merits of Huws's book is its emphasis on the effects of new technology on women's work. The impact is far from simple and cannot be contained wholly within the framework of job losses and deskilling. Both processes will certainly develop. Sales staff, for example, are being affected by the labour-saving and controlling electronic devices to deal with recording, monitoring and storing cash; and we have already discussed the effects of the word processor. But technologically derived deskilling can sometimes lead to the replacement of men by women. Huws gives the example of Hepworth's clothing factory in Leeds, where skilled, male cutting work has been replaced by computerised cutting of made-to-measure suits carried out by six women working at visual display unit (VDU) screens (1982: 51).

Such jobs are fewer in number, cheaper and deskilled, and herald a similar pattern in industries like printing, where new technology is eroding the material basis for traditional job and skill categories. The complex and contradictory features in current trends in women's work merely highlight the necessity to focus on explaining *why* employers bring women into the labour force and *how* they are used to carry out particular tasks within the labour process. We start by looking briefly at some more traditional answers.

The academically invisible woman?

A number of related factors has prevented conventional social science theory from coming to terms with these questions. There has been little interest shown in the pattern of women's work and conditions. This is not simply a result of *personal* bias by male writers. Mainstream discussions of class, work and stratification have assumed male workers. Pollert gives a classic example from the famous Hawthorne studies. Workers in two departments were shown to have

behaved very differently: the fact that one group was women and one men was just not investigated (1981: 74). A
modern example is the omission of women from analyses
of social mobility. This is repeated in the recent Oxford
studies (Halsey, 1978; Goldthorpe *et al.*, 1980) despite the
fact that the non-consideration of the effects of post-war
women's entry into employment gives an absurdly lop-sided
picture.

The presence of women must be acknowledged before
theory is able to distinguish between male and female wage
labour. Yet this is difficult when women are not simply
omitted, but analyses start from the position that the economy
is indifferent to gender. This is the starting point of standard
neoclassical economic theory,[2] which rests on the assumption
that economic behaviour is governed by the free choices of
individuals attempting to maximise their utility. Sexual
inequalities of participation and reward at work pose no
problem. People marry to increase their utility, and the
resulting division of labour between breadwinner and home-
maker is based on an assessment of the likely returns from
the work of either partner on the market. This circular des-
criptiveness is supplemented by *human capital* theory. From
this perspective sexual inequalities are not the result of structural discrimination, but of the *voluntary* smaller investments
in their own capital by women, which result from their
'choice' to spend more time in the family (see Mincer and
Polachek, 1980). Employers take note of this and place men
in the most skilled, senior and lucrative jobs.

Critics have pointed to the obvious weaknesses. It does
not explain why there are female ghettos even within particular skill categories. It fails to account for the substantial
differences in rewards and position even where qualifications,
training and productivity are equal. Most importantly it completely ignores the constraints on individual choice rooted in
women's place in the mode of production and reproduction
(for a full discussion see Amsden, 1980; and Siltanen, 1981).
The result of the above academic perspectives has been to
render women 'conspicuously invisible in the majority of
analyses of wage labour' (Siltanen, 1981: 26).

There have been exceptions, particularly in sections of

industrial sociology that have focused on factories where women work in substantial numbers. Inevitably such a focus highlights the different expectations and attitudes brought to work by women and men. Quite rightly this leads to recognition of the importance of the family and the associated life cycle which affect women's 'availability' for employment (see Beynon and Blackburn, 1972). Such studies, however, put most emphasis on the operation of the *labour market*: 'The fact that more women are going out to work has not in itself aided sexual equality but has served to reinforce their inferior status. While work remains segregated, work rewards will remain unequal' (Blackburn and Stewart, 1977: 437). Previous chapters have given considerable attention to the question of labour markets and their interrelations to the labour process. It is not difficult to see why theories of labour market segmentation have been attractive options. Research by writers such as Doeringer and Piore (1971) show that labour markets do not operate according to the principles of perfect competition, with the useful addition of a focus on actual discriminating practices.

Employers use the historical association between employment stability and differentiation by factors such as sex and race to direct women into the secondary labour market based on casual security and low rewards. Segmentation is reproduced by the patterns of institutionalised discrimination that follows: hence the 'ghetto effect'. For example, Cavendish reports that local labour markets were so rigidly compartmentalised by race in the area of London where she was researching that when she rang to apply for jobs, she got replies like 'but you don't sound Asian' (1982: 159). As we have seen, more radical versions of segmented labour market theory attribute its development to a further and partly contrasting cause: the functional use in dividing and controlling a labour force supposedly becoming increasingly homogeneous due to large-scale mass production (Edwards, Reich and Gordon, 1975). Edwards argues that race and sex are the most powerful differences available to create divisions among workers, and gives examples of blacks used as strikebreakers and women used to separate clerical from blue-collar occupations through the 'feminisation' process (1979: 196).

Criticisms have already been made in other chapters of both versions of labour market theory. The divisions between primary and secondary markets is being eroded by long-term deskilling and decline in job specificity. Even if some differences remain, there is no explanation of inequalities between men and women *within* each sector. Furthermore, little account is taken of the action of men in general — not just employers — to restrict women workers because they benefit from such restrictions. The same goes for race divisions, yet this is denied in the work of Reich (1978), whose views are summarised by his co-worker Edwards: 'racism strengthens employers . . . divides the working class and thereby weakens the ability of white (and black) workers to obtain higher wages' (1979: 196). This emphasises the major weakness of segmented labour market theory. It fails to examine the independent structures of stratification by sex or race which feed into the workings of markets. Describing discrimination and stereotyping does not fully explain it.

In some versions, such as Edwards's, the 'separate dialectics' of racial and sexual relations are recognised and accorded the necessity of independent analysis, although none is attempted.[3] More seriously, it is not enough to identify a separate structure of gender subordination 'out there' without seeking to *connect* its effects to differentiation in labour markets and processes. In the absence of such connections we are little nearer understanding why, when a labour market develops, women are unable to take on the attributes of a free wage labourer; nor are we any nearer understanding the origins as well as the mechanisms of the lower rewards of female labour power. The path to such explorations lies elsewhere.

The Application of Marxist Categories

Many feminists have turned to the adaptation of Marxist categories. Marx's use of the distinction between the social and technical divisions of labour means that women's position in the workplace or society is not taken as given. Furthermore, concepts such as deskilling, the cheapening of labour power, and the transition from formal to real subordination, can be used as an aid to understanding changes in the conditions of female wage labour. An emphasis on the dynamics of capital accumulation necessitates an examination of the motive forces underlying those changes, looking at what the advantages and disadvantages of women workers are for employers. For example, Barker and Downing (1980) use the concept of formal and real subordination to provide the primary explanation for current changes in patterns of control in the office related to the introduction of microelectronic technology, a process we shall return to later.

From the angle of the social division of labour, Marxism has asked important questions concerning the origins of the family and its interrelations with the economic structure. Even when reaching different conclusions, feminists have drawn from the idea used in Engels's pioneering study (1970) of the 'two-fold character' in a materialist analysis of the production and reproduction of immediate life (Bland *et al.*, 1978: 35). This is the notion that the conditions for producing commodities are bound together with the reproduction of people as social beings, particularly in the family. Nevertheless, the work of Marx and Engels has been subject to much criticism on these questions, which leads many commentators to argue that 'there are certain major problems with the wholesale application of Marxist conceptions onto a labour process which is primarily female' (Barker and Downing, 1980: 64–5). Why is this the case?

Marx and female wage labour

Difficulties immediately arise from Marx's belief — discussed in Chapter 1 — that capitalist development would erode the basis for differential rates of participation in the labour force by women and men. Central to this process were the equalising of types of work, deskilling, and reduction in heavy labour associated with mechanisation in the period of transition to large-scale industry. The material basis for interchangeability of labour having been laid, women could then be used to undercut and dilute the skilled character of male occupations.

Implicit in this conception of events was that the effect of increased participation in waged work would undermine the sexual division of labour. Admittedly the Factory Acts — resulting from social reaction to 'an excess of exploitation' — excluded many women. But this was said merely to hasten the conversion of domestic industries and other forms of manufacture into mechanised forms of production. Hence it did not halt the long-term tendency for capital to select from among 'free and equal' wage labourers 'labour power simply on the basis of its potential contribution to the production of surplus value' (Philips and Taylor, 1978: 2).[4]

Quite clearly these and similar events did not take place in such a straightforward way. Women have on numerous occasions replaced men, but not in any manner resembling equal participation. Marx failed to recognise this, not just because he overestimated the degree to which work was interchangeable, but because he simply failed to grasp the significance and staying power of the wider sexual division of labour. The ability of women to enter the labour force, particularly in male preserves, was constrained by the preventative action of male workers. The story does not stop there. A further factor was the advantage accruing to patriarchal power structures as a whole from women's confinement to the home as domestic labourers.

The reproduction of the labour force through services of care and maintenance at home came to be seen increasingly as a vital asset to overall societal stability. Unfortunately, Marx took little interest in this. His fragmentary comments in Volume One of *Capital* indicate that the reproductive role of the family was relegated to 'an a-historical and peripheral plane'. This was so particularly in the oft-quoted comment that: 'The maintenance and reproduction of the working class remains a necessary condition for the reproduction of capital. But the capitalist may safely leave this to the worker's drives for self-preservation and propagation' (1976: 718). Reinforcement of this perspective came from the equally wrong view — put forward in *The Communist Manifesto* and elsewhere — that capitalism was abolishing the family. It was agreed that in the disruptive context of the factory system the family was already 'practically absent' among the proletariat. The process would be consolidated by the trend to the expansion of social services, and the incorporation of household skills and tasks into commodity production. For Engels, the long-run effect was progressive.[5] Only the introduction of women as a whole into productive work could guarantee their emancipation and end the isolation of housework. Any remaining sexual inequalities would be eliminated under socialism through the further socialisation of housework tasks as the collective responsibilities of the community.

Once again, with hindsight, this scenario is seen to be misleading. The family has survived precisely because it continues to perform functions vital to its members, to capital and to patriarchal relations. Obviously Marx's general framework for understanding the position of women and work has proved seriously defective. Nevertheless, that has not stopped the continued application of the analytical methods, and more specific theories such as the reserve army of labour, to a renewed look at the question.

Braverman: the feminist critique

As we have seen, the most prominent attempt to renew Marx's categories has come from Braverman (1974). Feminist theorists have rightly praised the prominence given to female wage labour and the sexual composition of the working class within the changing structures of employment (Beechey, 1982: 54; Siltanen, 1981: 33). *Labor and Monopoly Capital* provides an explanation, in the diversification of the labour process and capitalist production, for the expansion of sectors that have *come to employ* women, notably retail, clerical and service occupations. Women are thus a crucial component of an expanded working class, although one that has suffered deskilling and proletarianisation of its conditions. In providing this explanation, Braverman sticks closely to the central tenets of Marx, discussed earlier, in three crucial respects.

First, he sees the expanded participation of women as an extension of the unfinished process of homogenisation of labour. Remaining distinctions on sex lines are recognised, but not theoretically integrated. Second, Braverman returns to the concept of the industrial reserve army of labour.

Changes in production discard as well as deskill workers, and female labour drawn from the home constitutes a crucial part of the growing industrial reserve. Third, the combined effects of the above tendencies accelerate the decline of the family. While the 'core' personal functions of provision of social and emotional needs are retained and even strengthened, the rest are incorporated into the 'universal market'.

Braverman provides a more sensitive and accurate reading of these trends than can be found in Marx. Nevertheless, the traditional concepts cannot be used without reproducing many of the weaknesses in old or new form. Job distinctions between office and factory work, or within occupational groups, are affected by prior sexual divisions. For that reason the feminisation of occupations cannot be explained merely by reference to deskilling as providing the *facility* to employ cheaper female labour. As Philips and Taylor (1978) point out, just as skill is a category distorted by employers and social scientists, so it is affected by the struggles of male workers to retain their market rewards, employment security and status within the workplace. This sets in motion counter-tendencies to simple deskilling and homogenisation, which on occasion have the effect of making jobs which otherwise might become similar into genuinely non-comparable tasks. Through the constant creation and reproduction of 'men's and women's work', 'job definitions are organised in and through gender differences' (Philips and Taylor, 1978: 7). This is one of the reasons why the Equal Pay Act cannot work. For example, an employer's representative justified the lower wages of a woman toilet cleaner compared to a man doing the same work in terms of the *housekeeping* approach expected of a female attendant, and the labouring orientation of her male equivalent! (quoted in Bland *et al.*, 1978: 70)

Related to the above points are a set of criticisms directed at Braverman's exclusive focus on women's waged work at the expense of the activities of domestic labourers. For some critics the emphasis is on the need to *extend* the labour-process perspective to domestic activity, either in terms of a parallel deskilling of the 'craft' of housework (Baxendall *et al.*, 1976),[6] or stress on the increased capitalist organisation of consumption work as a bridge between production and the reproduction of human relations (Weinbaum and Bridges, 1976). Contributions of this sort are within the general idea of the universal market. But in a sustained critique of Braverman, Beechey (1982) is critical of whether a consumption-orientated perspective is the best way to conceptualise the multi-faceted relationship of the family to production. It is true that certain services once produced for use by women in the home are now produced by women in the workplace for exchange on the market. But by 'hiving off' the discussion of the family to the sphere of the universal market, Braverman 'does not discuss the role of the family in supplying female labour to capital' (Beechey, 1982: 70).

This has an adverse effect on Braverman's discussion of the industrial reserve army. In the post-war period women are said to provide a flexible, disposable and cheap source of labour, mainly to the new service industries. Braverman relies wholly on Marx's own theory and therefore comes up against the same problem of insufficient attention to the ways in which women's role as domestic labourers conditions their availability, and enables them to 'float' in and out of waged work. Hence a discussion of **Braverman's** use of the concept is inseparable from a general evaluation of its explanatory value.

An industrial reserve army?

By using this term, Braverman indicates that he is also following Marx in his division of the industrial reserve army into three segments. A *floating* reserve is constituted from workers repelled from industry by movements of capital and technology, suffering periods of unemployment before being 'attracted' back into jobs often at a lower rung. Of the other two, *latent* refers to sections 'set free' by major changes in non-industrial sectors, the classic example being agriculture in Marx's time; whereas the *stagnant* sector is drawn from the economically disadvantaged, who find it difficult to find employment other than in a casual, irregular and marginal way. For Braverman, women represent an expansion of the floating and stagnant sectors in that there is a mass of women who previously did not work, but who are drawn into the expanding spheres of the economy by the pressures of survival on one wage (1974: 385—6).

However, it is not enough to talk of women becoming 'available' for waged work without indicating what social conditions determine that availability, and why capital may wish to employ them in preference to men. As Beechey points out, the 'reserve army of labour' is used to refer to a long-term, general trend without specifying the types of employment of women in particular historical circumstances; overall it is sexually undifferentiated. This is a weakness taken over from Marx, whose concern was with patterns of capital accumulation and their effects on the attraction and repulsion of the relative surplus population. Consequently the concept was not developed or employed for the purpose of explaining the specific formation and membership of that pool of potential labour.

For some critics, Marx's concept is therefore, *by definition*, 'sexually undifferentiated' (Anthias, 1980). Employing Marxist economic categories such as the industrial reserve army tells us little about the structures and processes — linked to the family and patriarchy — which determine the use of female labour. Anthias argues that in the use of the reserve army, the additional problem is that it refers only to those who have been *made* unemployed and then brought in as a reserve. In contrast, emphasis must be put on women's *inclusion* in the labour force as a central and relatively permanent feature, rather than as casual and irregular. It is certainly the case that an undifferentiated use of the concept does marginalise the importance of women's employment in advanced capitalism, a theme also taken up by other theorists such as Baudoin *et al.* (1978). She argues that the female labour force is elastic in its interrelations with home and production, but is not a general reserve. The latter assumes a single labour market, whereas women are not competitors with the traditional male working class, but rather constitute a reserve army only in relation to themselves. Anthias also appears to favour an explanation based on segmented labour markets (1980: 60).

The crucial point at issue here is whether the reserve army concept can be adapted and modified from its original purpose in Marx and usage by Braverman. Anthias and others are determined to rule out this possibility and severely criticise those like Beechey who attempt to do so. It seems to me that there is no necessary reason why the concept cannot be used, as long as the independent processes affecting women's availability for the labour market are examined, and the 'army' is broken down into specific components as they relate to different aspects of the employment of women. This can be illustrated in the case of the latent category. There seems no reason why this has to apply only to those who are displaced from agriculture. Changes in the nature of family life and income have meant that women, particularly those who are married, increasingly form a *reservoir* of potential labourers (Mackintosh *et al.*, 1977). The situation of declining agriculture is thus 'analogous' to the position of married women who can work for particular periods when they are free from child-rearing (Bland *et al.*, 1978: 64). It is also interesting to note that the notion of a latent reserve has been used to explain the position of *immigrant* workers in Europe, many of whom come from rural areas of Southern Europe and the Third World (Castles and Kosack, 1973).

An orientation of this sort is followed by a number of theorists who attempt to make a specific use of the concept. While it is true that it has a limited usefulness in relation to long-term shifts in the sexual composition of the labour force, there are very many circumstances where women continue to move in and out of the labour market, the classic examples being the period around the two world wars (Beechey, 1982: 66). Aside from the latent sector, others have referred to both floating and stagnant areas. In the former some young women may get jobs such as sales assistants in boutiques, receptionists and hairdressers, where their age and sexuality are the key characteristic. Once having left for child-bearing, they are largely unemployable on the previous terms, but often return to different jobs when they are older (Bland *et al.*, 1978: 63). As for the stagnant sector, this could be 're-cast' to include part-time work, particularly women with difficult domestic circumstances forced to work on an irregular basis, often during 'unsocial hours'. Night cleaning is a prime example (Siltanen, 1981: 36; Bland *et al.*, 1978: 64).

Of course, this does not necessarily explain why women are a preferred source for the reserve army. But there is considerable support for Beechey's argument (1977; 1982) that their labour power has a lower value *because* they are at least partially dependent on the male wage. Therefore the dominant social expectation, used by capital and internalised by women, is that women can be paid at a lower rate, excluding the costs of reproducing labour power in the home that the man receives in the so-called 'family-wage'. We will return to objections to this theory later, but it does show how Marxist categories *can* be transformed by reference to the reproductive relations in the family. Hence the 'reserve' in this case becomes one that refers specifically to the position of women, and furthermore one that does not treat women as a homogeneous category, but as constitued in each case as a reserve by that position and its use for capital.

Conclusion

There is a great deal of difference between applying certain Marxist categories in a critical and modified way and attempting to use concepts developed to analyse the whole of capitalist *production* as a means of understanding the totality of women's work. Part of the reservations surrounding the relevance of Marxism stems from the debate on 'domestic labour'. This was dominated by efforts to 'incorporate women's unpaid homework into the value schema of Capital' (Amsden, 1980: 33). In this first serious debate about female labour, the position was advanced that housework directly produced surplus value (Dalla Costa and James, 1973),[7] or at least contributed to its creation, as the price of labour embodied the costs of reproducing the labourer in the home (Seccombe, 1974; Gardiner, 1975).

As our concern is with waged work, this highly technical debate is outside our scope,[8] but a couple of points are worth making. The above position — a minority among feminists and Marxists — had the merit of challenging the predominant view in Marxism that domestic labour was a private and unimportant concern; and that liberation was synonymous with entry into the 'public' realm of production (Bland *et al.*, 1978: 38). But in extending the conceptual apparatus of exploitation and production to housework, it was confusing activities that are not comparable through the same terms of labour time, value, and so on (Political Economy of Women Group, 1975). An example of this is the way that capital uses the 'elasticity' of housework, in relation to its tempo and organisation, to bring women into the labour market in the ways just discussed (Coulson, Magas and Wainwright, 1975).[9] Subsequent analysis has shown that it is possible to take work in the home seriously — as consumption and reproduction — as a specific activity in its own right (e.g. Weinbaum and Bridges, 1976). The above debate appears not to be dead in the face of a consensus that women's work and oppression has to be examined in terms of domestic *and* wage labour. Emphasising the former has diverted our attention away from the inter-relationships of patriarchy and capital.

Patriarchy and Capital

Like some of the other forms of Marxist analysis, the domestic labour debate focused on the relation of women to the economic system, at the expense of their relations to men, assuming the latter could be explained by the former (Hartman, 1979a). Yet even in our particular sphere of *waged* work, it is necessary, as Bland puts it, to go 'outside' the relations of capital — particularly to the family — before returning to the sphere of production and an understanding of the place of the sexes within it (1978: 1).

The independent influence of patriarchal relations can be illustrated by extending an example from the previous chapter: that of the use of feminity as a means of control.[10] A number of other studies provide additional evidence of management recognition of the usefulness of this weapon. In office work companies often turn to programmed systems of gifts, material rewards and 'treats', which are not just 'bribes' to conform, but a way of connecting to the dominant themes of consumerism, family and sexual attraction in women's lives. An ideology of 'niceness' is reflected in these practices, which cement company identification (Langer, 1970; Glenn and Feldberg, 1979). Like the feminine culture and trappings of romance imported into the factory (Pollert, 1981), it helps women cope with the rigid format, supervision and general pointlessness of the work.

Sometimes the recourse to patriarchal ideology is very explicit, for example in Grossman's study of Third World electronics plants. Not only do they exploit traditionally defined feminine attributes such as passivity and sentimentality in the manner already described, but they reach out to identifiable components of previous experience. As one US manager put it, 'What we are doing resembles a family system in which I am not just the manager, but also a father to all those in Fairchild. This conforms to a very important Indonesian principle, that of the family' (Grossman, 1979: 32).[11] Girls are hired for other qualities beyond their willingness to be controlled. An official government brochure from Malaysia praises the manual dexterity of the 'oriental female', adding: 'Who, therefore, could be better qualified by nature and inheritance to contribute to the efficiency of a bench-assembly production line?' (quoted in Grossman, 1979: 34).

It is very common for employers to refer to the 'naturally nimble fingers' of women as a means of explaining their location in the skill hierarchy of the factory (Brecher, 1979: 229) or at the office typewriter (Davies, 1979: 259), thus ignoring the social learning of gender-related skills at home or school. A more accurate reason why men — in this case Mexican — do not wish to do the dextrous but tedious work of assembling tiny components is given by a US personnel manager: 'It goes against a man's macho pride' (quoted in Hilsum, 1982). However, in most cases capital's use of patriarchal relations is not *conscious*. Like the fetishism of capitalist production relations, the generation and reproduction of sexual differences comes to be regarded as a natural process.

This helps to explain a final example of patriarchal independence: the survival of gender inequalities after the transformation of economic or production relations. In Cuba, despite the theoretical belief and practical necessity for mobilising women into the labour force, women still work a 'second shift' at home. The 1974 Family Code makes shared domestic responsibilities a legal obligation. However, the law also restricts women from taking some 300 types of jobs. The Cubans continue to assert a 'scientific' biological differentiation between men and women, and the ruling 'gives the force of law to a systematised sexual division of labour' (Bengelsdorf and Hagelman, 1979: 293). The roots of patriarchy are deeper than the new economic structures, but it is not merely a case of the survival of past social relations. As Molyneux (1981) says of Eastern Europe, the sexual inequalities at work and particularly at home arise from a contradiction at the heart of such social formations. Entry into productive work is regarded as the path to equality. Yet the role of housewife and mother remains ordained within a 'natural' sphere. The result is an inevitable combination of the burden of domestic responsibilities and restriction of job opportunities, reinforced by 'protective legislation'.

The parameters of partnership
Despite its independence, patriarchy therefore interlocks with specific systems of production — in our case capitalism. But what are the defining features of this relationship as they affect female wage labour? One of the most notable and distinctive theoretical frameworks is that of Hartman (1979a: 1979b). Marxism is held to be a theory only of economic and class relations, in which the categories of wage labour or reserve army say nothing about the composition of the people concerned in the process: 'Capitalist development creates the basis for a hierarchy of workers, but traditional Marxist categories cannot tell us who fills which places. Gender and racial hierarchies determine who fills the empty places' (1979a: 13). As an analysis of capital relations, Marxism is necessarily restricted to its terrain: both are *sex-blind* (as well as race-blind, etc.).[12] A separate analysis of the origins and uses of sexual divisions is therefore required.

   Those spheres of production and reproduction necessarily coexist, changes in either creating movement, tension and contradiction in the other. To create partnership out of coexistence rests on the ability to find a level of common interest between men in general and men as capitalists over the *control of women's labour power*. It is the latter that Hartman conceives as the material base upon which patriarchy rests. She argues that 'before capitalism, a patriarchal system was established in which men controlled the labour of women and children in the family, and in doing so men learned the techniques of hierarchical organisation and control' (1979b: 207). As the emergence of capitalism threatened to create a 'free' market for labour, the problem for men was to maintain this control. They therefore acted either to exclude women from the labour force, or confine them through job segregation to a subordinate place within the labour market and process. While low wages kept women dependent on men in the family, encouraged marriage and the maintenance of domestic services, it benefitted capital in its search for cheaper production. The crucial theoretical point is that this historic mutual accommodation is said essentially to be determined by patriarchal relations. If capital is sex-blind, then while its interests coincide, the motive force derives from the 'necessity' for men to control women. As one of Hartman's supporters put it when discussing women and the reserve army, 'any analysis of women's employment must be at the level of the determinate social formation [i.e. patriarchy] rather than the mode of production' (Anthias, 1980: 51).

Other feminists are more optimistic about the uses of Marxism, arguing that there is nothing in principle in the dialectical and historical *method* that limits it to class relations, even if a lack of sensitivity has been shown in its application so far to an analysis of capitalist patriarchy (Eisenstein, 1979: 7).[13] A similar point is developed by Philips and Taylor. Hartman's theory delivers Marxism to its most mechanical and economistic interpretation, just as labour process writings are showing how work and workers are transformed through struggles over skill and control. While sexual hierarchies cannot be reduced to relations of production, the division of labour within waged work cannot be deduced from two separate 'laws of motion' which happen to coincide. Capital is only *abstractedly* sex-blind. In practice it must *immediately* confront the organisation by workers, and of society, as it exists. Hence, 'There are no pure "economics" free of gender hierarchies' (Philips and Taylor, 1978: 4). This orientation creates a better basis for recognising a more equal and historically based 'partnership' between patriarchy and capital, in which the latter consistently *develops through* existing patterns of social domination and subordination, reinforcing them in the process.

Nevertheless, Philips and Taylor remain critical of labour process theory for failing to give due weight to the influence of sexual hierarchies. We have already referred to the examples given of the definition of skills through the power of male workers. This is extended in a highly specific concept of the 'feminisation' of areas of work. The orthodox Marxist account suggests that feminisation takes place as a result of certain jobs being deskilled or degraded in a way which facilitates the employment of women as cheap, replacement labour. Like other writers, Philips and Taylor argue that it is rare for women to be introduced directly into male-defined jobs. More likely is the creation of jobs that are subordinate through the status of women who come to perform them, for example in the evolution of clerical work: 'The work is not so much feminised because it has been de-graded, as de-graded because it has been feminised' (1978: 6). The theoretical perspective is therefore still strongly orientated away from orthodox 'imperatives of capital'.

An approach closer to that orthodoxy is provided by Beechey, whom we have already discussed with reference to the reserve army and Braverman. In an earlier analysis (1977), she stresses the point that capitalism itself generates tendencies towards bringing women as wage labourers under the direct domination of capital. The employment of women, especially married women, is situated in the context of Marx's theory of capital accumulation, which posits the necessity for employers to search out ways of lowering the value of labour power to counteract the competitive pressures on their rate of profit.

An analysis of the family is not absent. Beechey is aware of the functions of the family in reproducing labour power through domestic services for the 'cost' of the male 'family wage'. Precisely because of the social assumption that women are dependent upon the male wage, they can be paid less and 'disappear' back inside the family when squeezed out of the labour market. The employment of women is therefore structured by the offensive of capital to lower the value of labour power.[14]

The above three perspectives are representative of the range of conceptions of the parameters of relations between patriarchy and capital.[15] To evaluate their usefulness it is necessary to take a brief look at more historical and empirical factors.

The Family, Wages and Work

When women entered the labour markets of early capitalism, they carried with them the disadvantage, in terms of skills, traditions of pay and organisation, inherited from the previous sexual division of labour in the family and from agriculture and the guild system. Nevertheless, their employment came to be seen as a threat, and as we have seen, unions in the UK and USA took action to exclude women or restrict the type of work they could do. Part of this struggle was the relatively successful attempt by male workers to secure a wage high enough to support their families. Hence the 'family wage' becomes the cornerstone of the precarious and subordinate position of women workers. This is the interpretation of the partnership of patriarchy and capital discussed earlier in the perspective of Hartman.

That this situation can benefit both men in general and employers is not in doubt. As Andrew Ure, the manufacturer, wrote in 1835, 'Factory females have also in general much lower wages than males, and they have been pitied on this account with perhaps an injudicious sympathy, since the low price of their labour here tends to make household duties their most profitable as well as agreeable occupation, and prevents them from being tempted by the mill to abandon the care of their offspring at home' (quoted in Hartman, 1979b: 239). In addition the state has consistently acted to support the reproduction of labour power in the family

through legislative changes ranging from the Factory Acts
to the Beveridge Report and subsequent welfare practices
(Bland *et al.*, 1978; Wilson, 1977). Yet to argue that the
family wage and the desire of men to ensure women continue to 'perform the appropriate tasks at home' *explains*
why the employment patterns of women are dangerously
one-sided. Male workers took their actions because of the
immediate threat women posed to the dilution of their
skills and rewards (Rubery, 1980; Humphries, 1980). After
all, the same workers took similar action against other
'dilutees', whether the unskilled or immigrants, *without*
their being any benefit in terms of domestic services. To
posit a direct unity, embracing men in general and between
actions inside and outside production, is to present events
in too conscious and conspiratorial terms. Furthermore it
underestimates the variety of motives on the part of both
men and women, including the possibility that the 'family
wage' strengthened the supportive role of the working-class
family (Humphries, 1980).[16]

The major problem with Hartman's analysis is that it
fails to account for why capital wishes to employ women,
and the subsequent pattern of exclusion and inclusion. In
fact it is interesting that rather than refer to the search for
cheaper labour and lowering the general value of labour
power, she uses the overly conspiratorial model of sex
segregation as a means of divide, control and conquer, associated with the research of Edwards, Gordon and Reich (Hartman, 1979b: 229). Male control of women in the home and
the requirements of capital are *not* incompatible, as indicated
in the useful case study by Goddard (1977). In examining
domestic industry in Naples, she shows how capital has decentralised production to women in the home to cheapen
costs. In turn this is supported by the husbands, who previously used to encourage women to give up factory work on
engagement, or marriage, as work could be a 'bad influence'.
The domestic industry was seen as an ideal mediation of the
dual role by the woman, as they could earn money while
fulfilling their 'duties'. What is really at issue is the *emphasis*
and *impetus* governing the employment of women, and this
problem is reproduced in the wider debate.

The feminisation of jobs

Feminisation refers to a process whereby an association develops between the low status and rewards of jobs, and the fact that they are performed by women. But it is extremely important for an analysis of the characteristics of female wage labour to determine at what point it occurs. We have seen the argument of Philips and Taylor that, reflecting job segregation, the devaluation largely takes place subsequent to jobs being defined as women's work. This is indeed the case in a number of circumstances. Most prominent are those jobs that are seen as a natural extension of women's role, for instance nursing, primary schoolteaching and cleaning, which are largely female ghettos. A similar process can occur in occupations like banking, where as women become established as cashiers, the former male preserve lost its status (Blackburn and Stewart, 1977).

But there is considerable evidence that work has more often been feminised *after* it has already been deskilled and degraded, and in circumstances where there was overlap with the employment of men. In both the electrical and clothing industries, technological change towards lighter machinery and standardised, fragmented operations have led to the replacement of men by less trained women. Within the latter industry, 'skilled tailors and hand sewers were eliminated and contractors were able to move to the cheap female labour force' (Lamphere, 1979: 262). Furthermore, electrical employers have actively initiated such processes. 'The degradation of jobs has been intimately connected with the allocation of male and female labour. Where possible employers have been eager to break down jobs into lower-paid women's work' (Brecher, 1979: 226). Rationalisation of such developments in terms of the 'feminine' virtues of dexterity and patience only came *afterwards*. Replacement is also hidden by shifts of plant and resources. My own research on telecommunications shows that a largely 'raw' female workforce was recruited from the local labour market for a new factory based on deskilled, semi-electronic technology. In the older plants in the company a large number of men were employed in assembly work who were both more expensive and troublesome.

On an international scale, it is also the case that production is shifted to the Third World, and to female labour, subsequent to technological change and deskilling in the metropolitan centres. It is interesting to note that where women are not prepared to act as cheap and docile labour, they themselves may be replaced, as was the case in the New England textile industry in the nineteenth century when Yankee girls were substituted by newly arrived Irish immigrants.

Contrary to what Philips and Taylor say, feminisation broadly followed the above pattern in the evolution of clerical work. The expansion of clerical labour associated with the growing complexity and scale of production pushed employers into drawing on a strata of women previously restricted to a few jobs like teaching.[17] New technology like the typewriter and the telephone helped women into the office by creating new categories of work not in direct competition with men. Considering that the office was formerly an all-male preserve, it was transformed relatively quickly, and was accompanied by a 'massive ideological shift', breaking down moral concern about the entry of women into the business world. Once again, an ideology developed stressing the 'naturally' ladylike qualities of obedience and dexterity. As Davies points out, 'The ideology is obviously connected to the feminisation of the clerical labour force . . . [but] . . . Women were originally employed in offices because they were cheaper than the available male labour force (1979: 259). This is reinforced by Barker and Downing: 'It was the fact that they were cheaper and more abundant than men which gave that ideological shift its impetus' (1980: 68). Even today, the development of new office machinery facilitates the stratification of occupations along sexual lines, and the recruitment of less well trained women (Reid: 1978).

It is quite possible that *both* types of feminisation take place, even within one sector. For example, women were responsible for pioneering computer programming. But once it gained in status, the work was redefined in creative terms and taken over by men. Only when such tasks later became subject to deskilling were women 'allowed to enter the occupation they had created' (Kraft, 1979: 5). However, while it is important to acknowledge the complex sources of feminisation, it remains useful to distinguish between the stimulus of the capital accumulation process and the subsequent development of the sexual division of labour in the workplace, which takes on a life of its own. For instance, decision-making hierarchies in the office are often a direct reflection of external patriarchal relations.

The consolidation of women's work

The partly independent development of the workplace sexual division of labour is reinforced and consolidated by a number of powerful factors equally important as the initial impetus for the employment of women. For many women, the interlocking nature of their low-skilled, low-paid jobs and the burden of domestic responsibility fits together in a way that becomes a vicious circle (Cavendish, 1982: 162). Moreover, it is a 'trap' that is frequently adapted to, as Reid points out in relation to routine clerical workers: 'the value of these clerical jobs lay in the relatively short and flexible hours, and the lack of responsibilities' (1978: 6). Reluctance to apply for higher jobs was based on the real constraints of circumstances at home and work. One of the results is that men and women *experience* even the same type of work differently, Pollert quoting one female operative as saying, 'Men'd go mad. It'd kill them with boredom' (1981: 99). Such conditions are tolerated because family and home are *relative* compensations (Cavendish, 1982: chapter 5). Both Pollert and Cavendish observe in their observational studies of women factory workers that the actuality or prospect of marriage governed the orientation to wages and work. Pollert notes: 'What was specifically female in the women's conception of their wage labour was the fact that they still considered themselves dependent on a man, and their pay as marginal to a man's — even if they were single' (1981: 84). This surely confirms Beechey's position that dependency on the male wage lowers the value of women's labour power, despite criticisms that she uses married women as a generic term for all women.[18]

The organisation of production itself builds in patriarchal assumptions which act as further sanctions against changes in

the sexual division of labour. From the outset women's cate-
gorisation as unskilled is not a purely technical one, but reflects the low value of existing domestic 'training' (Elson and
Pearson, 1981) and practised expertise in the factory setting
(Cavendish, 1982). Even specialist, skilled tasks such as
tobacco spinning are not regarded as equivalent to male crafts.
As Pollert shows, job evaluation is used as a specific tool of
sexual discrimination. The supposedly 'objective' system
regards qualities such as accuracy, close concentration and
dexterity — valued in men's work — as 'natural and untrained
"aptitudes" in women doing women's occupations' (1981:
62). This, of course, is something men are likely to collude in.
The above studies record hostility to women workers and a
male-orientated union structure and practices. Mutual disin-
terest between unions and women workers is reinforced by
the alien language and atmosphere of trade unionism,[19]
confirming its location in a 'public' world, less relevant to
women (see Beale, 1982, for a general discussion). The
resulting lack of solidarity between the sexes is charted by
Nichols and Armstrong (1976). Hostility is not an illusion or
merely imported prejudice. When the men expressed the
opinion that 'women fuck the job up' they were reflecting
the concrete divisions built into the labour process.

Recent trends
In the post-war period, economic expansion drew on the continuous supply of cheap female labour, particularly when
restrictions were placed on immigration. But a contradiction
developed between the need to expand the labour force,
raise the birthrate, and maintain stable conditions for child-
rearing and domestic services (Bland *et al.*, 1978: 52). Despite
attempts to manage the contradictory aspects of women's
'dual role' through state policies, the changes, parallel to new
forms of social and sexual repression, resulted in severe
tension inside the family and the social fabric in general
(Segal: 1982).

The recession is solving *some* of these problems for capital.
Women are losing jobs at twice the rate of men. Yet as women
are excluded from what is often full-time work, the part-time
sector continues to expand beyond the four million it reached

in 1981. The reserve of female labour is still being drawn on, but in the most exploitative manner. *At the same time*, women are forced by the cuts in welfare and health spending to increase their burden of time and energy in the home for no cost. Furthermore, the wages of women, reflecting the intensified job segregation enforced by capital accumulation, falls further behind that of men (Equal Opportunities Commission, 1982). The partnership of patriarchy and capital is truly strengthened.

Economic restructuring, including the introduction of microelectronic technology, is also providing employers with an opportunity to transform traditional structures of control as they affect women. Despite the advantages women's employment has had for capital, the use of femininity as a form of control has left a space which women have used to develop informal patterns of resistance and appropriation of time for themselves. In a very important article, Barker and Downing (1980) show how this is under attack in the context of new office technology such as work processors. The massive increases in productivity, shedding of labour, and its replacement by staff that is less trained and less expensive is aimed at 'squeezing out the lost labour power' untouched even by the application of Taylorist techniques to the office. They argue that: 'Word processors are an attempt to achieve this by the replacement of patriarchal forms of control by more direct capitalistic forms of control — the move towards the Real Subordination of office workers' (1980: 24).[20] The new industrial revolution based on microelectronics also heralds changes in the international division of labour. Whereas European expansion in the early post-war period was based on bringing labour *to* capital, in the current circumstances capital is moving to the cheaper labour in the Third World periphery (Sivandan, 1982: 144). Shifts are therefore taking place within the uses of female and immigrant wage labour on the global assembly line.

Conclusion: the Analysis of Stratification

Capital is *not* impervious to divisions of sex or race. When shipping employers replace UK seamen by Indians on one-quarter of their wages, they are not 'blindly' seeking the cheapest forms of labour. Rather, the logic of capitalist development is connecting to existing and recognisable forms of stratification. Therefore, as Philips and Taylor put it, 'the sexual division of labour in wage work cannot be seen either as a product of patriarchal imperative on the one hand, or of the long march of capital on the other' (1978: 7). In the study of capitalist production, Marxist categories are consequently not inevitably blind to those interrelations. Having originally expunged the family and sexual divisions from an analysis of the labour process, they can be reinserted, strengthened by an understanding of the wider patriarchal relations which 'capital takes over' in using female wage labour.

This is not to say that Marxism is, or ever could be, an adequate means of understanding the whole nature of sexual stratification, or a substitute for an independent theory of patriarchal relations. For example, developments in the family have too often been reduced to the functional requirements of capital. Yet the marriage 'contract' is not just an economic relation, and intra-familial relations have an important bearing on the variations in the nature and extent of domestic work (Wajcman, 1981: 19). Furthermore, changes in the *family economy* — including birthrates and structure of family — decisively affect the availability of women for employment.

The reverse is also the case. Patriarchal relations cannot explain everything about women's work. This is for an additional reason to those mentioned so far. While the dissimilarities between men and women at work have been emphasised, studies like those of Pollert and Cavendish show that women are not a wholly separate species of worker. Men and women are governed by many of the same changes in the organisation of work, even if they often experience them differently. In addition, too few of the studies differentiate sufficiently *within* women workers. Just as the working class as a whole is not homogeneous, neither is female wage labour. From the beginning of industrialisation there has been strong class differentiation in women's work. By the mid-nineteenth century an internal hierarchy had developed between and within industrial and professional sectors (Buhle, Gordon and Schram, 1971). This continues today. In the late 1970s, the US feminist magazine, *Ms*, participated in a Women's Career Convention where discussion topics included: bossing styles, achieving status as a secretary, moving up to management, and getting elected to the board of directors. With whom does the average women factory or clerical worker have more in common: class-privileged women or their fellow male workers? The answer, of course, is that it depends on the issue.

But the complications do not stop there, for as Tepperman reports of the USA, beneath female clerical work: 'Racism is . . . clearly visible to anyone who walks through a big company office. Pretty young white women work as private secretaries . . . Black clericals are mainly reserved for the key-punching room, the typing pool, or the data processing centre — the routine, pressurised, low-paid jobs' (1976: 49). For this reason, and because it is wrong to use production categories to explain wider social relations it is misguided to describe women workers as anything like a 'class fraction' (as in Phizachlea and Miles, 1980). It is necessary to recognise simultaneously the independence of different forms of stratification *and* their interpenetration. A one-dimensional approach distorts the ability to analyse the complexity of stratification. The debates on women and the labour process, however, have begun to open up ways of connecting the specific developments in this sphere to a clearer general picture.

PART THREE

The Theoretical and Practical Consequences

8

The Theory and Politics of Production

The debate on the labour process examined here has been complex and lengthy. In this final chapter I start by summarising the arguments that have been made in evaluating the diverse contributions, so as to clear the way for a discussion of the major problems they pose for a theory and politics of production. Aside from the many unresolved aspects of the labour process debate, there are also a number of unanswered questions that arise from omissions in the discussion. These unanswered questions are a vital component of a wider theory of work and society. Two particular areas are therefore tackled in this chapter. The first consists of an attempt to pose more direct questions concerning the distinctiveness of the capitalist labour process, through a comparative examination of the parallel situation in Eastern Europe.

The second tries to draw out some wider implications from the analysis of work trends for class, politics and social change, focusing on how these issues are tackled within a Marxist framework. Particularly in the latter instance, the conclusions reached are necessarily tentative in the hope that they may illuminate some practical and theoretical ways forward. As Hales notes, the important research on the labour process may differ in analytical content, but 'all converge in a radical commitment to making the politics of the capitalist division of labour more transparent and subject to rational criticism and change' (1980: 44).

Summary

I started by arguing that Marx provided a historical and theoretical framework for understanding work which has been largely absent in mainstream social science. This framework challenges prevailing notions of the neutrality of science and technology, the inevitability of hierarchy and division of labour, and the linear progression of production systems towards a relatively satisfied and integrated workforce. The Marxist alternative derives less from a disconnected series of concepts concerning work than from a comprehensive theory of what constitutes a capitalist labour process. In this context a broad dynamic is envisaged which posits the development of features such as deskilling and managerial control as integral parts of the process of capital accumulation as it affects work. The legacy left by Marx inevitably bears the imprint of the historical period and the limits of his own thought. He wrote at a time when capitalism was the only available model of industrialisation, and when many of the basic components of that process, such as mass production and systematic management, were only in embryonic form.

Any subsequent labour process theory would therefore have to deal with important omissions, ambiguities and contradictions, as well as encompassing the vital analytical resources. Unfortunately, in the adaptation of Marxist theory and practice inside and outside the workplace, the critique of the mode of production was largely abandoned for the terrain of distribution and exchange. Changes in the composition of the working class, and their reflection in the industrial struggle from the 1960s, provided the practical stimulus for the re-establishment of labour process theory in the face of a largely disinterested social science and Marxism. Although preceded by other contributions, the pivotal work of rediscovery was that of Braverman. *Labor and Monopoly Capital* stuck closely to the original ideas of Marx, while placing them brilliantly in a new context. Particular emphasis was placed on the further erosion of skills under the impact of capital's new uses of science and technology, the development of systematic management and control of the labour force through Taylorism and its attendant practices, the incorporation of a wider array of activities in a universal market place, and the consequent transformation of the composition of the class structure.

In renewing Marxist orthodoxy, Braverman inherited its weaknesses — notably a failure to account for the effects of worker resistance on the development of production, the assumption of homogenisation of labour, and the under-estimation of the varieties of control. This created a context for a body of criticism and alternatives within labour process theory which has substantially modified the original schema. The extent and consequences of deskilling have been questioned by reference to the effects of labour markets and the attempts of workers to retain control of job tasks and rewards. But despite the persistence of limits and constraints to deskilling, it is still the main tendency within the capitalist labour process, as can be seen in the latest forms of new technology. Similarly, the association of the capitalist organisation of work with types of direct and despotic authority like Taylorism is contested by evidence that employers have found it necessary in given periods to use forms of limited autonomy, job enrichment and bureaucratic integration so as to maintain their overall control. However, it is not the case that alternatives have eliminated the requirement for some level of direct control. Scientific management and responsible autonomy address different aspects of work organisation, which are therefore capable of coexistence within the trend to real subordination of labour. A frontier of control therefore depends on the combination of circumstances and struggles, rather than complete systems and conscious strategies of capital.

The most significant weakness of the orthodox arguments has been the assumption that the loss of skills and subjection to control was equivalent to a degradation of work. Too often the subjective and relational components of experience are passed over in the emphasis on the structural features of the labour process. Degradation is qualified by the positive participation in practices that arise from workers' adaptation to the conditions of work. Recent attempts to fill the gaps on this question and to grapple with the production of consent have been useful but not wholly satisfactory, particularly when counterposing consensual practices to worker resistance, the continued use of coercive methods, and the denial of significant external influences. Indeed, a related weakness in much of the labour process debate has been its separation of the workplace from wider pressures and concerns. Recent research on the relation between the sexual division of labour and women workers has emphasised the impossibility of understanding patterns of control or distribution of skills outside the context of stratification and culture as a whole. Despite unfinished and contradictory features of the debate on women and the labour process, it has highlighted important issues concerning the scope and explanatory power of Marxist theory.

There are therefore two important lessons arising from the whole debate. First, it has produced a series of powerful but partial insights. A unified paradigm in labour process theory is possible, but its completion must await further empirical studies which can test concepts against the continually changing situation, not just in one country but against the new international division of labour. Second, the relevance of labour process theory cannot be contained within the workplace, just as the workplace cannot be understood in isolation. Whereas the first point is outside the possibilities of this book, the rest of this concluding chapter aims at raising some of the key questions from these debates for adjacent theoretical territory.

The Distinctiveness of the Capitalist Labour Process

In the debates great attention has rightly been focused on the *essential* features of a specifically *capitalist* organisation of the labour process. One of the strongest statements comes from the Brighton Labour Process Group in their reference to three immanent laws of the division of intellectual and manual labour, hierarchy and fragmentation/deskilling. Each of them are carefully related back to the objectives of valorisation in the sphere of production. Such an interpretation has been hotly contested, and certainly any talk of 'laws' unhelpfully obscures the substantial variations in relations and circumstances. Nevertheless, despite this and the even more significant absences from labour process theory, I have offered a qualified defence of these features, at least as main trends within the evolution of work under capitalism.

There is, however, a greater if less obvious challenge. For all the features referred to as 'laws' by the Brighton LPG also exist in societies which are theoretically non-capitalist, or in sectors of capitalist societies — such as major parts of the education, medical and welfare services — which are not governed by the law of value. This poses a serious dilemma for a labour process theory which takes as its starting point statements like the following by Edwards: 'Hierarchy at work exists and persists because it is *profitable*' (1979: viii). References to Eastern European societies or sectors outside the law of value are invariably in footnotes or asides, or consist, in the former instance, of brief mention of 'things not having changed from capitalism'.[1] It would be useful, therefore, to look in some detail at the example of Eastern Europe, so as to return better informed to the question of the capitalist organisation of work.

The labour process in Eastern Europe

It is difficult to be informed through official sources, such as the figures pumped out regularly by the Soviet state on the skill composition of its workforce, although Matthews (1972) makes a valiant attempt to make sense of them. The figures purport to show a long-term rise in the proportion of skilled workers. But as in the West, such calculations are distorted by the functional use of skill by workers and management. For example, as there is no significant external labour market, skill gradings constitute an even greater path to rewards and status than they do within internal markets under capitalism. It is further complicated by official ideology, which is committed to maintaining the fiction that as there is a correlation between socialist industrialisation and the elimination of low grade labour, *existing* uses of technology are steadily resulting in progress towards this goal (see Matthews, 1972: 149).

We referred briefly in Chapter 3 to the similarities of work in capitalist and 'actually existing socialist' societies.[2] Evidence for this proposition exists in substantial form in the work of Western sociologists[3] (Lane, 1972) and Marxists, and more importantly writers from Eastern Europe with direct experience of working conditions. Based on a reading of one the most important works of the latter type (Haraszti: 1977) just how little experience of work differs in crucial respects is summed up as 'monotony, boredom, lack of control, coercion by piece-rate and bonus systems — in sum, alienation' (Corrigan, Ramsay and Sayer, 1981: 59). One of the most striking instances is the building of the Fiat factory in Togliattigrad, 'with if anything an even more hierarchical structure than in Turin' (Karol, 1979: 139). Houlbenko (1975) points out that the entire project was carried out on plans from Fiat technicians, and not only the technical equipment, but also the organisation of work was directly imported. Moreover, the previously mentioned Bolshevik admiration for Taylorism is reproduced at a general level in Soviet industry through an expanded use of scientific management techniques, including the latest 'psycho-sociological insights' (Houlbenko, 1975: 23—4).

The most detailed account is provided by Harastzi's participant observation study as a machine operator in a Hungarian piece-work plant. It is an account of piece rates, rate-fixing, output restriction, bonuses, norms and foremen, which, as Beynon points out, would be familiar to anyone who has read Roy's description of its Chicago equivalent (Beynon, 1977: 79). Even the images of a 'war' between 'us and them', undermined by the individual competitiveness of the daily battle against machines and time, appears little different. And, as usual, in Haraszti's words, 'the norms are a rip-off to hold down wages, while incessant attempts continue to increase productivity without equivalent payment. The whole apparatus of norms, targets and bonuses has the aim of producing a surplus over which workers have no control — evidence that the society 'quite clearly exhibits relations of exploitation very similar to ours' (Karol, 1979: 141).

The official answer is that the factories belong to the people. Yet the 'people' in the factory have to follow blindly the orders of the management, know nothing of the machines or structure of production, or why the products are produced and what becomes of them (see Gorz, 1976a: x). This structure reproduces one of the characteristic features of capitalism, i.e. that there is a separation of the direct producers from their means of production. It continues what Marx referred to as the instruments of labour employing the worker, rather than living labour making actual choices about the goals and practices of work. There cannot be 'socialist' property or a workers' state when they are forced to coexist with a labour process governed by relations of exploitation and alienation.[4] This is not simply because they are incompatible, but because the labour process 'indicates' the character of the wider society. The situation that exists in Eastern Europe implies a grouping that appropriates and determines the use of the surplus labour, and also a state apparatus that stands apart from the working population in a manner beautifully summed up by the ex-Prime Minister of Poland, Gierek, when addressing striking shipyard workers in Poland: 'You work well, and we will govern well' (quoted in Bahro, 1977: 15).

There is a simple explanation as to why work experience has remained similar, and to why there is still exploitation and alienation: they are still capitalist societies, albeit ones in which a new *state*, and a new ruling class, are defining features. This 'state capitalist' position is associated with widely differing but important strands in Marxist thought, such as Bettelheim (1976), Rossanda (1979) and Cliff (1970). I believe this explanation to be wrong. The societies of Eastern Europe do not operate according to the characteristics of the capitalist mode of production. This is based on generalised commodity production. All products and elements in the labour process are commodities. Goods and services are produced for exchange on the market, rather than for their use by the population. Generalised production of commodities and surplus values can only exist when regulated by the market and competition between enterprises. As Marx put it, 'By definition competition is the internal nature of capital . . . Capitalism does not and cannot exist except when divided into innumerable capitals: for this it is conditioned by the action and reaction of one upon the others' (1973b:

414).[5] In the Soviet union, the state monopoly has gradually eliminated any significant private ownership and competition.[6] Neither the bulk of goods nor labour power function as commodities. In the latter case, compulsory purchase takes place. The state is constitutionally obliged to provide work, while the worker is legally compelled to sell his or her labour power to the state.

There is another influential argument, stressing that the labour process is capitalist, within a society in transition to socialism. Such a situation is held to result from the Bolshevik-influenced failure to transform the relations of production discussed in Chapter 2. This concept that the work processes in Eastern Europe are a residue of the past is held by influential theorists like Braverman and Marglin. There is an important partial truth here. The Soviet state had to socialise key sectors of large-scale production, and was forced to construct productive forces not created by a previous phase of capitalist development. This was inevitably influential in reproducing existing capitalist forms of organisation of technology and work that carried over into the new society (Coombs, 1978: 81). But this rationale cannot be extended over six decades! Subsequent accumulation has not been driven forward by capitalist competition, but by political decisions based on a particular model of industrialisation. Marx made clear that work relations he observed resulted from the *unity* of the labour process and the valorisation process. Hence, if there is no capitalist mode of production, there is no capitalist labour process. We are dealing with something different and new, in which it is impossible to define the working class, labour or forms of domination in the same terms used as those of the West (Schmiederer, 1979: 162–3). *If* this is the case, then the experience of work cannot be the *same*, no matter how many *similarities* there are. To avoid simply counterposing theoretical models, let us look a bit more critically at that experience.

Ninety per cent of Soviet workers operate under a piecework system. To supplement these incentives, there are 'interminable output competitions' and management campaigns such as getting workers to participate in rationalisation and invention drives (Matthews, 1972: 126). Existing in parallel are workplace apparatuses whose function is to discipline the workforce and enforce the plan. This includes the trade unions, one agreement stating that: 'Management and the trade union committee undertake: to examine every infringement of labour discipline (absenteeism, lateness, breakdown of equipment, production of faulty goods, etc.) and breach of public order at meetings of trade union groups and shop trade union committees' (quoted in Haynes and Semyonova, 1979: 13). Behind them stand the repressive apparatuses of the state itself.

However, neither the incentives nor the coercion show any evidence of working. Or to be more precise, it is the workforce who give little indication of working. There is a very low rate of productivity, and a high rate of absenteeism, theft, drunkenness, labour turnover and restriction of output reported in many studies inside and outside the Soviet Union. Sweezy reports a cynical slogan in Eastern Europe, 'Communism is better than working' (1971: 101), and Houlbenko comments that 'the right not to work hard at the factory is one of the few remaining rights which the Soviet worker holds' (1975: 22). Much of the worker's energy is saved for jobs 'moonlighting' in the 'second economy' (Karol, 1979: 142). Neither does management operate in the same manner as its Western equivalent. Inefficient hoarding of labour, waste of resources and withholding of information about targets and quotas are all common practices.

These two tendencies are not contradictory; they are the direct result of the mode of production. As Schmiederer notes, 'there is no "inner nexus" giving cohesion to the society through the law of value' (1979: 163). No economic equivalent has been found to the mechanisms of accumulation and competition; nor under existing conditions could there be. 'The extraordinary rhythm of the plan dictates to industry' (Haynes and Semyonova, 1979: 6), but its despotic and centralised character — excluding the creative involvement of Soviet workers and consumers — precludes the finding of an alternative means of effectively regulating wages, prices, supply and demand. This is not to say that the economy has no governing impetus. The Polish Marxists Kuron and Modzelewski (1982)[7] once referred to this as 'production for the sake of production', although it would be more accurate to speak of production to ensure the maintenance of the domination and rewards of the ruling party-state group. The nature of the relations of production do not even give rise to the limited forms of common interest in accumulation that arise between capital and labour in the West, hence the excessive reliance on piece-work incentives (Burawoy, 1981).

Nevertheless there is a curious type of 'social contract' based on state guarantees of employment in return for formal participation in work and the plan. This 'contract' does not provide the means for management or workers to advance their interests effectively. Management continues to hoard labour because production quotas have to be filled and there is no labour market to discard to and draw from. In addition the labour laws make it very difficult for managers to shed labour, a further disincentive being that bonuses are calculated according to the gross wage bill (Fantham and Machover, 1979: 17). Defective machinery and low standards of work result in large-scale waste of raw materials and industrial capacity. It is estimated that the Soviet Union employs more people repairing machinery than making it (Ticktin, 1973: 35). But enterprises frequently conceal information on waste and productive capacity. Indeed, such is the level of misinformation engendered by the hierarchical authority that some commentators believe that the Soviet Union is 'structurally incapable of joining a real technical scientific revolution' (Plyushch, 1979: 43). It is difficult to alter workers' performances because even if extra money is earned, it is seldom able to be used to buy anything, given inefficiencies in the availability of consumer goods. Aside from strengthening the black market, it means that material incentives cease to have any significant effect.

Taking these factors into account, it is clear that waste, inefficiency and low productivity are *generic* to such systems (Rakovski, 1977). Furthermore, the nature of production relations precludes the party-state bosses and managers from solving the inherent crises through intensifying labour and establishing an equivalent form of real subordination. Of course, attempts are made to increase productivity, but the absence of the discipline of the market means that there is no consistent impetus to squeeze out 'lost labour time' and reduce the porosity in the working day. For example, it has been estimated by one Soviet economist that there are 15 million individuals who could be removed from production without affecting output (Ticktin, 1973: 30). These factors make it very difficult for even the most drastic attempts to increase labour productivity to succeed, as Arnot (1982) shows in his case study of the Shcheniko Experiment.[8] As part of the wider movement towards economic 'liberalisation', it had successes in reducing manning, absenteeism and the like; but it proved difficult to maintain the momentum and generalise the experiment due to the constraints of the external environment of Soviet industrial life. Trapped in its own social relations, such economic mechanisms would need massive labour shake-out and wholesale market norms to have lasting effects. Yet the right to work is enshrined in Soviet society, making a stark contrast to our own societies, where mass unemployment is regularly used to discipline the working class. Each class society is caught in its own contradictions. So, while there is a common experience of hierarchical work organisation, mass production and some managerial techniques producing overlapping experiences among Eastern and Western workers, in other respects they are crucially different. And those differences relate to separate labour processes under separate modes of production.[9]

One way the differences are manifested is in the way conflicts and demands are expressed. It is a common feature in Eastern Europe that workers' demands are addressed directly to the political authorities. What the response will be often depends on the location of the factory in geographic-political terms. Concessions can be swiftly agreed by party representatives, although if this fails repression is certain to follow (Houlbenko, 1975: 9).[10] This pattern of events is not merely a result of the lack of adequate forms of collective representation, although that is a factor. It arises from the basic *transparency* of the system (Houlbenko, 1975; Schmeiderer, 1979). Social inequality resulting from the distribution of wealth, services and power does not operate according to the hidden hand of the market, but through the visible mechanism of the party-state apparatus. As only the action of the state can sustain the species of forced labour in operation, the sources of power are also easily identifiable. Given that these are *planned* economies, the fact that many demands are concerned with prices and other aspects of economic-political management should be no surprise. Struggles cannot go beyond the bounds of the factory without confronting the all-encompassing rule of state political authority. This has been the course of events in Poland from the strikes over price increases in the early 1970s, through to the rise and suppression of Solidarity. It is not that Eastern European workers are more politically conscious than their Western counterparts, but the character of production relations makes them more *conscious of politics*.

Theoretical consequences

That the labour process, Eastern and Western, is not the same, does not let labour process theory off the hook. The recognition of two distinct industrial modes of production still creates important theoretical consequences.[11] Marx commented that it was necessary to judge one mode of production by comparison with another, and we have a situation where, despite crucial differences between East and West, there are clear overlaps in the features of work organisation and experience. The unavoidable lesson appears to be that whereas hierarchical control, division of intellectual and manual labour, and fragmentation of tasks have arisen under capitalism *because* they were profitable, they — and other features — can develop in a varied form under the impetus of different socio-economic pressures. There are thus two different meanings to the term 'essential' to capitalism: that which is an indispensable characteristic in some form under the capitalist mode of production, which clearly the above features are, and that which *belongs* distinctively to *a* specific mode of production, which the above features do not.

Similar guidelines can be applied to sectors of work under capitalism not governed by the law of value. On the face of it an office in a private company and one in a public-sector institution may not appear very different. It is likely that they will be working with fairly similar technology, and the

work will probably be organised in the conventional hierarchical manner. 'Organisation and method' studies have been
applied to the public service sector for some time, and Cooley
reports on the growth of programmes of scientific management techniques aimed at 'optimising efficiency' in education
(1981: 51–2). The reasons for the extension of techniques
developed in the capitalist labour process to other sectors is
less complicated than in Eastern Europe. Although such
sectors are not producing commodities for exchange, they
are part of the same overall mode of production, and developments cannot be contained within one sphere. Furthermore
we have to allow for some relative autonomy of science and
technology[12] and of managerial techniques. Concerning the
latter, we do not have to agree with Weber's view of bureaucracy as a rationality separate from a mode of production to
accept that bureaucratic models of organisation may be
used by public authorities in the belief that they are 'efficient',
regardless of the lack of a direct tie to profitability.

Nevertheless, once again the two labour processes are not
the same. The output of state services is directed towards a
distorted form of production of use values. The result is that
manning levels, work organisation and productivity have not
operated according to the restrictions of the product and
labour markets (Driver, 1981). Economists of varying persua-
sions have recognised that increased social spending is a drain
on already threatened profits (O'Connor, 1975; Eltis, 1979;
Aglietta, 1981). Until relatively recently, capital has accepted
the social costs of collective consumption because they
stabilised the provision of important needs within the extended post-war economy. Now, in a crisis, pressure is being
brought to bear to change the relation of the state service
sector to its private counterpart. This appears to be taking two
primary forms in Britain. First, a substitute for the 'discipline'
of the market has been found by imposing *cash limits* on the
amount of spending within particular sectors and institutions,
forcing them to 'rationalise' their resources. Second, there
has been a move towards what Aglietta calls the 'commodification of state services' as a means of revolutionising their
production conditions. This can be seen in the extensive
plans to *privatise* services in health, housing mangement,

refuse collection, hospital cleaning and many other instances.

There is a further theoretical consequence of accepting two industrial modes of production. That a society has come into being that is neither capitalist nor socialist challenges the strongly held view of some Marxists that historical development would be characterised by a linear succession of modes of production: feudalism → capitalism → socialism.[13] In current political circumstances of the unlikely short-term possibilities for socialism in the West, and the gigantic arms build-up between the superpowers, such questions may appear abstract at best. But there is a point of concern for labour process theory, because it is in production that the basis for a socialist society is said to develop. If we return to the idea of comparing modes of production, it can be seen that, under feudalism, capitalism took centuries to take root and develop *within* its framework. Socialism cannot develop in the same way, as the failure and marginalisation of utopian communities has shown. Marx believed that capitalism created the basis for its own replacement, in that the self-expansion of capitalism necessarily expands the proletariat, who become its own, inevitable gravediggers.

But as Sweezy (1971) points out, this omits crucial considerations. The proletariat that is impelled to destroy capitalism is the same one that is required to construct a socialist alternative, including new relations of production. There is a largely unrecognised problem here. Marx talked of the preparation for the new society rooted in the formation of the 'collective labourer', but did he not also write in depth about the detail-worker crippled by the fragmented work of modern industry? Which is of more importance in understanding the problems involved in the ending of capitalism and the creation of a socialist society? There are ways round the question, such as Lenin's theory that the political consciousness necessary for socialism has to be inserted from outside workplace experience. We can also say that, in changing society, the proletariat will also change itself, and will therefore be able to meet the challenge of new tasks. But this avoids the key problem, which is to set out the possible implications of the relationships between work and social change. This requires the raising of a number of very critical questions about Marxist analysis.

Remaking Class Society

Class analysis is directed towards searching out collective agents who may play a central part in social change, given their location in the functioning of an economy and social structure. Within such a framework Marxism has traditionally identified the working class as a pivotal force. But the growing complexity of advanced capitalist societies has inevitably led to an increased debate on the nature of the working class and class boundaries in general. Attention to the labour process is a vital part of that assessment, not simply because the work situation is the core economic experience, but as Hales says, 'Being a theory of production, labour process theory offers an angle on the pattern of how classes can be formed in specific practical circumstances' (1980: 112). History only tends to register classes when they make their mark as fully conscious and active agencies. What is needed is emphasis on class formation and action on a day-to-day level. The circumstances of changing forces and relations of production, skills and control structures discussed in this book therefore assume great significance in the debate.

The labour process and class analysis
This was not always recognised, particularly in the absence of critical perspectives on the productive forces and labour process discussed in Chapter 2. Prior to the emergence of such perspectives, occupational shifts which rapidly increased the proportion of wage and salary earners were held to represent a corresponding expansion of the working class (Budish, 1961; Szymanski, 1972; Hunt, 1975). Definitions remained structured around wage, rather than production relations, and were felt to be upholding a two-class model derived from Marx. Consequently those shifts were transposed into an elaboration of classes, *without* a detailed examination

of the nature of the work of new professional and white-collar jobs, particularly one that emphasised the control functions exercised on behalf of capital.

In addition, the orthodox position advanced the view that all the expanded scientific, technical and intellectual skills were valuable assets for the building of a socialist alternative. As Gorz pointed out, this drew on the mechanistic conception of neutral productive forces clashing with capitalist social relations. It was used to justify the identification of professionals — including engineers, technologists, supervisors and even managers — with blue-collar workers as part of the enlarged 'collective worker' whose labour combines in the modern process of production (see Azcarte, 1975).[14] As we saw in Chapter 3, even less orthodox analyses of the 'new' working class repeated the mistake of looking only at the relation of such occupations to the employers and the state, and not to other workers (as in Mallet, 1975). Nevertheless, such studies broke new gound in consciously applying an analysis of changes in work relations and the contradictions engendered by the new productive forces.

Those who developed new working-class theory, such as Gorz, later reshaped it to take account of those situations where 'scientific and technical workers, in performing their technical functions, are also performing the function of reproducing the conditions and the forms of domination of labour by capital' (1976c: 162). Contributions like this have become part of an important debate on the new class locations and boundaries (Poulantzas, 1975; Wright, 1978; Ehrenreich and Ehrenreich, 1979; T. J. Johnson, 1980; Carchedi, 1975). I am not particularly concerned with the detailed differences between the respective positions, which have been extensively discussed elsewhere (see Walker, 1979). What is notable is their common commitment to analysing class with reference to criteria which go beyond legal ownership, property and wage relations. Indeed, Braverman himself developed a model of the class structure from his wider theory. As Coombs notes, 'By attempting to dissect the concrete development of labour processes and by describing actual jobs, Braverman cuts through much of this discussion and attacks the question in a novel manner' (1978: 91).

As a theoretical framework, Braverman's contribution was less sophisticated than that of others. Poulantzas, for example, uses the concept of structural locations based on objective positions in the division of labour, which include political and ideological as well as economic criteria. On this basis, a *new petty bourgeoisie* is said to have developed. They are not part of the ownership of production, but are beneficiaries of the dispersal of the functions of capital and the separation of conception and execution. The Ehrenreichs use labour process material even more directly, with explicit reference to Braverman. They argue that new conditions of production have generated a class of *mental workers* whose functions rest on social control and the reproduction of capitalist relations of production. This *professional-managerial class* both institutes and benefits from processes such as deskilling. The political interests of such workers are contradictory. While the above factors separate them from the working class, they are also faced with the counter-tendency of increased interference with their autonomy by capital.[15]

The most fruitful direction has been developed by Wright, who argues that it is necessary to break down the tradition in Marxism that every position in the division of labour is assigned a definite class.[16] Class boundaries are governed by *contradictory class relations* linked to the effects of workers' progressive loss of control, more complex hierarchies of authority, and the differentiation of functions in the enterprise. The point is that many professional, technical and white-collar occupations are in an intermediate position between the working class and higher classes because they embody contradictory features deriving from their functions in the division of labour. This corresponds broadly with Braverman's own discussion of the 'middle layers'. The working class, on the other hand, is said to occupy a *determinate* class location, in which its class interest is fixed by its relations to the means of production. The above debate represents an important advance on earlier class analysis, but it does not significantly advance our understanding of the capacity of the working class to transform class society. All the discussions of what constitutes the working class *assume* that it is already constituted as a class acting according to its imputed interests. A similar point is made by the Ehrenreichs in a criticism of Wright:

> In his analysis . . . The working class occupies a 'determinate class location' — hostility to the bourgeoisie and a fundamental interest in achieving socialism is built in to its economic situation . . . this theoretical assignment of the working class . . . in one stroke 'solves' the most serious problem of the US Left — simply by *positing* that the working class is inherently socialist.
>
> (Ehrenreich and Ehrenreich, 1979: 331)

Work and social change

It must be said, however, that this theoretical 'leap' is firmly based on the traditional Marxist understanding of the relations between work, class and social change, taking us back to the problem that was approached in Chapters 4 and 6, that is, the relations between the analysis of the dynamics of change in the labour process towards deskilling, fragmentation, the emergence of the 'collective labourer' in large-scale socialised production, and the objective basis for class formation.[17] The orthodox projection has been that class antagonisms were simplifying and intensifying in the sphere of production, capital producing its own gravedigger in the proletariat which would become progressively more conscious of its historical tasks as capitalist social relations unfolded in a more transparent way.[18] This process is outlined with some clarity by Marx in *The Poverty of Philosophy*:

> Economic conditions had first transformed the mass of people of the country into workers. The combination of capital has created for this mass a common situation, common interests. This mass is thus already a class against capital, but not yet for itself. In the struggle, of which we have noted only a few phases, this mass becomes united, and constitutes itself as a class for itself. The interests it defends become class interests. But the struggle of class against class is a political struggle.
>
> (Marx, 1963: 173)

Burawoy interprets the traditional view as follows: 'Marxist programs for the transformation of capitalism involve a revolutionary agency which derives its identity through labour but realises its interests through politics' (1981: 83). The development of this political struggle and party formation is consequently seen by Marx as 'arising in a natural process from the everyday struggles under capitalism' (Carol Johnson, 1980: 81). In *The Communist Manifesto* it is made clear that although workplace struggles may be defeated and divided, the long-term advance is ensured by the centralising tendencies of modern industry: 'The organisation of the proletariat into a class, and consequently into a political party is continually being upset again by competition between the workers themselves. But it ever rises up stronger, firmer, mightier' (1968: 42).[19] Any observable barriers to the advance of revolutionary struggle in the major European countries were put down to factors like economic prosperity, poor leadership, and the lack of generalised bourgeois relations: for example, the continued importance of the petty-bourgeoisie and peasantry in Germany and France. Although most of these perspectives were developed in Marx's early writings, the mature works such as the *Grundrisse* and *Capital* did not alter the general views of the relation between production and the development of class consciousness, as Carol Johnson convincingly shows in an examination of Marx's later political writings (1980: 86—9).

Now it may be that there were complex theoretical-political considerations which led Marx to overestimate the possibilities. And certainly subsequent experience of trade unions, reformism and changes in capitalism has made all but the most dogmatic aware of greater problems. Yet these problems continue to be seen primarily in terms of political organisation, programmes and consciousness (see, for example, Blackburn, 1976). Within Marxist orthodoxy the objective conditions for revolution are still held to exist in the decay of the material foundations of the system and the location and conditions of the working class in production. After all, Marx did say that, 'It is not a question of what this or that proletarian, or even the whole proletariat, at the moment *regards* as its aim. It is a question of what the proletariat is, and what in accordance with that being, it will historically be compelled to do' (quoted in Meszaros, 1971: 85). Efforts are therefore directed towards the shaping of the 'subjective factor' to match the historical potential of a class brought into existence by capitalism and destined to produce the means of a 'universal liberation from all forms of oppression and exploitation' (Blackburn, 1976: 3).

Labour process theory has generally not confronted the problems of this theoretical legacy. In some cases, notably Braverman, there has been a refusal to deal with the consequences of analyses of changes in the nature of work. Others, like Edwards, clearly show the divisions inherent in the development of the capitalist labour process, but do not trace back the theoretical weaknesses to their source. However, despite this disjuncture between the analysis of work and its 'political' consequences, the overwhelming body of evidence can be used against the idea that the working class is constituted as a united class against capital by the production process. We have seen that deskilling does *not* result in the homogenisation of labour, but in an internally differentiated structure of dexterities and rewards with a variety of consequences for class formation.

It is also necessary to take seriously the consequences of trends in the division of labour. The increased fragmentation of tasks and the separation of conception and execution make the possibility of collective mastery of production processes considerably more difficult. Even simple factors like the capacity for increased communication between workers embodied in the concentration of capital — a factor often pointed to by Marx as an important foundation for a class-in-itself — can be limited in practice. Hales comments: 'Not only are different workers employed in subsequent stages of production, but also the necessity of direct communication between these distinct work groups is systematically extruded as labour becomes increasingly objectively ordered — notably by specialised instruments of labour, machines' (1980: 95). The division of labour does not obliterate the existence of class, but it does structure the experience of class in such a way as to limit its oppositional character. Hence trade union action continues to reflect a *sectionalism* which inhibits class consciousness and reflects work divisions (Hyman, 1980: 326).

Theoretically these 'negative' factors are contradicted by the parallel rise of the 'collective labourer'. Arguing against a pessimistic interpretation of Braverman, Coombs says,

> Simultaneously, these same relations of production create a working class which, as the degree of labour productivity increases, becomes a progressively more coherent and powerful collective labourer, measured in terms of its objective ability to shoulder the task of organising the administration of the entirety of society under new social relations.
>
> (Coombs, 1978: 94)

However, to measure the existence of the collective labourer by a hypothetical future capacity is to ignore the unfavourable existing terrain on which 'capital can develop its own form of socialised labour, articulated by the division of mental and manual labour' (Elger and Schwarz, 1980: 360).[20] As Hales notes, capitalist production develops no corresponding *subjective* socialisation of labour. The greater interrelationship of tasks under the value-form does widen the *potential* class forces for socialism. But that requires a long-term struggle to establish a practical collectivity based on a conscious alliance between different strata of the workforce.

Neither are these factors the only constraining ones. We have also seen the way patterns of external and self-control create forms of accommodation and positive attachment to work practices under capitalism. The 'manufacture of consent' was linked to the concealment of exploitation and oppression by the fetishisation of capitalist social relations as natural phenomena. This is a theme taken up by Carol Johnson, who argues that Marx failed to take into account the implications arising from mystifications from work for proletarian consciousness. Hence the misleading theory of work and class remained intact *despite* the power of the analysis of commodity fetishism. Finally, it has also been shown that divisions arising independently of the labour process — notably the sexual and ethnic divisions of labour — also point away from the simple idea of a homogeneous working class that can automatically unite around the same goals and means, thus throwing added doubt on the notion of the working class as universal liberator.

Concepts reconsidered

The above analysis is not intended to paint a pessimistic picture of the prospects for class struggle. Throughout this book examples have been given of how worker resistance persists through even the most comprehensive reorganisation of work, schemes of incorporation and methods of control. Clearly the workplace remains a crucial site of social conflict and, indeed, one that has increased in importance over the last two decades. Furthermore, changes in the labour process *have* resulted in new and often more advanced forms of organisation and demands, some of which were discussed in Chapter 3. For example, one social scientist described the types of struggle that developed around the semi- and unskilled workers in the large assembly plants in Italy:

> at the peak of cycles of disputes in 1969—70 workers in several plants organised changes in work organisation on their own initiative, cutting down on work rates, altering hours, reorganising job routines and refusing various jobs. By this means they actually achieved demands that had been set in the union platform at regional level.

(Dubois, 1978: 12)

Letteri (1976) gives a similar detailed example of the campaign by Italsider workers in 1970 to do away with the system of job classification then in use and collectively design one of their own which considerably reduced its hierarchical features.

These are not isolated examples of the way in which the restructuring of work can shape more advanced responses from the workforce. But how should such events be understood in terms of class formation? An influential account in Italy and Europe during this period theorised them through the concept of the *mass worker*, also referred to in Chapter 3. Such assembly workers were not only seen as the motive force of anti-capitalist struggle, but as embodying the rejection of wage labour, and the focus for redefining the nature of work under socialism. Furthermore, so far had this 'massification' process spread among manual and white-collar workers that an alliance between the working class and other social forces was no longer necessary (see Red Notes, 1979, for a fuller presentation of the perspectives).[21] This application of the homogenisation thesis typically covered over ideological and material differences in the working class. The complex political problems associated with maintaining the impetus of industrial action, advancing perspectives that could generalise class-wide demands beyond the industrial strongholds, *and* on to the state terrain, were systematically underestimated. Suffice it to say that the mass worker thesis has not survived the sharp decline in industrial struggles, marginalisation of many sections of the Left, and the general political impasse of the later 1970s and beyond.

This example has been used to illustrate one of the main points of theory that need reconsidering. The structure of the capitalist labour process continually reproduces the conditions of antagonistic class relations. Workers are compelled to resist in one form or another. There is no guarantee of anything more, even under the kind of favourable conditions mentioned above. Or as Aronowitz puts it, 'The logic of capital forces them to fight, even if their awareness of the stakes of combat does not translate into political terms' (1979: 226). Marx was therefore quite wrong to suggest that there is anything in the objective location of the working class in capitalist production that 'compels' it to transform and ultimately abolish class society. It may well accomplish that task, but if the proletariat is to be the gravedigger of capitalism, it will have to do more than work in the cemetery.

This recognition requires a re-evaluation of the nature of class-in-itself and class-for-itself. If these terms were used to describe the opposite poles of class formation — at one end the objective model of class approximating to the relations of production, at the other a fully conscious actor on the historical stage — they would be satisfactory. Unfortunately, the traditional usage tends to imply that class-in-itself is already constituted against capital by virtue of its economic conditions. Class-for-itself becomes the political 'icing on the cake'. In the normal circumstances of capitalist society, class is reflected in a much more fragmentary and uneven way. To believe otherwise is to ignore the real historical processes through which a class actually develops. Even to reach the position of a class against capital — prior to a full consciousness of its identity — the working class has to be subject to cultural, ideological and political factors outside the immediate sphere of production which act on the ability of highly divided workers to find common interests and a unity of purpose.[22] We are therefore beginning to address the problem of finding an adequate framework for a politics of production.

Resistance and Transformation

It follows from the discussion of work and social change that if we are to make sense of the limits and possibilities of work-place action, then it is necessary to distinguish between struggles of resistance and transformation. Unfortunately the two have frequently been confused. Following the hypothetical model of orthodox Marxism concerning the development of class consciousness in work, social scientists have expected too much of workplace struggles. They have been judged from the standpoint of their capacity to achieve full class consciousness, even in the most sensitive discussions (Salaman, 1981: 27–35). In the often subsequent denial of the capacity of class struggle to transform society, many social scientists concluded that the prospects for such struggle and for the working class as an oppositional force have been considerably reduced, in the worst interpretations to the point of disappearance. For some, this tied in with supposed 'trends' such as rising skills, increased affluence, and a shift from work to home concerns, which reinforced a general picture of working-class acquiescence and integration. But as Meiskens-Wood points out, 'While the concentration of working class battles on the domestic front may detract from the *political* and *universal* character of these struggles, it does not necessarily imply a declining militancy' (1981: 94).

Types of politics

When not faithfully reproducing Marx's conceptions of the

relations between capitalist production and class conscious-ness, Marxists *have* utilised a distinction between resistance and transformation. This has followed Lenin's dictum that the workplace can only generate trade union consciousness. The problem with this formulation is that it *denies* — through a rigid separation of political and economic spheres — any radical significance to action at the point of production. Friedman comments: 'While labour process struggles may be insufficient for transforming the working class into a revolu-tionary class . . . they are not insufficient for changing the organisation of work or investment patterns under capitalism' (1977b: 45). A specific political framework thus exists which cannot be equated with a *particular* type of trade unionism. For example, Clements employs a useful distinction between micro- and macro-level trade unionism, arguing that:

> issues of job control do transcend economism in so far as work groups do unilaterally seek to *impose* their own definition of key aspects of their own employment situa-tion. Micro-level trade union consciousness as manifest through issues of job control provides a complex interface of economic and political factors in which the plant becomes an arena of class conflict at the point of production.
>
> (Clements, 1977: 320)

In this light, it makes more sense to talk of *two types of politics*, corresponding initially to the distinction between resistance and transformation. This is not meant to imply that the former is solely defensive, or necessarily sectional and economistic. It is a question of the social relations that the respective struggles correspond to. I find Burawoy's differentiation between *global* and *production* politics a useful one. In a modified usage from the original, the former would refer to the *relations of production and reproduction* — for example, ownership, appropriation and distribution of the surplus product — at the level of capitalist society as a whole; the latter would correspond to the manifestations of exploita-tion, control and the wage-effort bargain as *work relations*.[23] As Burawoy argues, by defining a politics associated with the labour process, it is possible to break with the orthodoxy of

Lenin and others that the only 'real' political struggles are those directed at the state (1981: 122).

Nevertheless, the two types of politics are not equal. The capitalist organisation of work is a key site for the potential development of radical class consciousness. In the commodity nature of labour, the worker experiences a number of very important features of the hierarchical class society he or she lives in. To challenge the degree to which skills and human capacities are treated as things to be exchanged according to the needs of the market and dictates of management requires the beginnings of a vision of a new order and consciousness of ability of self-rule necessary for any social transformation. But the commodity nature of labour is not spontaneously transparent. When workers enter into collective self-activity to protect their working conditions and living standards, there is no automatic connection to the wider social relations and inequalities. Nor are even the most advanced forms of action easily transferred to a struggle at a societal level.

Questions of the transformation of capitalist society can never be successfully posed unless global relations are brought to bear on production politics. For example, a genuine movement for workers' control requires that issues be addressed — of ownership and purposes of production — that *job* control leaves largely untouched. Furthermore, global politics may actually *challenge* the dominant articulation of politics in the workplace.[24] One instance of the latter is the acceptance of a sexual hierarchy of skills and rewards in the labour process, and the subsequent marginalisation of women in trade union bargaining policies (Campbell, 1982). Production politics therefore tends to reflect the existing structure of labour power created by capital. These express vital sources of resistance. But to transcend its limits, means have to be found to 'bridge' the two spheres. Attention needs to be paid to practices, demands and forms of organisation that are *transitional* between factory and state, and between immediate and long-term goals.

The major labour process writings seldom *directly* address the problem,[25] but others locating the labour process inside wider concerns have begun to provide some theoretical guidelines. As Meiskens-Wood suggests, the 'tenacity of working class economism' derives from the real way that essentially political issues of domination and exploitation are transformed into more limited economic concerns because they 'appear' to be separately located in the workplace, apart from capitalist social relations (1981: 67). To unite what has traditionally been 'economic' and 'political' requires what Carol Johnson calls forms of struggle that can *de-fetishise* bourgeois relations of production by stressing their historically and socially specific nature. She mentions Marx's praise of the exemplary role played by the producer co-operative movement, and more modern workers' control tactics (1980: 95). A further contemporary example could be the attempt to link the defence of jobs and services in the public sector to an extension of their use-value character through schemes to decentralise the services, introducing forms of neighbourhood and worker control (Shield, 1982). These examples need to be situated inside a more practical context.

Workplace practices and strategies

Questions of social transformation may seem distant when the 1980s is likely to be characterised by a wholesale onslaught on even the limited forms of resistance in the workplace. As we have seen, traditional organisation, job controls and restrictive practices are increasingly the focus of attack. They are not the sole source of the profits crisis of British industry as employers conveniently assert, drawing attention away from evidence on their own financing procedures, investment policies and incompetence (see Manwaring, 1981, on the British Steel Corporation). But such practices do represent 'real but limited and sectional gains for workers, particularly in terms of relative security in the labour market and restraints on the intensification and de-skilling of work' (Hyman and Elger, 1981: 140–1). Capital is therefore taking advantage of the recessionary economic climate to go beyond holding down wages, substantially to restructure the labour process.

The resultant heavy stress on management's 'right to manage' strengthens the case against those theorists such as Bosquet, Pignon and Querzola, and Burawoy, who argued that participation, integration and job enrichment were essential ingredients of the modern enterprise. As was shown in

Chapters 5 and 6, the situation was always more complex than that. The key question is *context*. For instance, Nichols notes that in Britain in 1977 the balance of class forces was such that employers felt strong enough to reject even the relatively tame proposals on industrial democracy contained in the Bullock Report (Nichols, 1980a: 277).[26]

Employers' strength is being reinforced throughout the industrialised world by two previously discussed factors. First, the long-term changes towards capital-intensive plant, encompassing gradual deskilling and the erosion of traditional crafts and defensive practices. Second, the impact of the new technological revolution which is an added weapon of restructuring. In the USA, intensive mechanisation and scientific management have led to a reorganisation of the postal service, destroying tightly knit informal work-groups (Rachleff, 1982); and in the car industry, external pressures are leading to lighter cars and a transformation of the productive process eroding union controls over work pace and output standards (Fabar, 1979). However, restructuring and its effects on workplace practices take different *forms* in particular national and sectoral conditions.

In Italy and the USA, a significant trend has been the *relocation* of plant. Italy's 'new entrepreneurship' involves decentralised production in smaller plants, the turning out of components for large firms in small workshops, and even a growing number of home-based women workers (Mattera, 1980). This is not a return to pre-capitalist methods, as decentralisation is intimately tied to the large corporations. Nevertheless, it *is* a response — in the form of a new 'primitive accumulation' — to advances in shopfloor power. As the sociologist, Massimo Puci, put it, 'Just as Taylorism was the response to the autonomy of skilled workers, so the current tendency towards the fragmentation of the productive cycle in "islands" and in small firms is the response to the autonomy won by assembly-line workers' (quoted in Mattera, 1980: 71). Mattera (1980, 1981) also shows that although production in the USA remains highly centralised, restructuring has taken the form of a geographical shifting of investment from the old industrial areas to the 'sun-belt' states.

What the relocation has in common is the attempt to take

advantage of low tax, low wage, non-union conditions, where workers have to work without the collectively won rights and securities of the previous decades. Such a trend is not entirely absent from Britain. Aside from the much publicised 'enterprise zones' of Sir Geoffrey Howe, there has been a longer-term flight of large-scale plants from the central conurbations towards a small, multi-plant model in rural areas (Lane, 1982). While the greater strength of the British trade union movement ensures a higher level of unionisation, there is a definite challenge to workers' union traditions and job practices. As Lane comments,

> we can be quite sure that a new rural plant belonging to a multi-plant firm has been provided with carefully designed labour processes. Equipped with supervisory workers long experienced in the habits, ruses and dodges of urban workers, firms can establish from scratch their ideal job descriptions and work rhythms.

> (Lane, 1982: 9)

Taking all these factors into account, important articles by Hyman and Elger and Manwaring suggest that informal job control and restrictive practices are proving seriously inadequate as defence mechanisms. The ideological representation of restrictive practices and overmanning become crucial levers in the employers' offensive to restore 'general directive control' (Hyman and Elger, 1981: 117). In the steel industry the main union, the Iron and Steel Trades Confederation, still has a fragmented power base resting on industry-specific skills. But that power 'has been established in the different context of bargaining over productivity in a relatively high-wage industry in which jobs were secure and foreign competition limited' (Manwaring, 1981: 86).

Roughly the same story is revealed in case studies of four industries by Hyman and Elger. Thus any workplace strategy based on a simple defence of 'parochial and precarious' job controls is rightly described as romantic and ultimately disastrous. Unions will be required to move off their traditional terrain if they are to challenge capital on its own terms of planning, investment and resources, even to provide adequate forms of resistance on issues of jobs, skills and living standards. This is not just rhetoric. Unions *are* being forced into a wider and more conscious bargaining stance, increasingly incorporating 'alternative strategies', based largely on attempts to extend the scope of collective bargaining to include corporate planning, disclosure of information and new technology agreements (Lane, 1981).

Nevertheless, these are in their early stages, indicating important divergences between the Anglo-American tradition of business unionism and the exclusion of *informal* job controls from the collective bargaining process, and their European equivalents. In the latter case radical new strategies have emerged to respond to changes in the economy and labour processes (Kelly, 1982a). The Scandinavian trade union movement — notably in Sweden and Norway — has long produced perspectives on industrial democracy and work organisation, recently consolidated in agreements on new technology which incorporate initiatives like specialised shop stewards. Similar developments have taken place in Italy at both official and unofficial level, and more recently in France.

It is likely that such initiatives will grow in Britain, particularly in the context that the Lucas Combine Plan for alternative products, design of work and use of resources has stimulated discussion and proposals among workers at Vickers, Parsons, Rolls-Royce, Chrysler, Dunlop and Thorn (Cooley, 1981:55). There is no reason why this counter-planning cannot be extended to changing the character of the public and co-operative sectors. Finally, both trends have taken place in a context of alternative strategies at a state level connected to more radical thinking in the Labour Party (see CSE London Working Group, 1980). Existing in a number of forms, typical features include attempts to provide a framework for Labour governments or councils to extend control simultaneously over the state and private capital — through measures such as planning agreements and controls over the movement of capital and imports — *and* the working environment through the encouragement of new forms of bargaining and industrial democracy. As Manwaring argues, shopfloor and sectoral union initiatives need a nationally supportive framework. At the British Steel Corporation, a guarantee of sustained reflation would have provided greater market stability for a different form of expansion. In more general terms, forward central planning is necessary to avoid competition for a given demand for a single product around which workers may develop plans.

The combined elements of these initiatives could form the basis for a more viable politics of production which integrates resistance and transformation, although it would require appropriate organisational forms such as combine committees with access to their own information resources. While it is possible to argue that workers' plans form the micro level of a macro alternative state strategy (Hodgson, 1980), even those sympathetic rightly point to the tensions involved between the three structures of shop floor, official union and central or local government. Existing shopfloor counter-planning by combine committees has met resistance from national unions concerned at maintaining their monopoly of political initiative (Wainwright, 1979). Previous attempts by Labour governments to provide a framework for state intervention through the National Enterprise Board did not have a happy relationship with workers in the companies concerned, as is made clear in the excellent report by a number of Trades Councils (1980). Such experiences have made rank and file representatives wary of incorporation in the formal machinery of the state and employers.

'It is not realistic to depend on State agencies to defend the jobs of motor industry workers or to develop social planning for the long term future of the industry . . . this highlights the essential need for workers to develop an autonomy of ideas and action. The prerequisite for this is to maintain the total independence of the labour organisations from the company structures and then as an organisation to develop our own strategy for the industry concerned, without waiting for imminent disaster before any action.'

(Jim Shutt of AUEW-TASS at Talbot Motors, 1979: 3)

Even more importantly for our discussion, macro-level strategies have given scant attention to existing job controls of workers (Hyman and Elger, 1981: 143). Employers want to expand their operations on the basis of the destruction of such practices. If any national alternative economic strategy accepted the same premise of an intensification of labour, then it is hardly likely to involve workers positively in its implementation. Even the expansion of collective bargaining runs the danger of drifting away from immediate shopfloor issues. And counter-planning itself tends to draw on the more technical and skilled sectors of the workforce, with problems of majority involvement. These dilemmas are not only built into the interrelationships between the respective structures; they will persist because circumstances will continue to compel employers to take restructuring initiatives.

This is even the case in what appears to be the dead issue of democracy and authority in the workplace. Assertions of the 'right to manage' do not solve the most fundamental problem of management, which is the need to *engage* and *control* the workforce simultaneously. Managerial policies will continue to vary according to circumstances and sector. Even in a period of recessionary restructuring, forms of participation may be retained. For example, Pilkingtons have opened a new, high technology glass-making plant in St Helens, with a central emphasis on job enrichment in the hope of integrating workers and extending the 'flexibility' necessary for new work practices. As Cressey and MacInnes (1980) note, the traditional response has been to reject any scheme of participation and industrial democracy as the road to incorporation, counterposing strong shopfloor unionism.[27]

There has been a good deal of justification for suspicion, as examples from Leyland and elsewhere have shown. But in current circumstances the continuation of a 'strategy of refusal' carries the danger of an inability to respond with independent initiatives, and thus avoids workers' organisations being put on a wholly defensive footing. Cressey and MacInnes argue that there is a need to use the spaces available within 'capital's contradictory aims in the workplace'. Emphasis should be put on prefiguring new relations of production by subverting and changing forms of hierarchy and organisation of production (1980: 20–1). The same could be said in relation to exploiting spaces available inside the state apparatus at national and local level. One example is the development of local-authority-backed trade union centres that can act as a focus for counter-planning in industry and community. An orientation of this nature undoubtedly carries considerable dangers. But the kind of changes in the labour process and economic environment discussed in this book suggests that a strategy of refusal may be a 'luxury' no longer available. The theoretical and practical challenge is there to be taken up.

End-notes

Chapter 1

1. Rose's account, although widely referred to and containing useful detail, is dismissive of most strands of thought. Yet the alternative he finally espouses, that of a non-political Marxism, is barely mentioned throughout the book! Salaman (1981) is more useful and has the additional merit of charting the impact of some of the better known labour process theory on a newer sociology of work.
2. The fragmentation of the study of work has been attacked for growing narrowness, divorce from wider concerns of patterns of power, and for paying too little attention to the changing nature of work. See Esland and Salaman (1975) and Nichols (1980b).
3. A number of contributions to the recent compilation of Esland and Salaman (1980) disuss Kerr, particularly that of Weeks. In this chapter the emphasis will be on the themes raised by Kerr that are connected to work, rather than to wider aspects of power and societal organisation.
4. Taylor was referring to a piece-work system as a means of dividing common interest as well as providing an incentive to work harder. An account of Taylor's battle to impose his system is contained in Braverman (1974). We will return in detail to Taylorism in Chapters 3 and 5.
5. The Western Electric research was considerably more complicated and diverse, with divisions of approach among those carrying out the study, than can be expressed here. For a detailed account see Rose (1975, Pts II and III).
6. Just how the results of this research have been incorporated into the consensus of social science can be seen in a further quote from Argyle: 'Elton Mayo, one of the founders of the Human Relations Movement, maintained that all that was needed to improve the effectiveness and happiness of working organisations was to improve the social skills of those who ran them' (1972: 135).

7. Like a number of other writers in this period, Sayles considered himself to be a reformer of human relations theory, rather than an opponent of it. One of his major modifications was to reject the notion of motivations to work being mainly social, preferring a return to an emphasis on economic influences.

8. Although the Blauner study appeared in 1964, it was actually part of the 1950s generation of technologically influenced research. He relied mainly on a job attitude poll conducted over a dozen years before he wrote the book (Rose, 1975: 209).

9. Noted in Salaman (1981). He also points out the defects of Blauner's use of the concept of alienation. There is an unacknowledged collapse of alienation into the Durkheimian idea of anomie, relying more on subjective feeling states than objective features of work.

10. The Tavistock Institute was founded in 1947 as an agency of applied social science that could provide research of use to industry and industrial problems.

11. It is interesting to note that in schools of management, courses on work study and those relating to managerial skills are normally completely separate, further emphasising the practical division of labour that exists between the fundamental organisation of labour process and 'man management'.

12. Rosenbrock is Professor of Control Engineering at the University of Manchester Institute of Science and Technology, (UMIST). He is therefore one of the few people from that tradition to be concerned with the social relations and effects of technology; in 1981 he convened a Working Party on New Technology for the Council for Science and Society.

13. One of the few older studies to challenge the established wisdoms was Friedmann (1961). He attacked both the human relations theory and 'technicism' for separating technology and social relations. It is no accident that his work developed in France outside the Anglo-American approaches. Friedmann anticipated some of the later labour process theory, although his own view of future technological trends was confused and ambiguous.

14. It is remarkable that despite all the attention given to modifying styles of supervision and work, there is no proven correlation between 'satisfaction' and productivity (Argyle, 1972: 241). Perhaps 'happy' workers do not work harder because alienation reaches a little deeper than surveys uncover.

15. Some writers ignore economic factors altogether. Maslow's famous 'hierarchy of needs', for example, simply assumes that economic wants have been met.

16. This list is taken from Argyle (1972: 3–6). Both Rose and Salaman note that functionalist theory stressing an essential consensus in work and society provides an underlying theoretical framework for much of industrial sociology. This functionalist approach derives from Durkheim, but was consolidated in early post-war US sociology.

17. Marxism retains a distinction between the *social* and *detailed* (or technical) division of labour. The former operates at the level of society as a whole, the latter in the sphere of production. By explaining the origin and differences in various forms of hierarchy, Marxism is able to avoid the level of abstraction common in sociology that the division of labour is a universal and undifferentiated phenomenon. This relates to the debate between Marx and Smith referred to in Chapter 2.

18. The Frankfurt School is generally taken to mean a group of German neo-Marxists, which also included Habermas and Adorno. Habermas also made a critique of Weber's concept of rationality, but went even further than Marcuse in moving on from Marxism in the process (see Hamilton, 1980).

19. It is interesting to note the theoretical direction of Salaman. From the 1975 collection to the 1980 compilation edited jointly with Esland, there is a considerable shift from radical Weberianism to Marxism under the impact of labour process theory. Fox has also moved, though in a different manner, from pluralism to a more Marxist approach (see his contribution to the latter compilation).

20. For a critique of the dominant pluralist theory of industrial relations, see Fox (1977) and Goldthorpe (1977). As industrial relations theorists seldom deal directly with work, further commentary on these debates is beyond our scope. But see Hill (1981: chapters 7 and 8).

21. The view that extrinsic needs are more important to work satisfaction than intrinsic needs contrasts sharply with human relations theory and its successors, e.g. Herzberg and Maslow.

22. The study by Wedderburn and Crompton did, however, also provide useful material on differences in attitudes and behaviour related to skills and position in the work process. They also made the qualification to Goldthorpe and Lockwood that instrumental attitudes were not confined to 'new' workers, their own sample being based on traditional manual groups.

23. Gouldner took the existence of external ideologies a little too far. Attempting to explain workers' ribald comments on the new management (for instance, 'He is a guy that wants the men to work on their job and stick a broom up their ass and sweep the floor at the same time') he reached the unfortunate conclusion that, 'for some men, the strike was motivated on a very deep and unconscious level, by a desire to ward off homosexual attack' (1955: 73). Nor was this the only example of such psychological gobbledygook.

Chapter 2

1. Marx's discussion of the labour process is underlaid by his wider economic theories. In this case the impetus for capitalists to control working conditions is strongly related to his labour theory of value,

in which Marx argued that as the common feature of commodities is that they are the product of labour, the relationships of exchange could be analysed from the viewpoint of the labour time necessary to produce the commodities. It is a general problem that while Marx's discussion of the labour process can be understood in its own terms as a body of concepts, the economic theory is relevant to a full explanation. For the non-economist, Marxist economic theory can be a daunting experience. Ben Fine (1975), however, provides a useful short introduction.

2. The detailed concepts for understanding the forms and means of the subordination of labour are developed in an Appendix to *Capital, Volume One*. Known as the 'Resultate', this section of Marx's writings forms an important bridge between the first two volumes of *Capital*. It was only published in 1933, and was published for the first time in English as an Appendix of *Capital, Volume One* by Penguin in 1976. See the introduction by Mandel for further details of its history and character.

3. In economic terms, Marx described the difference between increasing productivity through extending the duration of work and the more sophisticated methods of increasing the intensity of labour as a shift from *absolute* to *relative* surplus value.

4. This is to be found primarily in chapters 13, 14 and 15 of *Capital, Volume One*.

5. Berg has performed a very useful service by gathering together historical documentation usually referred to second-hand in other historical sources. Some useful material on technological change and the nature of work also exists in conventional historical studies, notably Hobsbawm (1968), Dobb (1963), Pollard (1965), Bendix (1963) and Landes (1969).

6. The rural discontent in the 1830s was sometimes referred to as the 'Swing' riots because threats and petitions were often signed 'Captain Swing'. The best discussion of these events is in Hobsbawm and Rudé (1969).

7. This statement, quoted in Young (1976), was made by the industrialist Josiah Wedgwood.

8. This extract is from an essay by J. Swift entitled 'Engineering', and is quoted in Berg (1979: 190).

9. Marx distinguished between living and dead labour. When workers act to transform objects, they are performing living labour. Once these actions have been embodied in products, machines and so on, then it passes over into dead labour, existing objectively and externally to the worker.

10. The term collective worker was also meant to indicate that some mental as well as manual labour was *productive*. Defining the difference between productive and unproductive labour was central to Marx's theory of value, any labour which is indispensable to the production of the final article being counted as productive. This meant the inclusion of technologists, engineers and even some

managers. Furthermore, the distinction is also relevant to a theory of class. Despite deskilling and fragmentation, the trend towards interchangeable collective work widens the class forces which make the overthrow of capitalism possible. However, these questions have been the subject of some controversy (see Chapter 8).

11. See Marx (1976), pp. 553–64.

12. Although not writing specifically about the labour process, historians have made a notable contribution to an understanding of changes in the character of work, particularly Hobsbawm ((1968), Dobb (1963), Landes (1969), Pollard (1965) and Thompson (1967). See Salaman (1981) for the best summary of that contribution.

13. Craft workers were often described as a 'labour aristocracy'. For the debate about the nature of their struggles and class consciousness, see Foster (1974), Morris (1979) and Gray (1976).

14. Such arrangements drew on the traditions of master–apprentice relationships, established in the guild system and early periods of industrialisation.

15. See the essay by John Day, 'The Boot and Shoe Trade', in Berg (1979) for an account of the industry.

16. Ibid., p. 173.

17. Marx (1976), pp. 599–610. He argued that their rapid conversion into modern industry was due mainly to the influence of the restrictions imposed under the Factory Acts to super-exploitation of women and children, and to the demands of expanded markets, competition and technical innovation.

18. The concept of the reserve army of labour as a means to understanding the economic position of women has come under increasing criticism from Marxist feminists. This debate is dealt with in detail in Chapter 7 of this book.

19. See the essay by W. Glenny Crory, 'Iron Shipbuilding', in Berg (1979) for further explanation.

20. Burawoy's (1979) study is one of the few to deal extensively with the problem of ideology and consent within the labour process. I discuss the book and others on the same theme in detail in Chapter 6.

21. Kumar uses the perceptive concept of 'premature conceptualisation' to describe the over-generalisation embodied in understanding the progress of industrialisation. Nevertheless, there is a problem in the use of the term 'industrialism'. It is wrong to associate the 'arrival of industry' with a particular form of management or productive apparatus. Scientific management and the assembly line may have marked a particularly important point of maturity in the system, but that system is capitalism not industrialism, and that had arrived well before the twentieth-century developments referred to by Kumar.

22. One problem in deciding how much of Marx's economic theory is necessarily connected to a specific study of the labour process is that important parts of the theory are themselves subject to major

debate among modern Marxists. For example, see Elson (1979) and Fine and Harris (1976).

23. The work of Marglin and of Gordon is part of a debate about the origins of hierarchy, and the precise relations between efficiency, profitability and capitalist control. The formulations of the two authors are by no means generally accepted, as will be seen in the debate in Chapter 5.

24. In a useful, if dense, study of the 'Class Structure of Machinery', Bahr notes that: 'Neither the spinning-jenny and mechanical loom, nor the steam engine arose in direct connection with either the discoveries or technical apparatus of theoretical physics' (1980: 103). Mackenzie (1981) gives a useful summary and assessment of the science and social relations debate.

25. Braverman has a brief discussion (pp. 9–13) of why the labour process was neglected. He correctly identifies as central factors the impact of labour movement activity and the Russian experience, although they are given rather cursory treatment.

26. Syndicalism was centred on a belief in the role of industrial unions using the basis of craft skills and job control to take over the running of production and society after a general strike. They were completely hostile to 'politics'. In other countries the Workers' Council Movement developed ideas of self-management, which were also 'inextricably linked to the technology of the labour process' (Bologna, 1976: 70). The orientation of these movements to the sphere of production explains in part the hostility of Lenin and the Bolsheviks, who believed that they ignored the question of state power. The Bolsheviks' own interest in workers' control was a short-lived affair that arose out of the necessity to use factory organisation as a means of appropriating the means of production from capital, rather than from an entirely genuine concern with the work process (Goodey, 1974).

27. Some of these writers, particularly Hyman and Clements, make a critique of the rigidity of Lenin's categories of consciousness, suggesting modifications which would establish more flexible ideas of ideology and work experience without entirely rejecting the distinction between 'politics' and 'economics'.

28. In the first part of this century there was less distinction than today between the Communist and Socialist parties. Even after the split that produced the Second (reformist) and Third (revolutionary) Internationals, many of the former regarded themselves as Marxists. Therefore interpretations of Marxism could and did cross political boundaries, and while Bolshevism was a sharp break with reformist currents on questions of power and the state, strong overlaps remained on conceptions of the organisation of socialist society.

29. In doing so they were highly influenced by the writings of Marx's partner, Engels, who wrongly attempted to incorporate technological developments into general laws of nature transcending the

social relations of any particular mode of production. For a rather complex discussion of the origins and varieties of 'technicist' Marxism, see Slater (1980). This discussion involves an evaluation of some of the early critics such as Luxemburg, Lukács, Korsch and Gramsci.

30. The general distortion in Marxism is often labelled 'economism' and refers to the reduction of all social processes to economic factors, reflecting a narrow interpretation of the distinction between base and superstructure in Marx. In this case it is the failure to consider the social relations in the work process. Converts to Marxism in the past have often thought they were embracing a technologically based theory of society. The famous archaeologist Gordon Childe believed that: 'Marx and Engels were the first to remark that this technological development is the foundation of all history, conditioning and limiting all other human activities' (1949: 70).

31. Both are dissident Marxists and have ended up in prison for their views, Haraszti in Hungary and Bahro in East Germany, although the latter was eventually expelled to the West.

32. Cotgrove (1972), for example, wrongly asserted that Marx's usage of alienation had nothing to do with factors such as the character of technology and fragmentation of work, believing it to be solely concerned with the socio-economic *context* of work. This belief was used absurdly to argue that Goldthorpe and Lockwood's concept of instrumentalism leant back towards Marx.

33. One of the few exceptions was the work of the first major post-war labour process theorist, the Italian writer Panzieri (1976 and 1980). Writing in the 1950s, he and other dissident socialists and communists argued that Lenin and the dominant Marxist tradition had reduced the primary contradiction of capitalist society to one *between* factory and society, because the struggle for profitability took place only in production. Socialism is therefore identified with economic planning leaving the social relations of work untouched. Such perspectives have failed to understand the changes in the capitalist world. The system once characterised by Marx as combining despotism in the factory and anarchy in society has extended planning from the workplace as a means of regulating wider socio-economic structures. Changes of this kind have also forced a parallel crisis for reformist parties. For what is socialism beyond the mixed economy and welfare provision? Most of the answers seem to point to an extension of state planning, ownership and intervention based on the existing productive forces. This was exemplified by the Wilson government's promise in 1964 of a technological revolution, and is reproduced in a more radical form in orthodox versions of Labour's current *Alternative Economic Strategy*.

Chapter 3

1. Many radical and academic journals have also devoted special issues to the labour process, for example *Capital and Class* (Spring 1977), *Politics and Society* (nos 3—4, 1978) and *Monthly Review* (July—August 1976). Following their conference in 1976 on the labour process, the Conference of Socialist Economists have played the most consistent role in promoting debate on the issue, particularly in their journal *Capital and Class*. See also their influential collection of articles in the pamphlet, *The Labour Process and Class Strategies* (1976).

2. The concept of 'labour aristocracy' referred to materially privileged sections of the working class, with a consequent weakening in class consciousness. It was used by Lenin and other Marxists to explain trends in the working-class movement most strongly supporting reformist politics, and was linked to a theory concerning the effects of imperialist domination on the population of the metropolitan countries.

3. This repeated another mistaken interpretation of the contradiction between the collective forces of production and the private character of ownership and control. Once again the forces of production are seen as neutral. This led Mallet to argue that it was in the interest of the modern working class that technological development continued, reforms only dealing with such consequences as expanded possibilities for reduction in working hours and greater mobility.

4. The theorists who combined together in the early 1960s through the journal *Quaderni Rossi* to do research work on working-class politics and the labour process held a variety of viewpoints and were later to go separate ways politically. Hence they are not strictly a 'school of thought'. They had little influence outside Italy and perhaps France, where the journal *Le Temps Moderne* later took considerable interest. In Britain the pamphlet produced by the Conference of Socialist Economists (1976) popularised the work of Panzieri, Bologna and Tronti, but this was after labour process theory had come to the fore through Braverman, Gorz and others. An anthology of Italian writings is provided by Red Notes and CSE Books (1979), although it concentrates on those writers adhering to particular extreme left positions. For a critical commentary, see Lumley (1980).

5. For the roots of these struggles see Partridge (1980). There is little available in English on the later period, though see Red Notes/CSE (1979: 167—95).

6. Braverman strangely does not use the concept of the difference between formal and real subordination, although the process is clearly inferred.

7. Both Stone and Marglin are briefly referred to by Braverman, but their work is parallel and supportive of each other, rather than a direct influence.

8. It is interesting to note that many banners of craft unions depicted scenes showing the clasped hands of worker and employer. This was not meant to indicate subservience, but the 'equal partnership' based on the knowledge and skills of the workforce.

9. Sohn-Rethel's aim of developing a critique of scientific management was unfortunately limited by some mistaken characterisations of Taylorism. Although constrained by its capitalist usage, Sohn-Rethel believed that scientific management could be used alternatively as a basis for work organisation in a socialist society. This belief was based on the notion that the new methods to measure and compare labour in a conscious way could be used to economise on time, and minimise effort in a general scientific sense. In fact he contrasted the 'scientific' planning of the labour process at the level of 'plant economy' with the anarchy in the competitive market as a whole. These judgements of scientific management clearly underestimate the degree to which it is based on the specific context of capitalist social relations and methods derived from the necessity to intensify labour under managerial control. For critical commentaries on Sohn-Rethel, see Taylor (1979) and Kapferer (1980).

10. Ford's five dollar day prefigured, in a period of depression, later attempts to develop an economy in which higher wages were linked to consumption as a means of stimulating demand and encouraging competitive efficiency. However, the assumed compatibility between high wages and profits only worked in the favourable context of economic expansion. The high wage economy tended to suffer the same fate as Taylor's 'scientific incentives' schemes. Their failure caused Taylor to complain bitterly that employers used them as a means of rate-cutting when competitive pressures threatened profitability levels.

11. This recognised, of course, that it was methods of work under *capitalism*. Taylor realised that his methods could not have been a more general 'scientific workmanship', even though skills and knowledge had been appropriated from the workforce. He said that workers had neither the time nor the money to run production, and that the workforce would willingly subject themselves to the loss of jobs or higher rates of exploitation resulting from application of his methods.

12. In Britain, Ford was the first motor company to use a 'measured day work' rate instead of piece work, a payment system which well organised workers could exploit. Other manufacturers were later to pay dearly to buy out piece-work systems and replace them with the day rate, which provides a better basis for managerial control of earnings.

13. Features common to the monopoly stage of capitalism are generally thought to be: centralisation of capital into fewer, but larger units within each country; greater internationalisation of capital within an expanded imperialist world market; and an expanded role for the state. With specific reference to the labour process, there has

been some debate on whether monopoly capitalism is also a fourth era following manufacture and large-scale industry. Aspects of this debate will be examined in Chapter 5.

14. Braverman has co-operated with Baran and Sweezy in *Monthly Review*, an independent Marxist journal of long-standing influence in the USA.

15. The entire section in question consists of only thirty-eight pages, and many of the passages on changes in urban and family life appear to be merely critical reinterpretations of basic sociological material. The detail provided on changes in production is largely absent. In addition there is no attempt to provide any substantial political economy concerning the socialisation of capital and the role of the state, which is assumed to be mainly a result of shifts in production. Political and economic changes arising from the effects of social conflicts on the terrain of unemployment, welfare provision, and the like are given little attention.

16. Some Italian theorists refer to this phenomenon as the development of a 'social factory'. Little has been published in English on this, but for some of the background see Red Notes/CSE (1979).

Chapter 4

1. The others are said to be the division of mental and manual labour, and hierarchy.

2. The Wood (1982) collection is a compilation of papers from the Nuffield-sponsored Conference on Deskilling held by the British Sociological Association in 1978. My own chapters were written prior to the publication of the 1982 compilation, and attempts to update the references have been made difficult by the changes subsequently made in many of the articles. Some of them are shorter, one is new, and in another case two previously separate articles — by Rosemary Crompton and Stewart Reid — have been combined. Given the unavailability of the Nuffield papers in their original form, I have tried, where possible, to update the references. Where this has proved impossible I have retained the 1978 references, and readers can check them against the new versions, which are in all cases broadly similar.

3. Sadly, Braverman's death in 1976 precluded any extension of the debate into areas of working-class organisation and consciousness.

4. For a similar view from a different perspective of Italian labour process theory, see Bologna (1976).

5. More (1978) makes the point that Marx's analysis of the relations between modern industry and the destruction of craft skills was inevitably limited by the small proportion of industry affected at the time.

6. On a wider note, Gartman argues that 'Braverman's brilliant analysis of the degradation of work . . . confirms Marx's theory in every respect' (1979: 194).

7. Monds's attack is directed against the work of the Marxist historians mentioned earlier — Stone, Montgomery, Hinton, and others — which he describes as suffering from a 'workerist illusion'. But in making his case against the political significance of the craft tradition, Monds appears to confuse the objects of historical study. He judges a history of the struggle between capital and labour in the workplace by criteria designed to evaluate the struggle between classes in society as a whole. It therefore becomes an easy, but misguided task to point to the political weaknesses of the craft tradition with respect to political clarity and organisation. Hinton makes a reply to Monds in the same issue of *New Left Review*.

8. Some commentators criticise *Labor and Monopoly Capital* both for romanticising craft work, and for ignoring the effect of worker resistance on retaining skills. This is not necessarily a contradiction. Having overestimated the power and skill of the craft workers, Braverman then goes on to underestimate their capacity to use that power to limit the degree of deskilling and loss of market rewards.

9. In addition, Rubery correctly notes that without an analysis of the bargaining process, Braverman cannot explain why he found a tendency towards a progressive polarisation of earnings in industries which have been most affected by deskilling and the homogenisation of labour. Such trends would appear to point towards equalisation of wage levels (1980: 257).

10. Lee's theoretical orientation appears to be the development of an expanded neo-Weberian theory of the operation of the labour market at a macro level. This would deal with class structuration beyond individual market capacity, in the direction indicated by Giddens (1973). It is therefore apparent that Lee's interest in the labour process is clearly secondary to a concern with the development of an adequate theory of the market.

11. Sources used by Lee include statistics published by the Industrial Training Boards and the Department of Employment. The idea that these are in part socially constructed skills is dismissed by Lee on the grounds that union power is inadequate to create skills of this type (see the discussion later in this section). A good critique of such official statistics on skills can be found in the pamphlet on *New Technology* by the Council for Science and Society (1981).

12. In fact Rubery argues that Braverman's account of deskilling necessarily questions elements of labour market theory which assume that in the primary sector job-specific skills are increasing. The deskilling trend is breaking down some of the distinctions between the sectors and making it likely that many primary sector jobs have secondary sector characteristics (1980: 254–5).

13. The wider context of political economy tends to be dealt with rather haphazardly in labour market theory. For example, Lee refers to deskilling being determined by 'the underlying rhythm of the trade cycles' (1978: 24). The active role of capital in shaping

productive processes tends to be underestimated, for instance in shifting products through 'runaway shops', thus changing the location of skills within the international division of labour.

14. A number of commentators have also put this down to the distorting effects of the North American situation on Braverman. In the absence of a strong tradition of trade unionism and socialist politics, the dominance of capital appeared to be untrammelled (Mackenzie, 1977; Burawoy, 1978). In a further article Braverman quite wrongly extends this absence of significant class struggle to other industrialised countries (1976: 123).

15. For example, compare Lee's 'optimistic' comments on the retention of skills in the machine-tool sector with the evidence collected by the Coventry Machine Tool Workers' Committee on the loss of jobs and skills (1979).

16. As Elger points out, problems in the concept of real subordination of labour are partly rooted in ambiguities in Marx's own treatment of trends in large-scale industry (1979: 66). But it should be remembered that Marx clearly stated that real subordination involved a 'constantly repeated' revolution in the means of production to itensify productivity and increase relative surplus value, and was not therefore a static or finished process.

17. Two of the more prominent examples — Fiat and Volvo — have mainly used robot *welders*, despite extravagant claims like 'built by robots'. In 1981 there were an estimated 8,000 robots being used in the world, with only just over one hundred in Britain. But obviously this is the beginning of an expanding market.

18. The next stage of development beyond the independent NC machine is the flexible manufacturing system (FMS), where a group of machines is clustered around a robot and controlled by a microcomputer. The precise effects of this, beyond job reduction, are unclear, as it is largely in the development stage, even in Japan. Some employers are presenting FMS as a means of turning work into a light and supervisory type. But this is doubtful, as the excellent discussion by the Council for Science and Society (1981: 26—7) makes clear. The pamphlet contains some remarkable material on the effect of NC machinery in general on work. This includes reports from employers in the USA of the successful employment of mentally retarded workers on NC machines because of their patience and persistence.

19. Although Yarrow describes the labour process in traditional mining as a 'deviant case from Braverman's theory' (1979: 170), he later goes on to make a more general point: 'This is the side of the knowledge—power dialectic Braverman did not explore: not only is skill a crucial resource for giving power over the work process, but workers' power over the work process increases the skill content of the jobs by allowing them to make more decisions' (185). An important distinction can be drawn from this between job control

as a means of increasing market rewards, and as a means of increasing areas of discretion. Only the latter sense can be described as part of genuine skill.

20. Like other critics of Braverman, Jones makes the point that there is a substantial difference between what the technical literature exhorts management to do in terms of skills and control, and what they are actually able to achieve given the constraints of workers' organisation. However, it could be argued that Jones, as with other writers, is partly confusing claw-back of the ability to control aspects of working conditions to retain rewards, and actual retention of skills.

21. The techniques in question cover a variety of processes, but can be grouped under the headings of:
   job enrichment — addition to tasks requiring greater initiative, participation and responsibility.
   job enlargement — previously fragmented tasks aggregated to make a more meaningful whole.
   job rotation — jobs remain the same, but movement of workers from one to the other.
   semi-autonomous work groups — arrangements for aspects of work decided by a group of workers within the constraints of the technology, patterns of ownership and labour process as a whole.

22. The point being made is that deskilling is neither inevitable, nor merely one tendency among others, as Friedman suggests.

23. In most other aspects the Gagliani article is very poor. It consists of an attack on the proletarianisation concept almost solely by reference to rewards (which he rightly notes are still likely to be higher for non-manual workers), with nothing on the labour of such occupations, which is a crucial aspect of genuine proletarianisation. Ironically he refers to himself as a 'labour economist'.

Chapter 5

1. This distinction between control and co-ordination is used by some Marxist writers as the basis for a critique of the sociological argument that hierarchy and bureaucracy are an inevitable consequence of large-scale organisation and division of labour (see Johnson, 1972).

2. According to Littler, the emergence of foremen created a tradition with many parallels to the function of sub-contractors, with the crucial difference that foremen were directly employed wage labourers. Their power was modified early on at the turn of the century by the previously discussed trend towards new work methods involving 'feed and speed' and quality control inspectors. Thus the resistance of foremen to new patterns of control was also a factor alongside that of craft workers.

3. Palmer accuses Braverman of failing to see the connections between technical innovations and reorganisation of the labour process. But this mistakes Braverman's insistence on the *origins* of Taylorism as a management method, and the *consequences* when it is applied to different levels of technology. In terms of the latter, Taylorism is definitely seen as having a close relationship with the design of the instruments of production. See chapter 8 of *Labor and Monopoly Capital* (Braverman, 1974) for examples.

4. The Industrial Workers of the World (IWW) was a radical syndicalist union whose efforts in organising among all skills, sectors and races sharply contrasted with the conservative, craft-orientated American Federation of Labor (AFL).

5. This view has been reinforced by reactions against the inflated claims made by Taylor for the potential and actual success of his methods. For example, he commented that there had not been any strikes during a thirty-year period of operating scientific management. Whenever there were problems of implementation, he blamed the incompetence or short-sightedness of management!

6. Many of Taylor's disciples were not as anti-union and took up 'progressive' stances on joint co-operation, particularly influenced — as in Britain — by the joint planning experiences during the First World War. This tendency was increased by the influence of Taylorists during the New Deal period in the USA in the 1930s. They saw a direct relationship between the necessity for interventionist planning in the factory and in society as a whole, thus providing further grounds for accommodation between the progressive agencies of capital and 'responsible' trade unionism.

7. Friedman's 'responsible autonomy' concept gets explicit support as an alternative to Taylorism from Littler (1978: 12) and Burawoy (1981: 92).

8. The gang system represented sectional combinations of workers, under which a gang leader would negotiate an informal deal with management. The leader and the gang generally would then ensure the effective distribution and enforcement of work. This differed from traditional sub-contracting in that the gang leader was elected by the workers and responsible to them (Friedman, 1977a: 213).

9. We have already mentioned the rise and fall of the Coventry Toolroom Agreement in Chapter 4. The links to the labour process are illustrated by this quote from an employer: 'I am not exaggerating when I say that the Coventry Toolroom Agreement is the single biggest restricting factor in the modernisation of methods of working and payment in the West Midlands area' (quoted in *The Times*, 2 March 1971).

10. Roy's article deals with the variety of tactics used by employers in the southern USA to resist unionisation. The 'sweet stuff' of relaxed supervision and partnership is paralleled in other firms by the 'fear stuff' of repression and ideological blackmail, and the 'evil stuff' of

ideological offensives of an anti-union, racist and anti-communist nature.

11. This featured strongly in management attitudes revealed in my own research into the telecommunications industry. A training officer at one plant told me that 'the biggest problem is motivation' (quoted in Thompson, 1981: 210). The workforce had no apparent militancy, and no new managerial methods were planned that would be directed at bringing about changes in the conditions affecting motivation.

12. The type of policy and relations between sections of management will depend very much on factors like the size of the firm. Larger companies are more likely to experiment in 'progressive' management methods. Even then, the introduction of such schemes may lead to considerable cynicism by managers, or a 'pineing for the days when a manager's job was to manage' (Jones, 1978: 14).

13. A part of the debate about responsible autonomy and job enrichment not discussed in this chapter concerns the implications for patterns of conflict and trade union strategy in the workplace. Some theorists argue that new methods carry the danger for capital that they open up genuine possibilities of a shift in the frontier of control. This argument will be examined in Chapter 8.

14. The panel consists of AT&T, IBM, Ford, General Electric, Polaroid, Pabst Brewing, Pullman and US Steel. They provide useful sources of information on broad changes in the labour process and control, although there is very little revealed of the actual organisation of work in a detailed sense.

15. Edwards draws on examples like the strikes at Pullman and US Steel, and uses radical history sources such as Montgomery in a similar way to other labour process theorists.

16. To give equal weight to scientific management, welfare and company union schemes in the light of subsequent development is not realistic. Neither does Edwards detail their interrelationships. For example, it was very much part of Taylor's vision that the need for 'external' unions would be eliminated through factors such as individualised payment systems and the acceptance of 'scientific' work norms. In one of the few available discussions of 'contested terrain', Burawoy (1981) is highly critical of Edwards's account of this period. While it was a period of experimentation, he argues that Edwards does not provide an adequate theorisation of the transition from competitive to monopoly capitalism, and that his work lacks any substantial political economy.

17. Quoting from an earlier article by Edwards, Burawoy implies that Edwards owes more to Weber than Marx in his concept of bureaucratic control. This appears to be accurate. In arguing that bureaucratic control tended to legitimise the firm's exercise of power and translate it into authority, he not only uses Weber's language, but repeats the mistake of conceiving of power and control from the

viewpoint of the 'rationality' of management. Counter-controls and influences exerted by the workforce are underplayed or ignored.

18. Edwards considers the segmentation of the labour market almost wholly in terms of distinct systems of control in the firm (1979: 178). The inadequacy of such analysis will be discussed further in Chapter 7.

19. This is not to suggest that hierarchy cannot exist for any other reason under a different mode of production. The question of hierarchy in Soviet-style societies will be discussed in Chapter 8.

20. One of the problems with analyses such as Marglin's is that it is very difficult to discuss efficiency in a general sense. Confusion arises from trying to compare efficient production under capitalism, with a hypothetical non-hierarchical alternative. The analysis tends to lose its sense of the purpose of efficiency, discipline or hierarchy in its specific context in a particular mode of production. Nevertheless, distinctions between profitability and efficiency are very important for maintaining the basis for a critique of existing forms of technology and organising production.

Chapter 6

1. Marx states in *The German Ideology* (Marx and Engels, 1964) that the ideas of the ruling class are in every epoch the ruling ideas. The book, however, contains a more developed discussion of ideology and its connections to capitalist social relations in and out of the workplace.

2. There has obviously been a considerable debate about the nature of ideology within the Marxist tradition. The notion of ideology as a lived experience is taken from the work of the French Marxists, Althusser (1969) and Poulantzas (1975), and some of this debate is contained there.

3. Burawoy makes a distinction between consent, which has to be organised, and the more general concept of legitimacy, which he takes to be a subjective state of mind carried around by individuals. It is therefore a social relation, not a form of consciousness (1979: 27). The problems of defining consent are dealt with in greater detail in the conclusion to this chapter.

4. A class-in-itself is regarded as being formed from common material relationships to the means of production in terms of wealth, ownership and control, place in the division of labour, social composition and background, and so on. Class-for-itself refers to a self-consciousness, not merely of existence as a class, but a 'higher' stage of realisation of historical goals and means of remaking society. This concept can be found in both Marx's political texts, such as 'Class Struggles in France' (1973a), and also in theoretical writings like *The Poverty of Philosophy* (1963) and *The German Ideology* (Marx and Engels, 1964).

5. Naturally, sociological attention has largely been focused on providing more negative reasons why there is a lack of class consciousness. But given the acknowledged debate 'with the ghost of Marx' concerning class and capitalism, discussion has often been a more conservative version of 'why no revolution?' See Salaman (1981, ch. 7) for some discussion of this.

6. Gramsci's writings on hegemony are to be found in his *Prison Notebooks* (1976). There are some fragmentary comments on work and consent in his essay included in the *Notebooks* on 'Americanism and Fordism'. A critical commentary is provided by Elger and Schwarz (1980).

7. Traction was one of the categories of 'relative satisfactions' referred to by Baldamus (1961). The others were inurement, based on acclimatisation to experience of physical discomfort, and contentment, which is said to be a form of adaptation to the weariness and fatigue of work determined by its coercive nature.

8. Burawoy uses the concept of the 'simultaneous obscuring and securing of surplus value' to define the essence of the capitalist labour process. Even when the value process is obscured by the relations of production, capital still needs to secure the surplus, and this can only be done through mechanisms in which workers participate. This leads on to the concept of the labour process as a series of 'games', which is discussed in the rest of the chapter.

9. The idea of 'games' flows from the literature on restriction of output. In one sense it is a misleading term, as it implies coherent, conscious and even frivolous activity. But games are meant to refer to *practices* which reflect the battle workers have with the conditions of work, such as beating the clock, outwitting the foreman, setting their own targets to pace the time, and so on.

10. Hales widens the analysis of design workers by using the Ehrenreichs' (1979) concept of a professional-managerial class to situate the experience of these workers within a wider class-cultural context. This kind of connection between work and class location will be discussed in Chapter 8.

11. Given their position as unorthodox and libertarian Marxists, there is a rather disingenuous use of Lenin by the Ehrenreichs to justify a shift away from workplace organising, on the grounds that political consciousness can only come from without. The Ehrenreichs are not the first American-based leftists to abandon the view that the workplace is capable of generating class consciousness due to changes in society and production — see Marcuse (1964) and Lasch (1973).

12. Corporatism is generally defined as the development of state structures which incorporate trade unions and business associations within economic administration and policy-making. For an account of its post-war rise, see Harris (1972), while a more theoretical discussion is contained in Panitch (1981).

13. The Donovan Commission reported in 1968 and was a major focus for the debate on the causes of the 'problems' of British industrial relations. It received considerable academic input. It was concerned particularly with the prevalence of unofficial organisation and action, and the role of shop stewards in the workplace.

14. The Employment Bill (1982) gives employers the right to ignore previous agreements concerning the provision of a closed shop and the use of non-union labour for contract work. The Conservative government has set an example by tearing up its own agreements such as the provision for use of arbitration to settle wage disputes which led to the Civil Service strike of 1981. They have also encouraged employers such as Michael Edwardes of BL and Peter Parker at British Rail to break procedures and bypass union structures by going straight to the shop floor. In the National Union of Railwaymen strike of 1982, Parker broke an agreement on the closed shop by promising strike-breakers the retention of their jobs if they turned up for work. These developments seriously question the idea of permanent bureaucratic structuring and institutionalisation of trade unions.

15. Burawoy uses Nichols and Beynon as evidence for a supposed move by British corporations to move to his US model, without informing his readers that they carefully qualify any idea that corporatism is a general trend that avoids class conflict (Burawoy, 1979: 189 and 244).

16. This belief leads Burawoy into a strange alliance with the early industrial sociologists like Mayo, who also thought it was possible to study workplace behaviour without reference to so-called external factors. He gives his explicit blessing, with his normal qualification that they didn't know why they were right! (1979: 135—6).

17. This phrase comes from the famous passage where Marx gives a short exposition of many of his basic theoretical and methodological concepts, the *Preface to A Contribution to a Critique of Political Economy* (1971).

18. Burawoy refers critically to the development of a Marxist psychology by the Frankfurt School (Marcuse, 1955) and more favourably to Heller (1976). Other discussions of the basis for a Marxist psychology include Fromm (1973), Brown (1973), Reich (1972) and Sève (1969).

Chapter 7

1. Basic labour process writing has said little about gender, and even less about race. On the latter, one of the exceptions is Burawoy 1980), although without much apparent effect on his main analysis (1979).

2. 'Neoclassical' is the term used to describe the central school of mainstream economic thought, which takes the social and economic institutions of capitalism as natural and eternal social forms.

3. The 'separate dialectics' of sex and race referred to by Edwards appears to be downgraded or even denied by his attempt to identify segmentation in labour markets with 'distinct systems of control' within the firm (1979: 178).

4. Marx and Engels state in *The Communist Manifesto* that: 'Differences of age and sex no longer have any distinctive validity for the working class. All are instruments of labour, more or less expensive to use, according to their age and sex' (1968: 40). The more detailed presentation of Marx's conception of the impact of modern industry on the sexual division of labour can be found mainly in chapter 15 of *Capital, Volume One*.

5. To be fair to Marx and Engels, their analysis of the 'disappearing family' made considerable sense in its context of female and child labour. They were also motivated by a strong moral critique of the effects of the industrial revolution on the family, in the form of prostitution, exploitation of child labour and the oppression of women in the home.

6. Baxendall *et al*. argue that 'As the home was re-organised into an internal market for capitalist penetration, the actual work was transformed from artisan—craftswomanship to a definition not unlike "machine-minding" ' (1976: 8).

7. The political consequences for these authors of their belief that housewives were exploited in a value-relationship was that they should be paid a wage. 'Wages for housework' was rejected as a perspective by most feminists on the grounds that it would institutionalise housework as women's work on an even stronger basis.

8. Bland *et al*. (1978) and Wajcman (1981) discuss the domestic labour debate. But the most comprehensive review and bibliography is in Himmelweit and Mohun (1977).

9. I would agree with the majority position that housework only produces use-values. For example, domestic labour acts upon commodities bought with part of the household income, e.g. food, cleaning materials and clothes, to provide goods or services directly consumable within the household, and not for exchange on the market. This is not to say that housework can only be explained in terms of the functional requirements of capital for unpaid labour. Marriage and intra-familial factors are also important (see conclusion to the chapter).

10. The concept of patriarchy has been used to describe a wide variety of sex—gender relations. Its vagueness and implication that the oppression of women is rooted in an ahistorical biology has led some feminists to argue for avoiding the concept (Rowbotham, 1979). A reply by Alexander and Taylor (1980) puts a convincing case for its retention, given the inability of existing stratification

theory — Marxist or otherwise — to explain hierarchical sexual structuring independent of specific economic systems.

11. There is a certain tension between the Western images of femininity inculcated by the companies and the traditional submissive forms associated with Indonesian family life. The attempt to link the concept of the 'company family' to the kinship form is aimed at bridging that culture gap. Parental approval is also sought through rituals such as 'parents' day', and through promises of control over extra-plant activities. On the whole, however, the cultural imperialism connected to the global assembly line does gradually erode the national traditions, constituting a further means of control.

12. Hartman says that racial hierarchies can be understood in the same context as manifestations of the 'reproduction of people'. The attempt to identify ethnicity on the same terms as gender is quite misleading. While capital has needed both cheap female and immigrant labour, the material structures governing their respective availability have been very different.

13. Oddly, this is also the position of Anthias, who is also more optimistic about the eventual use of Marxism in its 'marriage' with feminism, *if* the former can be rid if its 'economist-technicist' bias (1980: 61).

14. Beechey qualifies her position in an end-note by admitting that she probably underemphasises the significance of the domestic labour aspect to the family's relationship to capitalism (1977: 64).

15. I have not discussed the radical feminist theory that women constitute a 'sex-class' within a 'domestic mode of production' (Delphy, 1977). This is because the position of women is examined largely distinct from capital, and therefore concentrates on the family, rather than wage labour. Delphy repeats the mistake of applying Marxist categories developed in production, thus describing the domestic sphere in rigidly economistic terms, marginalising issues of sexuality, ideology, etc. A previous attempt to invert traditional Marxist concepts to apply them to a 'mode of reproduction' was made by Firestone (1971).

16. Equally it is the case that many men have, however reluctantly, come to accept women working and two-wage families, even sometimes with the woman as main 'breadwinner'. Many feminists have attacked Humphries's views about the working-class family. But she recognises that the family wage reinforces sexual inequalities. The point is that the analysis helps us to go beyond an unbalanced functionalism that interprets the family and other social formations in terms of the needs of capital alone.

17. Even here, the traditional pattern was followed. One study recorded that 'If women had not been cheaper than men, they would not have replaced nine-tenths of the men in American public schools' (quoted in Davies, 1979: 251).

18. This is one of a number of criticisms levelled at Beechey by Anthias

(1980). It seems to me that while the expectation of marriage clearly does not have the same effects right across the board — for instance in professional 'dual career families' — Beechey's point is accurate since most women are in low-grade jobs. A further point made by Anthias is that dependency on the male wage does not alter the *value* of labour power, as capital has to pay more to men. This surely ignores the competitive and individualistic nature of commodity production and the ability of the family to assume additional financial burdens.

19. There was no evidence that women were anti-union or less militant, once motivated. In both factories strike action took place during the course of the studies; in one case it was the biggest dispute for twenty years, and women played an important part in it.

20. To argue that these 'technical' means of control will wholly *replace* the traditional ones is probably to underestimate the continuing significance of patriarchal relations. Nevertheless, the article is a useful illustration of how labour process theory can be applied without losing sight of the specificity of female wage labour.

Chapter 8

1. See, for example, Edwards (1979: 17), Brighton Labour Process Group (1977: 4), Marglin (1976: 15). Of course, there has been considerable mention of the effects of Lenin's admiration of Taylorism, but this has not generally led to a discussion of alternative analyses of labour processes.

2. This is a term used by Bahro. He does not believe they are socialist, but to avoid complicated debates on labels, he settles for an ironical use of the official 'actually existing socialism' (see Bahro, 1977: 5).

3. I am not referring here to the theory of 'convergence' propagated by functionalist sociologists such as Kerr *et al.* (1962). This was discussed briefly in Chapter 1. A critique can be found in Lane (1972) and Parkin (1971).

4. There is a number of currents within orthodox Marxism that continue to apply the label socialist — deformed, degenerated or otherwise — to Soviet-style societies. It is normally held that they are transitional between capitalism and communism, combining contradictory elements. For the Trotskyists the economic base is broadly socialist in that it has nationalised property relations, while the political superstructure is regarded as non-socialist (Mandel, 1978). Ignoring the old-style Stalinist worship of the Soviet Union, modern Euro-communism manages to be critical of aspects of economic and political relations without questioning their ultimately socialist character (Purdy, 1976; Corrigan, Ramsay and Sayer, 1981). As Claudin — himself a prominent Left Euro-communist — critically points out, there is now little difference between the two perspectives (1979: 222).

5. The fact that modern capitalism does not require a completely 'free' market, relying on state intervention and planning to survive and function efficiently, is not enough to change the character of the system. Such measures are carried out precisely to ensure the survival of capitalism within a competitive market structure.

6. In the Soviet Union, there *are* small sections under exchange relations, ranging from the black market, residues of private ownership and parts of agricultural production, to small artisan production. With the exception of the first example, they operate largely within the contours of the plan. For example, private agricultural units must give to the state what it orders them to produce (Carlo, 1974). Similarly, any elements of 'competition' between enterprises are strictly controlled through the apparatus of central planning. For a fuller explanation of why such societies are not capitalist from a similar perspective to my own, see Carlo (1974) and Fantham and Machover (1979).

7. This pamphlet is a re-issue of the famous 'Open Letter to the Polish Communist Party' from two Marxist dissidents in 1965. Kuron went on to become one of Solidarity's key advisers, and has been imprisoned on a number of occasions. In the course of events he appears to have dropped, or at least modified, his original Marxism.

8. Although providing very useful detail concerning the Shcheniko Experiment, Arnot's article also attempts to outline a preliminary analysis of the general characteristics of Soviet society. I only came across the article after I had virtually finished this section of the chapter, but its perspectives are very similar and the analysis is a very effective combination of theoretical and empirical material.

9. Elsewhere I have described this new mode of production as *state collectivist*, in that the character of such societies resides in the collective ownership and control of economic resources through a fused party-state apparatus (Thompson and Lewis, 1977). There is a growing number of writers who share some variation on the position that Soviet-style societies are of a new type, neither capitalist nor socialist. For example, see Rakovski (1977), Bahro (1977, 1978), Carlo (1974), Fantham and Machover (1979) and Sweezy (1971). For a hostile review of such perspectives see Binns and Haynes (1980).

10. The best details of the extent and pattern of industrial conflict are given in Houlbenko (1975) concerning the Soviet Union. For documentation from the small but significant free trade union movement, see Haynes and Semyonova (1979).

11. This refers to capitalism and state collectivism. Socialism, of course, makes a third!

12. How autonomous science and technology are, and what constraints they place on creating a differently designed and organised labour process, is still a matter of debate. As Cooley says, the Left is 'remarkably ignorant' about science and technology (1981: 55). There is a real danger that the healthy recognition of the *social*

influences on such processes is reduced to a notion that they are simply a mirror image of existing social relations. This would result in a relativism useless both to scientific knowledge and knowledge of science. A good discussion of these issues can be found in Mackenzie (1981) and Burawoy (1978).

13. For example, Balibar says that Marx showed that capitalist production relations were 'the last possible relation of exploitation in history . . . you can neither return to former modes of exploitation . . . nor go forward to a "new" mode of exploitation' (1977: 140).

14. Szymanski argues that: 'A socialist regime would not undermine the role of scientists, teachers, engineers and doctors, etc. (although it would re-direct their energies) . . . even lower managers would not suffer greatly in the short run' (1972: 56). Statements like this make the failure to transform the labour process in 'actually existing socialism' understandable!

15. The Ehrenreichs' theory has the merit of attempting, not altogether satisfactorily, to show proof of a coherent social and cultural existence for the 'professional-managerial class', linking it to the dominant concerns of the US left. The PMC theory has generated a lot of comment and criticism which is collected together in Walker (1979).

16. Wright's positions were originally very strongly influenced by and reacted against those of Poulantzas, of whom he makes a specific critique in an earlier article (1976).

17. The orthodox formulation is represented in the introduction to the influential CSE pamphlet on the labour process:

> For Marx the analysis of the labour process has a further significance. His discussion of the possibility of transition from capitalism to socialism, and ultimately to communism, rests heavily on the thesis that the changes brought about in the labour process are producing new forms of class organisation and struggle, which at last will be able to challenge the existence of class society. The deskilling and fragmentation of labour which capital seeks to introduce into production may eliminate the power of the individual worker, but at the same time brings into existence what Marx calls the 'collective labourer' — the proletariat which both makes possible and demands the overthrow of capitalism.

(Conference of Socialist Economists, 1976: 1—2)

18. An example of the kind of statement Marx was prone to make comes from *The Communist Manifesto*: 'But with the development of industry the proletariat not only increases in number; it becomes concentrated in greater masses, its strength grows and it feels that strength more. The various interests and conditions of life within the ranks of the proletariat are more and more equalised, in proportion as the machinery obliterates all distinctions of labour, and

nearly everywhere reduces wages to the same low level' (Marx and Engels, 1968: 41—2).

19. This has not been the view of all Marxist theoreticians. A more accurate comment on class composition and party formation was made by Bukharin in 1927: 'It is the *heterogeneity* of class which makes a party indispensable' (quoted in Matthews, 1972: 39, emphasis added).

20. This is partly a reference to Lenin's specific interpretation of the collective labourer. The quote continues: 'there is an unconvincing depiction of a homogeneous working class, duped into reformism by a labour aristocracy which has been bought off by the bourgeoisie' (1980: 360).

21. The anti-alliance perspective was directed against the Italian Communist Party's notion of the road to socialism being based on a 'class bloc' within which the working class would be hegemonic, a concept deriving ultimately from Gramsci.

22. Burawoy puts forward a similar perspective which has influenced my own thinking on this question:

> According to the traditional view, class as a historical force — class for itself — can only emerge out of a particular intervention of certain 'superstructural' (political and ideological) or 'subjective' factors, situated outside the economic realm, upon an already pre-existing 'class in itself' defined in 'objective' economic terms. But as we have seen, there is no such thing as a class in itself defined in 'objective' 'economic' terms. The so-called economic realm is itself inseparable from its political and ideological effects, and from specifically political and ideological 'structures' of the work place. There is no 'objective' notion of class prior to its appearance on the stage of 'history'.
>
> (Burawoy, 1978: 274—5)

In my view this makes the mistake of confusing the historical processes through which a class develops, and the existence of class. The latter's objectivity does have an historical dimension, for a class cannot come into being without the emergence of an overall structure of class relations of which it is a part. This is the starting point of class. The subsequent historical development provides the additional dimensions.

23. Burawoy's own formulation of the distinction is that global politics are based on the relations *of* production (appropriation, distribution, etc.), while production politics correspond to the relations *in* production: 'the relations of cooperation within the process of production itself' (1981: 89). There are two things wrong with this. First, production politics is too closely identified with his specific theory of *consent* ('relations of cooperation'). Second, global politics should take in the relations of reproduction discussed

in Chapter 7, otherwise they take on an unnecessarily narrow class character.

24. This is not to imply that there is any particular or fixed notion of global politics which necessarily challenges workplace hierarchies. The dominant politics of 'labourism' in the working-class movement would manifest an identity between politics at production and global levels. The statement simply signifies the *potential* for such a challenge.

25. The American writers — Braverman, Edwards and Burawoy — present a situation where workers are so closely controlled and divided that a significant production politics appears to be excluded. Braverman did not deal with the question at all; Edwards believes that the terrain of struggle is for the 'fractions' of the working class to unite in defence of representative democracy (1979: chapter 11); while Burawoy sees the problem, but is limited by his belief that, 'To insist on the centrality of working class resistance is an exercise in cloud kissing' (1981: 106). British theorists we have discussed give a much more balanced account of working-class struggles at the point of production, but seldom spell out the wider political consequences. For one attempt, see Nichols (1980a: 263—82).

26. The full title of the Bullock Report was the *Report of the Committee of Inquiry on Industrial Democracy*. Appointed by the Labour government, it was eventually shelved after pressure from the CBI, who threatened to withdraw co-operation on investment if it was implemented.

27. Cressey and MacInnes argue that the rigidity of attitudes to industrial democracy can be located within 'the way Marx's theory of the formal and real subordination of labour to capital has been taken up by contemporary Marxists' (1980: 6). Whether their complex theoretical case is correct or not, such a link seems unnecessarily restrictive in understanding the relations between theory and practice on this issue.

Guide to Labour Process Literature

The aim of this short guide is to provide a means of distinguishing the most important contributions within the large and ever-growing body of labour process writing discussed in the book as a whole. The full references can be found in the bibliography. Rather than simply produce a list of books and articles, I have attempted to group particular works in a smaller number of overlapping categories.

Marx

Harold Wilson once boasted that he could never get past the first page of *Capital*. In fact, Marx's major work is at its most accessible where he deals — drawing on contemporary writers and sources such as reports of factory inspectors — with the development of the capitalist labour process. Chapters 13 to 15 of Volume I are the essential basis for labour process theory, with the addition of the *Resultate*, which forms an appendix to the 1976 Penguin edition.

Braverman and After

Braverman's *Labor and Monopoly Capital* (1974) was not the first example of the re-awakening of labour process theory, but it has been the most influential. He was not an academic, and his background as a skilled worker greatly aided the clarity and directness of the book. Its influence can also be understood in terms of the sharpness of emphasis on his key themes: a merciless attack on the mystifications of conventional social science concerning the 'upgrading' of skills, the presentation of Taylorism as the major addition to the armoury of capital in reshaping work in the twentieth century, and the search for practical evidence on the growing degradation of work. *Labor and Monopoly Capital* should be taken together with its most direct American off-shoot, the collection of articles by Zimbalist (1979). These *Case Studies on the Labor Process* are a conscious and powerful defence of Braverman against his critics, by the most effective means: the application of his perspectives to a wide range of industries. Like their inspiration, the articles are well written and a mine of valuable information about jobs as different as computer programming, coal mining and electrical assembly.

In Britain, the articles collected by Stephen Wood (1982) represent the most obvious reaction to Braverman. Originally deriving from a British Sociological Association Conference on deskilling, most of the contributions are more critical. They are also more academic and specialist, coming largely from a sociological rather than activist tradition. Nevertheless, the collection offers an important and wide-ranging set of commentaries on the issues raised through Braverman, including sexual divisions in the valuable article by Beechey, as well as the extensive material on deskilling. There is also a particularly strong emphasis on the varieties of *historical* development of skill and work in British industries. A highly idiosyncratic contribution to the post-Braverman debate in Britain came with the publication of Hales's *Living Thinkwork*. An often curious mixture of personal politics, analysis of the design work he did for ICI, and high theory, it is worth ploughing through the more abstruse sections to find a sensitive attempt to think through key labour process concepts in a practical context. A new book by Cynthia Cockburn (1983), *Brothers: Male Dominance and Technological Change*, also takes up and extends a number of crucial themes from the Braverman debate.

The Control Debate

The major works of Friedman (1977a), Edwards (1979) and Burawoy (1979) are frequently taken to be direct rivals to the perspectives of Braverman. Yet with the partial exception of Friedman, Braverman is not extensively discussed in what are highly distinctive theories and accounts of historical and contemporary structures of control. Their common feature is a rejection of the orthodoxy of Marx and Braverman concerning the necessity for capital to control the labour force *directly*. Instead, there is a stress on the need for capital to *accommodate* worker resistance and involvement through more complex means of control and integration. Friedman's perspective is based upon the concept of *responsible autonomy*, while Edwards talks in terms of the evolution of distinct structures of control: from *simple* to *technical* and finally *bureaucratic* methods. The most radical challenge is provided by Burawoy. Despite an overestimation of the degree of worker integration into the functioning of the labour process, his analysis genuinely breaks new ground by introducing the theme of *consent* and positive participation in 'self-control' by workers.

More recent contributions by British writers promise to open up further dimensions of the control debate. Kelly (1982b) provides a fresh look at Taylorism and job design, arguing strongly against the idea that job enrichment is a genuine attempt to provide an alternative to worker alienation. *The Challenge to Management Control* by John Storey (1982) details the variety of influences from workers and employers on the shifting frontier of control. A useful cross-cultural perspective is offered by Craig Littler in *The Development of the Labour Process in Capitalist Societies* (1982b).

Other Compilations

A number of other books bring together articles on the above debates. The most important, and earliest, is that of Gorz (1976a). This is particularly interesting in that its French edition predates Braverman, and shows how European Marxist and sociological thought was beginning to move in a similar direction. The influence of radical workplace struggles in Italy and France is noticeable, especially in the political links drawn by Gorz, who has long been a pivotal figure in Europe for analysing work. In his new work, *Farewell to the Working Class: An Essay in Post-Industrial Socialism* (1982) Gorz retains his reputation for original and provocative analysis in arguing that changes in the labour process have broken the power of industrial workers. The original collection contains the influential article by the American writer, Marglin, on the origins of hierarchy in capitalist production. This article is also contained in the compilation by Nichols (1980a), although in shortened form. Nichols has collected together a very interesting set of articles which have a much wider range than the subtitle, *Studies in the capitalist labour process*, would indicate. While this is often valuable, the sheer diversity of the contributions sometimes lessens their impact, although the articles by Bosquet, Ramsay, Haraszti and Nightingale are particularly useful, as are the extracts from Marx and Braverman. I have drawn extensively on Berg's (1979) collection of documents from the nineteenth century in Chapter 2. This is an indispensable source of information, often with uncanny similarities to contemporary debates and issues on the transformation of work. Finally, there is the volume of essays on *Science, Technology and the Labour Process* edited by Levidow and Young (1981). It draws on the valuable work done by the *Radical Science* journal, and the Conference of Socialist Economists. Rosenberg's article is a useful short introduction to Marx's views on technology, and Cooley gives a valuable insight into Taylorism and technical white-collar work. Not all the articles are as accessible or relevant, and Duncan's contribution on new technology can be seen in more detail in the CSE Microelectronics Group book on that issue 1980).

Industrial Sociology

The work of Beynon, and Nichols and Beynon, on Ford and on ChemCo, is the best of British industrial sociology. Although Marxist, it is not overtly theoretical. The influence of Braverman can be seen in the ChemCo study, but the book is valuable precisely for what he and other labour process writers leave out — a complex and sensitive discussion of the relations between work, ideology and consciousness. The influence of labour process theory can also be seen in the useful collection of sociological research by Esland and Salaman (1980). Articles by Hyman, Nichols and T. J. Johnson are particularly important. In a similar vein, attempting to incorporate labour process insights, are the more general works of Salaman (1981), and Hill (1981). Both show an orientation to combine radical Weberian perspectives with the newer Marxist writings.

Sexual Divisions

As Chapter 7 makes clear, there has been a considerable debate on women and work, some of it in direct response to Braverman. Unfortunately, some of it is in inaccessible sources and difficult styles of debate. Aside from Beechey's contribution mentioned earlier, there have been two observational studies of women factory workers that the above description does not apply to. Ruth Cavendish's *Women on the Line* (1982) and Anna Pollert's *Girls, Wives, Factory Lives* are valuable attempts to provide a practical context for discussing gender and the labour process. Neither draw out the theoretical conclusions effectively enough, but Pollert in particular plots the inseparability of experiences inside and outside work, which provide a very effective accompaniment to the more abstract theoretical discussions from other sources. There are two additional articles which are not as easy to get hold of, but which are excellent examples of the necessity for an independent emphasis on gender. Barker and Downing's discussion of new technology and the office is a unique attempt to combine theoretical concepts like real subordination of labour with a particular case study of the transformation of women's work. Grossman's article, 'Women's Place in the Integrated Circuit', is a fascinating description of femininity and control within the new international division of labour, notably Malaysian electronics factories. The former article can be found in the journal *Capital and Class* (no. 10), and the latter originated in *Radical America*.

Workplace Experience and Struggle

Although difficult to get hold of, the two volumes of essays on European class conflict edited by Crouch and Pizzorno (1978) represent an important source of information on struggles which have provided the practical stimulus for labour process theory. Goodrich's famous study of the frontier of control in an earlier period in Britain retains its significance, as do the essays and interviews on work by Frazer (1968 and 1969) and Terkel (1977). Beynon's new book *Born to Work* (1982) promises additional direct insight from workers themselves. Interesting insights are also provided in a rare example of theoretician becoming factory worker: Robert Linhart's *The Assembly Line*, an account of his time working for Citroën in France. Finally, my own book with Eddie Bannon tries to link labour process theory with changes in workplace organisation in telecommunications plants on Merseyside.

These sources of labour process theory by no means exhaust the useful contributions. I have not listed articles and contributions that would be particularly difficult to find, notably those in journals. Nevertheless, journals like *Capital and Class* in Britain — reflecting the invaluable role played by the Conference of Socialist Economists in introducing labour process writings — and *Radical America* and *Monthly Review* in the USA have been a vital location for new writings and perspectives in this area; and readers should certainly try to look out for future contributions in these and other sources.

Bibliography

Aglietta, M. (1981) *A Theory of Capitalist Regulation: the US Experience*, London, New Left Books.

Ahsan, R. (1981) 'Retreat on the Shop Floor', *New Left Review*, no. 129.

Albrow, M. (1981) 'The Dialectic of Science and Values in the Study of Organisation', in Salaman, G. and J. Thompson, K. (eds).

Alexander, S. (1975) 'Women's Work in Nineteenth Century London', in Oakely, A. and Mitchell, J. (eds), *The Rights and Wrongs of Women*, Harmondsworth, Penguin.

Alexander, S. and Taylor, B. (1980) 'In Defence of Patriarchy', *New Statesman*, vol. 99, p. 161.

Althusser, L. (1969) *For Marx*, London, Allen Lane.

Amsden, A. (ed.) (1980) *The Economics of Women and Work*, Harmondsworth, Penguin.

Anthias, F. (1980) 'Women and the Reserve Army of Labour: a Critique of Veronica Beechey', *Capital and Class*, no. 10.

Anthony, P. D. (1975) *The Ideology of Work*, London, Tavistock.

Argyle, M. (1972) *The Social Psychology of Work*, Harmondsworth, Penguin.

Argyris, C. (1957) *Personality and Organisation*, New York, Harper & Row.

Arnot, B. (1982) 'Soviet Labour Productivity and the Failure of the Shchekino Experiment', *Critique*, no. 15.

Aronowitz, S. (1979) 'The Professional-Managerial Class or Middle Strata?', in Walker, P. (ed).

ASTMS (1980) *Technological Change and Collective Bargaining*, discussion paper, London, ASTMS.

Azcarte, M. (1975) 'The New Role of Science', in *Class Structure*, pamphlet, London, Communist Party of Great Britain.

Bahr, H.-D. (1980) 'The Class Structure of Machinery', in Slater, P. (ed.).

Bahro, R. (1977) 'The Alternative in Eastern Europe', *New Left Review*, no. 106.

Bahro, R. (1978) *The Alternative in Eastern Europe*, London, Verso.

Baldamus, W. (1961) *Efficiency and Effort: an Analysis of Industrial Administration*, London, Tavistock.

Balibar, E. (1977) *On the Dictatorship of the Proletariat*, London, New Left Books.

Baran, P. and Sweezy, P. (1968) *Monopoly Capital*, Harmondsworth, Penguin.

Baritz, L. (1960), *The Servants of Power*, Middletown, Wesleyan University Press.

Barker, J. and Downing, H. (1980) 'Word Processing and the Transformation of the Patriarchal Relations of Control in the Office', *Capital and Class*, no. 10.

Baudoin, T. *et al.* (1978) 'Women and Immigrants: Marginal Workers?' in Crouch, C. and Pizzorno, A. (eds).

Baxendall, R. *et al.* (1976) 'The Working Class Has Two Sexes', *Monthly Review*, vol. 28, no. 3.

Beale, J. (1982) *Getting it Together: Women as Trade Unionists*, London, Pluto.

Beechey, V. (1977) 'Some Notes on Female Wage Labour', *Capital and Class*, no. 3.

Beechey, V. (1982) 'The Sexual Division of Labour and the Labour Process', in Wood, S. (ed.).

Bell, D. (1974) *The Coming of Post-Industrial Society: a Venture in Social Forecasting*, London, Heinemann.

Bendix, R. (1963) *Work and Authority in Industry*, New York, Harper & Row.

Benet, M. K. (1972) *Secretary*, London, Sidgwick & Jackson.

Bengelsdorf, C. and Hagelman, A. (1979) 'Emerging from Underdevelopment: Women and Work in Cuba', in Eisenstein, Z. R. (ed.).

Berg, M. (ed.) (1979) *Technology and Toil in Nineteenth Century Britain*, London, CSE Books.

Bettelheim, C. (1976) *Class Struggles in the USSR 1917–23*, New York, Monthly Review Press.

Beynon, H. (1973) *Working for Ford*, Harmondsworth, Penguin.

Beynon, H. (1977) 'The Carcase of Time', *New Society* review, 13 October 1977.

Beynon, H. (1982) *Born to Work*, London, Pluto.

Beynon, H. and Blackburn, R. M. (1972) *Perceptions of Work*, Cambridge, Cambridge University Press.

Binns, P. and Haynes, M. (1980) 'New Theories of Eastern European Class Society', *International Socialism*, no. 7.

Blackburn, R. (1976) 'The Politics of Marx and Engels', *New Left Review*, no. 97.

Blackburn, R. M. and Stewart, A. (1977) 'Women, Work and the Class Structure', *New Society*, 1 September 1977.

Bland, L. *et al.* (eds) (1978) 'Women Inside and Outside the Relations of Production', in Women's Studies Group (eds).

Blau, P. M. (1972) *The Dynamics of Bureaucracy*, Chicago University Press.

Blauner, R. (1964) *Alienation and Freedom*, Chicago University Press.

Boggs, C. (1976) *Gramsci's Marxism*, London, Pluto.

Bologna, S. (1976) 'Class Composition and the Theory of the Party at the Origin of the Workers Councils Movement', in Conference of Socialist Economists (eds).

Bosquet, M. (1980) 'The Meaning of Job Enrichment', in Nichols, T. (ed.).

Branson, N. and Heinemann, M. (1971) *Britain in the 1930s*, St Albans, Panther.

Braverman, H. (1974) *Labor and Monopoly Capital: the Degradation of Work in the Twentieth Century*, London, Monthly Review Press.

Braverman, H. (1976) 'Two Comments', *Monthly Review*, vol. 28, no. 3.

Brecher, J. (1972) *Strike! The True History of Mass Insurgence in America from 1877 to the Present*, San Francisco, Straight Arrow Books.

Brecher, J. (1979) 'The Roots of Power: Employers and Workers in the Electrical Products Industry', in Zimbalist, A. (ed.).

Brighton Labour Process Group (1977) 'The Capitalist Labour Process', *Capital and Class*, no. 1.

Brown, H. (1981) 'The Individual in the Organisation', in Salaman, G. and Thompson, K. (eds).

Brown, J. A. C. (1954) *The Social Psychology of Industry*, Harmondsworth, Penguin.

Brown, P. (ed.) (1973) *Radical Psychology*, London, Tavistock.

Budish, J. M. (1961) 'The Changing Structure of the US Working Class', *Political Affairs*, October.

Buhle, R., Gordon, A. and Schram, N. (1971) 'Women in American Society', *Radical America*, vol. 5, no. 4

Bulmer, M. (ed.) (1975) *Working Class Images of Society*, London, Routledge & Kegan Paul.

Burawoy, M. (1978) 'Towards a Marxist Theory of the Labour Process: Braverman and Beyond', *Politics and Society*, vol. 8, nos 3–4.

Burawoy, M. (1979) *Manufacturing Consent: Changes in the Labour Process under Monopoly Capitalism*, University of Chicago Press.

Burawoy, M. (1980) 'Migrant Labour in South Africa and the United States', in Nichols, T. (ed.)

Burawoy, M. (1981) 'Terrains of Contest: Factory and State under Capitalism and Socialism', *Socialist Review* (USA), vol. 11, no. 4.

Campbell, B. (1982) 'Power not Pin Money', *New Socialist*, no. 6.

Carchedi, G. (1975) 'On the Economic Identification of the New Middle Class', *Economy and Society*, vol. iv, no. 1.

Carlo, A. (1974) 'The Socio-Economic Nature of the Soviet Union', *Telos*, November.

Castles, S. and Kosack, G. (1973) *Immigrant Workers and the Class Structure in Western Europe*, London, Oxford University Press.

Cavendish, R. (1982) *Women on the Line*, London, Routledge & Kegan Paul.

Centre for Alternative Industrial and Technological Systems (1981) *CAITS Quarterly*, September.

Child, J. (1973) 'Organisation, Structure and Environment: the Role of Strategic Choice', in Salaman, G. and Thompson, K. (eds).

Childe, G. (1949) *History*, London, Cobbett Press.

Chinoy, E. (1955) *Automobile Workers and the American Dream*, Garden City, Doubleday.

CIS (1980) *Report on New Technology*, Counter Information Services pamphlet, London.

Clarke, T. and Clements, L. (eds) (1977) *Trade Unions under Capitalism*, Glasgow, Fontana.

Claudin, F. (1979) 'Eurocommunism and the Antagonistic Societies of a New Type', in *Power and Opposition in Post-Revolutionary Societies*, London, Ink Links.

Claudin-Urondo, C. (1977) *Lenin and the Cultural Revolution*, Brighton, Harvester.

Clegg, H. (1972) *The System of Industrial Relations in Great Britain*, Oxford, Blackwell.

Clements, L. (1977) 'Reference Groups and Trade Union Consciousness', in Clarke, T. and Clements, L. (eds).

Cliff, T. (1970) *Russia: a Marxist Analysis*, London, Pluto.

Cockburn, C. (1983) *Brothers: Male Dominance and Technological Change*, London, Pluto.

Colletti, L. (1972) *From Rousseau to Lenin*, London, New Left Books.

Conference of Socialist Economists (eds) (1976) *The Labour Process and Class Strategies*, London, Stage One.

Cooley, M. (1980) *Architect or Bee?*, Slough, Langley Technical Services.

Cooley, M. (1981) 'The Taylorisation of Intellectual Work', in Levidow, L. and Young, B. (eds).

Coombs, R. (1978) 'Labour and Monopoly Capital', *New Left Review*, no. 107.

Coriot, B. (1980) 'The Restructuring of the Assembly Line: a New Economy of Time and Control', *Capital and Class*, no. 11.

Corrigan, P., Ramsay, H. and Sayer, D. (1978) *Socialist Construction and Marxist Theory: Bolshevism and its Critique*, London, Macmillan.

Corrigan, P., Ramsay, H. and Sayer, D. (1981) 'Bolshevism and the USSR', *New Left Review*, no. 125.

Cotgrove, S. (1972) 'Alienation and Automation', *British Journal of Sociology*, December 1972.

Coulson, M., Magas, B. and Wainwright, H. (1975) 'The Housewife and Her Labour under Capitalism — a Critique', *New left Review*, no. 83.

Council for Science and Society (1981) *New Technology: Society, Employment and Skill*, pamphlet, London CSS.

Coventry Machine Tool Workers' Committee (1979) *Crisis in Engineering: Machine Tool Workers Fight for Jobs*, pamphlet jointly with Institute for Workers' Control.

Cressey, P. and MacInnes, J. (1980) 'Industrial Democracy and the Control of Labour', *Capital and Class*, no. 11.

Crompton, R. (1978) 'The De-Skilling of Clerical Work', Nuffield Paper.

Crompton, R. and Reid, S. (1982) 'The De-Skilling of Clerical Work', in Wood, S. (ed.).

Crouch, C. and Pizzorno, A. (eds) (1978) *The Resurgence of Class Conflict in Western Europe*, two vols, London, Macmillan.

Crozier, M. (1964) *The Bureaucratic Phenomenon*, London, Tavistock.

Crozier, M. (1971) *The World of the Office Worker*, University of Chicago Press.

CSE London Working Group (1980) *The Alternative Economic Strategy: A Labour Movement Response to the Crisis*, London, CSE Books.

CSE Microelectronics Group (1980) *Microelectronics: Capitalist Technology and the Working Class*, London, CSE Books.

Cutler, A. (1978) 'The Romance of Labour', *Economy and Society*, vol. 7, no. 1.

Dahrendorf, R. (1959) *Class and Class Conflict in an Industrial Society*, London, Routledge & Kegan Paul.

Dalla Costa, M. and James, S. (1973) *The Power of Women and the Subversion of the Community*, Bristol, Falling Wall Press.

Daniel, W. W. (1969) 'Industrial Behaviour and Orientations to Work', *Journal of Management Studies*, no. 6.

Davies, M. (1979) 'A Woman's Place is at the Typewriter', in Eisenstein Z. R. (ed.).

Davis, L. E. and Taylor, J. C. (1972) *Design of Jobs*, Harmondsworth, Penguin.

Davis, M. (1975) 'The Stop Watch and the Wooden Shoe: Scientific Management and the Industrial Workers of the World', *Radical America*, vol. 8, no. 6.

Delphy, C. (1977) *The Main Enemy*, Women's Research and Resource Centre, London.

Dickson, P. (1974) *Alternative Technology*, Glasgow, Fontana.

Dickson, P. (1977) *Work Revolution*, London, Allen & Unwin.

Ditton, J. (1976) 'Moral Horror versus Folk Terror: Output Restriction, Class and the Social Organisation of Exploitation', *Sociological Review*, no. 24.

Dix, K. (1979) 'Work Relations in the Coal Industry: The Handloading Era, 1880–1930', in Zimbalist, A. (ed.).

Dobb, M. (1963) *Studies in the Development of Capitalism*, London, Routledge & Kegan Paul.

Doeringer, P. B. and Piore, M. J. (1971) *Internal Labour Markets and Manpower Analysis*, Lexington, Mass., D. C. Heath.

Donovan Report (1968) *Royal Commission on Trade Unions and Employers' Associations*, 1965–8, London, HMSO.

Driver, C. (1981) 'Review of Aglietta', *Capital and Class*, no. 15.

Dubin, R. (1956) 'Industrial Workers' Worlds: a Study of the Central Life Interests of Industrial Workers', *Social Problems*, no. 3.

Dubois, P. (1978) 'New Forms of Industrial Conflict', in Crouch, C. and Pizzorno, A. (eds) vol. 2.

Duncan, M. (1981) 'Microelectronics: Five Areas of Subordination', in Levidow, L. and Young, B. (eds).

Dunlop, J. T. (1958) *Industrial Relations Systems*, New York, Holt.

Edwards, R. (1979) *Contested Terrain; The Transformation of the Workplace in the Twentieth Century*, London, Heinemann.

Edwards, R., Reich, M. and Gordon, D. M. (eds) (1975) *Labour Market Segmentation*, Lexington, Mass., D. C. Heath.

Ehrenreich, B. and Ehrenreich, J. (1976) 'Work and Consciousness', *Monthly Review*, vol. 28, no. 3.

Ehrenreich, B. and Ehrenreich, J. (1979) 'The Professional-Managerial Class', in Walker, P. (ed.).

Eisenstein, Z. (1979) 'Developing a Theory of Capitalist Patriarchy and Socialist Feminism', in Eisenstein, Z. (ed.), *Capitalist Patriarchy and the Case for Socialist Feminism*, London, Monthly Review Press.

Eldrige, J. E. T. (1971) *Industrial Disputes*, London, Routledge & Kegan Paul.

Elger, T. (1979) 'Valorisation and De-skilling: a Critique of Braverman', *Capital and Class*, no. 7.

Elger, T. and Schwarz, B. (1980) 'Monopoly Capitalism and the Impact of Taylorism: Notes on Gramsci, Braverman, Lenin and Sohn-Rethel', in Nichols, T. (ed.).

Elson, D. (1979) *Value: the Representation of Labour in Capitalism*, London, CSE Books.

Elson, D. and Pearson, S. (1981) 'The Subordination of Women and the Internationalisation of Factory Production', in Young, K. *et al.* (eds).

Eltis, W. (1979) 'How Rapid Public Sector Growth Can Undermine the Growth of the Gross National Product', in Beckerman, W. (ed.), *Slow Growth in Britain: Causes and Consequences*, Oxford, Clarendon Press.

Engels, F. (1970) 'The Origins of the Family, Private Property and the State', in Marx, K. and Engels, F., *Selected Works in One Volume*, London, Lawrence & Wishart.

Equal Opportunities Commission (1982) *Annual Report*, London, EOC.

Esland, G. (1980) 'Professions and Professionalism', in Esland, G. and Salaman, G. (eds).

Esland, G. and Salaman, G. (eds) (1975) *People and Work*, London, Open University Press.

Esland, G. and Salaman, G. (eds) (1980) *The Politics of Work and Occupations*, London, Open University Press.

Etzioni, A. (1961) *A Comparative Analysis of Complex Organisations*, New York, Free Press.

Fabar, A. (1979) 'Auto in the Eighties: Uncars and Uncarworkers', *Radical America*, vol. 13, no. 1.

Factfolder (1972) 'The Coventry Toolroom Dispute', London, Factfolder.

Falk, R. (1970) *The Business of Management*, Harmondsworth, Penguin.

Fantham, J. and Machover, M. (1979) *The Century of the Unexpected: a New Analysis of Soviet-Type Societies*, London, Big Flame pamphlet.

Faunce, W. A. (1968) *Problems of an Industrial Society*, New York, McGraw-Hill.

Feickert, D. (1979) 'Of Men and Minos', *Computing Europe*, 22 November.

Fine, B. (1975) *Marx's 'Capital'*, London, Macmillan.

Fine, B. and Harris, L. (1976) 'Controversial Issues in Marxist Economic Theory', in *Socialist Register*, London, Merlin.

Firestone, S. (1971) *The Dialectic of Sex*, London, Paladin.

Flanders, A. (1964) *The Fawley Productivity Agreements*, London, Faber.

Flanders, A. (1970) *Management and Unions*, London, Faber.

Foster, J. (1974) *Class Struggle and the Industrial Revolution*, London, Methuen.

Fox, A. (1971) *A Sociology of Work in Industry*, London, Collier-Macmillan.

Fox, A. (1974) *Man Mismanagement*, London, Hutchinson.

Fox, A. (1977) 'The Myths of Pluralism and a Radical Alternative', in Clarke, T. and Clements, L. (eds).

Fox, A. (1980) 'The Meaning of Work', in Esland, G. and Salaman, G. (eds).

Fraser, R. (ed.) (1968, 1969) *Work*, 2 vols, Harmondsworth, Penguin.

Freedman, F. (1975) 'The Internal Structure of the American Proletariat', *Socialist Revolution*, vol. 5, no. 26.

Fridenson, P. (1978) 'Corporate Policy, Rationalisation and the Labour Force: French Experiences in International Comparison, 1900 to 1929', Nuffield Paper.

Friedman, A. (1977a) *Industry and Labour: Class Struggle at Work and Monopoly Capitalism*, London, Macmillan.

Friedman, A. (1977b) 'Responsible Autonomy versus Direct Control over the Labour Process', *Capital and Class*, no. 1.

Friedman, A. (1978) 'Worker Resistance and Marxian Analysis of the Labour Process', Nuffield Paper.

Friedmann, G. (1961) *The Anatomy of Work*, London, Heinemann.

Fromm, E. (1973) *The Crisis of Psychoanalysis: Essays on Freud, Marx and Social Psychology*, Harmondsworth, Penguin.

Gagliani, A. (1981) 'How Many Working Classes?', *American Journal of Sociology*, September.

Gallie, D. (1978) *In Search of the New Working Class: Automation and Social Integration in the Capitalist Enterprise*, Cambridge University Press.

Gardiner, J. (1975) 'Women's Domestic Labour', *New Left Review*, no. 89.

Gartman, D. (1979) 'Origins of the Assembly Line and Capitalist Control of Work at Ford', in Zimbalist, A. (ed.).

Giddens, A. (1973) *The Class Structure of the Advanced Societies*, London, Hutchinson.

Glaberman, M. (1976) 'The Working Class', *Radical America*, vol. 1, no. 1.

Glenn, E. K. and Feldberg, R. L. (1979) 'Proletarianising Office Work', in Zimbalist, A. (ed.).

GMWU (1980) *New Technology Report to Congress*, Surrey, GMWU.

Goddard, V. (1977) 'Domestic Industry in Naples', *Critique of Anthropology*, issue 9—10.

Goldthorpe, J. H. (1977) 'Industrial Relations in Great Britain: a Critique of Reformism', in Clarke, T. and Clements, L. (eds).

Goldthorpe, J. H. *et al.* (1980) *Social Mobility and Class Structure in Modern Britain*, Oxford, Clarendon Press.

Goldthorpe, J. H., Lockwood, D. *et al.* (1968) *The Affluent Worker: Industrial Attitudes and Behaviour*, Cambridge University Press.

Goodey, C. (1974) 'Factory Committees and the Dictatorship of the Proletariat', *Critique*, no. 3.

Goodrich, C. (1975) *The Frontier of Control*, London, Pluto.

Gordon, D. M. (1972) *Theories of Poverty and Underdevelopment*, Lexington, Mass., D. C. Heath.

Gordon, D. M. (1976) 'Capitalist Efficiency and Socialist Efficiency', *Monthly Review*, vol. 28, no. 3.

Gorz, A. (1965) 'Work and Consumption', in Anderson, P. and Blackburn, R. (eds), *Towards Socialism*, Glasgow, Fontana.

Gorz, A. (1967) *Strategy for Labour*, Boston, Beacon.

Gorz, A. (ed.) (1976a) *The Division of Labour: the Labour Process and Class Struggle in Modern Capitalism*, Brighton, Harvester.

Gorz, A. (1976b) 'The Tyranny of the Factory', in Gorz, A. (ed.).

Gorz, A. (1976c) 'Technology, Technicians and Class Struggle', in Gorz, A. (ed.).

Gorz, A. (1982) *Farewell to the Working Class: An Essay in Post-Industrial Socialism*, London, Pluto.

Gouldner, A. (1954) *Patterns of Industrial Bureaucracy*, New York, Free Press.

Gouldner, A. (1955) *Wildcat Strike*, London, Routledge & Kegan Paul.

Gramsci, A. (1976) *Selections from the Prison Notebooks*, London, Lawrence & Wishart.

Gray, R. (1976) *The Labour Aristocracy in Victorian Edinburgh*, Oxford, Clarendon Press.

Green, K. and Bornat, A. (1978) 'Group Technology in Small Batch Engineering', Nuffield Paper.

Greenbaum, J. (1976) 'Division of Labour in the Computer Field', *Monthly Review*, vol. 28, no. 3.

Grossman, R. (1979) 'Women's Place in the Integrated Circuit', *Radical America*, no. 14, no. 1.

Hales, M. (1980) *Living Thinkwork: Where Do Labour Processes Come From?*, London, CSE Books.

Halmos, P. (1970) *The Personal Service Society*, London, Constable.

Halsey, A. H. (1978) *Origins and Destinations: Family, Class and Education in Modern Britain*, Oxford, Clarendon Press.

Hamilton, P. (1980) 'Social Theory and the Problematic Concept of Work', in Esland, G. and Salaman. G. (eds).

Harastzi, M. (1977) *Worker in a Worker's State*, Harmondsworth, Penguin.

Harman, C. (1979) *Is a Machine After Your Job?*, London, Socialist Workers' Party pamphlet.

Harris, N. (1972) *Competition and the Corporate Society*, London, Methuen.

Hartman, H. (1979a) 'Marxism and Feminism, Towards a More Progressive Union', *Capital and Class*, no. 8.

Hartman, H. (1979b) 'Capitalism, Patriarchy and Job Segregation by Sex', in Eisenstein, Z. R. (ed.).

Haynes, V. and Semyonova, O. (1979) *Workers Against the Gulag: the New Opposition in the Soviet Union*, London, Pluto.

Heller, A. (1976) *The Theory of Need in Marx*, London, Allison & Busby.

Herzberg, F. (1968) *Work and the Nature of Man*, London, Staples Press.

Hill, S. (1981) *Competition and Control at Work*, London, Heinemann.

Hilsum, L. (1982) 'Uncle Sam's Jobs South of the Border', *The Guardian*, 19 March.

Himmelweit, S. and Mohun, S. (1977) 'Domestic Labour and Capital', *Cambridge Journal of Economics*, vol. 1.

Hinton, J. (1971) 'The Clyde Workers' Committee and the Dilution Struggles', in Briggs, A. and Saville, J. (eds), *Essays in Labour History*, London, Macmillan.

Hinton, J. (1973) *The First Shop Stewards Movement*, London, Allen & Unwin.

Hinton, J. (1976) 'Rejoinder to Monds', *New Left Review*, no. 97.

Hobsbawm, E. J. (1968) *Labouring Men*, London, Weidenfeld & Nicolson.

Hobsbawm, E. J. and Rudé, G. (1969) *Captain Swing*, London, Lawrence & Wishart.

Hodges, D. (1971) 'Old and New Working Classes', *Radical America*, vol. 5, no. 1.

Hodgson, G. (1980) 'Britain's Crisis', *International Socialism*, no. 7.

Houlbenko, M. (1975) 'The Soviet Working Class', *Critique*, no. 4.

Hughes, E. C. (1963) 'Professions', in Esland, G. and Salaman, G. (eds) (1975).

Humphries, J. (1980) 'Class Struggle and the Persistence of the Working Class Family', in Amsden, A. (ed.).

Hunt, A. (1975) 'Class Structure in Britain Today', in *Class Structure*, Communist Party of Great Britain pamphlet, London.

Huws, U. (1982) *Your Job in the Eighties: A Woman's Guide to New Technology*, London, Pluto.

Hyman, R. (1971) *Marxism and the Sociology of Trade Unionism*, London, Pluto.

Hyman, R. (1974) 'Workers' Control and Revolutionary Theory', *Socialist Register*, London, Merlin.

Hyman, R. (1975) *Industrial Relations: a Marxist Introduction*, London,

Macmillan.

Hyman, R. (1979) 'Shop Stewards as Full-Time Officials', *Revolutionary Socialism*, no. 3.

Hyman, R. (1980) 'Trade Unions, Control and Resistance', in Esland, G. and Salaman, G. (eds).

Hyman, R. and Elger, T. (1981) 'Job Controls, the Employers' Offensive and Alternative Strategies', *Capital and Class*, no. 15.

Ingham, G. (1967) 'Organisational Size, Orientations to Work and Industrial Behaviour', *Sociology*, vol. I, pp. 239—58.

Ingham, G. (1970) *Size of Industrial Organisation and Industrial Behaviour*, Cambridge University Press.

Johnson, C. (1980) 'The Problem of Reformism and Marx's Theory of Fetishism', *New Left Review*, no. 119.

Johnson, T. J. (1972) *Professions and Power*, London, Macmillan.

Johnson, T. J. (1980) 'Work and Power', in Esland, G. and Salaman, G. (eds).

Jones, B. (1982) 'Destruction or Redistribution of Engineering Skills: the Case of Numerical Control', in Wood, S. (ed.).

Jones, G. (1978) 'Ideological Responses to De-skilling of Managerial Work', Nuffield Paper.

Kapferer, N. (1980) 'Commodity, Science and Technology: a Critique of Sohn-Rethel', in Slater, P. (ed.).

Karol, K. S. (1979) 'How to Change Things for Good', in *Power and Opposition*, London, Ink Links.

Kelly, J. (1982a) 'Useless Work and Useless Toil', *Marxism Today*, vol. 26, no. 8.

Kelly, J. (1982b) *Scientific Management, Job Redesign and Work Performance*, New York, Academic Press.

Kerr, C. *et al.* (1962) *Industrialism and Industrial Man*, London, Heinemann.

Kraft, P. (1979) 'The Industrialisation of Computer Programming', in Zimbalist, A. (ed.).

Kumar, K. (1978) *Prophecy and Progress: the Sociology of Industrial and Post-Industrial Societies*, Harmondsworth, Penguin.

Kuron, J. and Modzelewski, K. (1982) *Solidarnosc: the Missing Link?* London, Bookmarks.

Lamphere, L. (1979) 'Fighting the Piece-Rate System: New Dimensions of an Old Struggle in the Apparel Industry', in Zimbalist, A. (ed.).

Landes, D. S. (1969) *The Unbound Prometheus*, Cambridge University Press.

Lane, D. (1972) *Politics and Society in the USSR*, London, Weidenfeld & Nicolson.

Lane, T. (1974) *The Union Makes us Strong*, London, Arrow.

Lane, T. (1981) *Parallel Management and Planning Agreements: an Approach to Industrial Democracy*, Liverpool, TGWU.

Lane, T. (1982) 'The Unions: Caught on the Ebb Tide', *Marxism Today*, vol. 26, no. 9.

Langer, E. (1970) 'Inside the New York Telephone Company', *New York Review of Books*, 12 March.

Lasch, C. (1973) *The Agony of the American Left*, Harmondsworth, Penguin.

Lee, D. (1978) 'De-skilling, the Labour Market, and Recruitment to Skilled Trades in Britain', Nuffield Paper.

Lee, D. (1980) 'Skill, Craft and Class: a Theoretical Critique and a Critical Case', *Sociology*, vol. 15, no. 1.

Lenin, V. I. (1963) *What Is To Be Done?*, Moscow, Progress.

Letteri, A. (1976) 'Factory and School', in Gorz, A. (ed.).

Levidow, L. and Young, B. (eds) (1981) *Science, Technology and the Labour Process*, London, CSE Books.

Likert, L. (1967) *The Human Organisation: Its Management and Value*, New York, McGraw-Hill.

Linhart, R. (1976) *Lenine, Les Paysans, Taylor*, Paris, Editions Du Seuil.

Linhart, R. (1981) *The Assembly Line*, London, John Calder.

Lipietz, A. (1982) 'Towards Global Fordism', *New Left Review*, no. 132.

Littler, C. J. (1978) 'De-skilling and Changing Structures of Control', Nuffield Paper.

Littler, C. J. (1980) 'Internal Contract and the Transition to Modern Work Systems: Britain and Japan', in Dunkerley, D. and Salaman, G. (eds), *Organisational Studies Yearbook*, London, Routledge & Kegan Paul.

Littler, C. J. (1982a) 'De-skilling and Structures of Control', in Wood, S. (ed.).

Littler, C. J. (1982b) *The Development of the Labour Process in Capitalist Societies: A Comparative Analysis of Work Organisation in Britain, the USA and Japan*, London, Heinemann.

Lockwood, D. (1958) *The Blackcoated Worker*, London, Allen & Unwin.

Lockwood, D. (1975) 'Sources of Variation in Working Class Images of Society', in Bulmer, M. (ed.).

Lozovsky, A. (1935) *Marx and the Trade Unions*, London, Martin Lawrence.

Lumley, B. (1980) 'Working Class Autonomy and the Crisis: Italian Marxist Texts 1964–79', *Capital and Class*, no. 12.

Lupton, T. (1963) *On the Shop Floor*, Oxford, Pergamon.

McGregor, D. (1960) *The Human Side of the Enterprise*, New York, McGraw-Hill.

Mackenzie, D. (1981) 'Notes on the Science and Social Relations Debate', *Capital and Class*, no. 14.

Mackenzie, G. (1974) 'The "Affluent Worker" Study: an Evaluation and Critique', in Parkin, F. (ed.), *The Social Analysis of the Class Structure*, London, Tavistock.

Mackenzie, G. (1977) 'The Political Economy of the American Working Class', *British Journal of Sociology*, June.

Mackintosh, M. *et al.* (1977) 'Women and Unemployment', unpublished paper.

McShane, H. (1978) *No Mean Fighter*, London, Pluto.

Mallet, S. (1975) *The New Working Class*, Nottingham, Spokesman.

Mandel, E. (1978) 'On the Nature of the Soviet State', *New Left Review*, no. 108.

Mann, M. (1973) *Consciousness and Action Among the Western Working Class*, London, Macmillan.

Manwaring, T. (1981) 'Labour Productivity and the Crisis at BSC', *Capital and Class*, no. 14.

Marcuse, H. (1955) *Eros and Civilisation*, Boston, Beacon.

Marcuse, H. (1964) *One Dimensional Man*, Boston, Beacon.

Marglin, S. (1976) 'What Do Bosses Do? The Origins and Functions of Hierarchy in Capitalist Production', in Gorz, A. (ed.).

Martin, R. and Fryer, R. H. (1975) 'The Deferential Worker', in Bulmer, M. (ed.).

Marx, K. (1963) *The Poverty of Philosophy*, New York, International Publishers.

Marx, K. (1971) *Preface to A Contribution to a Critique of Political Economy*, London, Lawrence & Wishart.

Marx, K. (1973a) 'The Class Struggles in France', in Marx, K., *Surveys From Exile*, Harmondsworth, Penguin.

Marx, K. (1973b) *Grundrisse*, Harmondsworth, Penguin.

Marx, K. (1976) *Capital, Volume One*, Harmondsworth, Penguin.

Marx, K. and Engels, F. (1964) *The German Ideology*, London, Lawrence & Wishart.

Marx, K. and Engels, F. (1968) *The Communist Manifesto*, Peking, Foreign Languages Press.

Maslow, A. H. (1958) *Motivation and Personality*, New York, Harper & Row.

Mattera, P. (1980) 'Small is Not Beautiful: Decentralised Production and the Underground Economy in Italy', *Radical America*, vol. 14, no. 5.

Mattera, P. (1981) 'From the Runaway to the Sweatshop', *Radical America*, vol. 15, no. 5.

Matthews, M. (1972) *Class and Society in Soviet Russia*, London, Allen Lane.

Mayo, E. (1945) *The Social Problems of an Industrial Civilization*, Harvard University Press.

Meiskens-Wood, E. (1981) 'The Separation of the Economic and Political in Capitalism', *New Left Review*, no. 127.

Merton, R. (1957) *Social Theory and Social Structure*, Chicago, Free Press.

Meszaros, I. (1971) 'Contingent and Necessary Class Consciousness', in Meszaros, I. (ed.), *Aspects of History and Class Consciousness*, London, Routledge & Kegan Paul.

Mills, H. (1979) 'The San Francisco Waterfront: the Social Consequences of Industrial Modernisation', in Zimbalist, A. (ed.).

Mills, C. W. (1956) *White Collar*, New York, Oxford University Press.

Mincer, J. and Polachek, S. (1980) 'Family Investments in Human Capital', in Amsden, A. (ed.).

Molyneux, M. (1981) 'Women in Socialist Societies', in Young, K. *et al.* (eds).

Monds, J. (1976) 'Workers' Control and the Historians: a New Economism', *New Left Review*, no. 97.

Montgomery, D. (1976) 'Workers' Control of Machine Production in the Nineteenth Century', *Labor History*, no. 17.

Montgomery, D. (1979) 'The Past and Future of Workers Control', *Radical America*, vol. 13, no. 6.

More, C. (1978) 'De-skilling in Historical Perspective', Nuffield Paper.

More, C. (1982) 'Skill and the Survival of Apprenticeship', in Wood, S. (ed.).

Morris, R. J. (1979) *Class and Class Consciousness in the Industrial Revolution*, London, Macmillan.

Mulcahy, S. D. and Faulkner, R. R. (1979) 'Person and Machine in a New England Factory', in Zimbalist, A. (ed.).

Myrdal, A. and Klein, V. (1956) *Women's Two Roles*, London, Routledge & Kegan Paul.

Nadworny, M. (1955) *Scientific Management and the Unions*, Cambridge, Mass., Harvard University Press.

Nichols, T. (ed.) (1980a) *Capital and Labour*, Glasgow, Fontana.

Nichols, T. (1980b) 'Management Ideology and Practice', in Esland, G. and Salaman, G. (eds).

Nichols, T. and Armstrong, P. (1976) *Workers Divided*, Glasgow, Fontana.

Nichols, T. and Beynon, H. (1977) *Living With Capitalism: Class Relations in the Modern Factory*, London, Routledge & Kegan Paul.

Nightingale, M. (1980) 'UK Productivity Dealing in the 1960s', in Nichols, T. (ed.).

Noble, D. F. (1979) 'Social Choice in Machine Design: the Case of Automatically Controlled Machine Tools', in Zimbalist, A. (ed.).

Oakeshott, G. (1979) 'Women in the Cigar Trade in London', in Berg, M. (ed.).

O'Connor, J. (1975) *The Fiscal Crisis of the State*, New York, St. Martin's Press.

Palloix, C. (1976) 'The Labour Process from Fordism to Neo-Fordism', in Conference of Socialist Economists (eds).

Palmer, B. (1975) 'Class, Conception and Conflict: the Thrust for Efficiency, Managerial Views of Labor, and the Working Class Rebellion', *Review of Radical Political Economics*, vol. 7, no. 2.

Panitch, L. (1981) 'Trade Unions and the State', *New Left Review*, no. 125.

Panzieri, R. (1976) 'Surplus Value and Planning: Notes on the Reading of Capital', in Conference of Socialist Economists (eds).

Panzieri, R. (1980) 'The Capitalist Use of Machinery: Marx Versus the "Objectivists" ', in Slater, P. (ed.).

Parkin, F. (1971) *Class, Inequality and Political Order*, London, Mac-Gibbon & Kee.

Partridge, H. (1980) 'Italy's FIAT in the 1950s', in Nichols, T. (ed.).

Penn, R. (1978) 'Skilled Manual Workers in the Labour Process', Nuffield Paper.

Perrow, C. (1972) *Complex Organisations: a Critical Essay*, Glenview Illinois, Scott, Foresman.

Philips, A. and Taylor, B. (1978) 'Sex and Class in the Labour Process', Nuffield Paper.

Phizachlea, A. and Miles, R. (1980) *Labour and Racism*, London, Routledge & Kegan Paul.

Pignon, D. and Querzola, J. (1976) 'Dictatorship and Democracy in Production', in Gorz, A. (ed.).

Plyushch, L. (1979) 'Forward Together or Down Together', in *Power and Opposition*, London, Ink Links.

Political Economy of Women Group (1975) *On the Political Economy of Women*, CSE pamphlet, London, Stage One.

Pollard, S. (1965) *The Genesis of Modern Management*, London, Edward Arnold.

Pollert, A. (1981) *Girls, Wives, Factory Lives*, London, Macmillan.

Poulantzas, N. (1975) *Classes in Contemporary Capitalism*, London, New Left Books.

Purdy, D. (1976) *The Soviet Union: State Capitalist or Socialist?*, Communist Party of Great Britain pamphlet, London.

Putnam, T. (1978) 'Skill and Technical Education: Getting Beyond Braverman', Nuffield Paper.

Rachleff, P. (1982) 'Working the Fast Lane: Jobs, Technology and Scientific Management in the US Postal Service', *Radical America*, vol. 16, nos 1/2.

Rakovski, M. (1977) 'Marxism and Soviet Societies', *Capital and Class*, no. 1.

Ramsay, H. (1980) 'Participation: the Pattern and its Significance', in Nichols, T. (ed.).

Reckman, B. (1979) 'Carpentry: the Craft and Trade', in Zimbalist, A. (ed.).

Red Notes (1976) *A Battle for Power — the Motor Industry Crisis in Britain 1975—76*, pamphlet, London.

Red Notes (1979) *Working Class Autonomy and the Crisis: Marxist Texts of a Class Movement: 1964—79*, London, Red Notes/CSE Books.

Reeves, T. K. and Woodward, J. (1970) 'The Study of Managerial Control', in Woodward, J. (ed.), *Industrial Organisation, Behaviour and Control*, London, Open University Press.

Reich, M. (1978) 'The Evolution of the United States Labor Force', in Edwards, R., Reich, M. and Weisskopf, T., *The Capitalist System*, Englewood Cliffs, N. J., Prentice-Hall.

Reich, W. (1972) *Dialectical Materialism and Psychoanalysis*, London, Socialist Reproduction.

Reid, S. (1978) 'Computers and De-skilling: Some Preliminary Observations from a Case-Study in Local Government', Nuffield Paper.

Rice, A. K. (1958) *Productivity and Social Organisation*, London, Tavistock.

Rose, M. (1975) *Industrial Behaviour*, London, Allen Lane.

Rosenberg, N. (1981) 'Marx as a Student of Technology', in Levidow, L. and Young, B. (eds).

Rosenbrock, H. (1979) 'The Re-direction of Technology', Research Paper, Council for Science and Society.

Rossanda, R. (1979) 'Power and Opposition in Post-Revolutionary Societies', in *Power and Opposition*, London, Ink Links.

Rowbotham, S. (1979) 'The Trouble With Patriarchy', *New Statesman*, vol. 98, pp. 970–1.

Roy, D. F. (1973) 'Banana Time, Job Satisfaction and Informal Interaction', in Salaman, G. and Thompson, K. (eds).

Roy, D. F. (1980) 'Fear Stuff, Sweet Stuff and Evil Stuff: Management Defences Against Unionisation in the South', in Nichols, T. (ed.).

Rubery, J. (1980) 'Structured Labour Markets, Worker Organisation and Low Pay', in Amsden, A. (ed.).

Salaman, G. (1981) *Class and the Corporation*, Glasgow, Fontana.

Salaman, G. and Thompson, K. (eds) (1973) *People and Organisations*, London, Longman.

Salaman, G. and Thompson, K. (eds) (1981) *Control and Ideology in Organisations*, London, Open University Press.

Sayles, C. R. (1958) *Behaviour of Industrial Work Groups*, New York, Wiley.

Schmiederer, U. (1979) 'Politics and Economics in Capitalism and in Already Existing Socialism', in *Power and Opposition*, London, Ink Links.

Scott, W. H. (1963) *Coal and Conflict*, Liverpool, Liverpool University Press.

Seccombe, W. (1974) 'The Housewife and Her Labour Under Capitalism', *New Left Review*, no. 94.

Seeman, M. (1959) 'On the Meaning of Alienation', *American Sociological Review*, vol. XXIV, pp. 783–91.

Segal, L. (1982) 'Unhappy Families', *New Socialist*, no. 6.

Sève, L. (1969) *Marxism et Théorie de la Personalité*, Paris, Editions Sociales.

Shaiken, H. (1979) 'Numerical Control of Work: Workers and Automation in the Computer Age', *Radical America*, vol. 13, no. 6.

Shapiro-Perl, N. (1979) 'The Piece Rate: Class Struggle on the Shop Floor: Evidence From the Costume Jewelry Industry in Providence', in Zimbalist, A. (ed.).

Shield, R. (1982) 'De-centralisation and Socialism', *Chartist*, no. 91.

Shutt, J. (1979) 'Workers' Organisation and Planning in the Motor Industry', CAITS Conference on Workers' Plans, unpublished paper.

Siltanen, J. (1981) 'A Commentary on Theories of Female Wage Labour', in Cambridge Women's Studies Group (eds), *Women in Society*, London, Virago.

Sivandan, A. (1982) 'Imperialism and Disorganic Development in the Silicon Age', in Sivandan, A., *A Different Hunger*, London, Pluto.

Slater, P. (ed.) (1980) *Outlines of a Critique of Technology*, London, Ink Links.

Sohn-Rethel, A. (1976) 'The Dual Economics of Transition', in Conference of Socialist Economists (eds).

Sohn-Rethel, A. (1978) *Intellectual and Manual Labour*, London, Macmillan.

Stone, K. (1973) 'The Origins of Job Structures in the Steel Industry', *Radical America*, vol. 7, no. 6.

Storey, J. (1982) *The Challenge to Management Control*, London, Kogan Page.

Sukharevsky, B. (1974) *Soviet Economy Under Advanced Socialism*, Moscow, Novosti.

Sweezy, P. (1971) 'The Transition to Socialism', in Sweezy, P. and Bettelheim, C., *On the Transition to Socialism*, London, Monthly Review Press.

Szymanski, A. (1972) 'Trends in the American Working Class', *Socialist Revolution*, vol. 1, no. 10.

Tannenbaum, A. (1967) *Control in Organisations*, New York, McGraw-Hill.

TASS/NDC (1979) *Computer Technology and Employment*, Technical and Supervisory Section of AUEW pamphlet, London.

Taylor, P. (1979) 'Labour Time, Work Measurement and the Commensuration of Labour', *Capital and Class*, no. 9.

Tepperman, J. (1976) 'Organising Office Workers', *Radical America*, vol. 10, no. 1.

Terkel, S. (1977) *Working*, Harmondsworth, Penguin.

TGWU (1979) *Micro-Electronics: New Technology, Old Problems, New Opportunities*, Transport and General Workers' Union pamphlet, London.

Thompson, E. P. (1967) 'Time, Work and Discipline, and Industrial Capitalism', *Past and Present*, no. 38.

Thompson, P. (1981) 'Class, Work and the Labour Process in Marxism and Sociology: a Survey and Evaluation', unpublished PhD, Liverpool University.

Thompson, P. and Bannon, E. (forthcoming) *Working the System: Workplace Organisation and the Labour Process in Telecommunications*, London, Pluto.

Thompson, P. and Lewis, G. (1977) *The Revolution Unfinished: a Critique of Trotskyism*, pamphlet, Liverpool, Big Flame.

Ticktin, H. (1973) 'Towards a Political Economy of the USSR', *Critique*, no. 1.

Trades Councils' Report (1980) *State Intervention in Industry: a Workers' Inquiry*, Coventry, Newcastle, Liverpool and North Tyneside Trades Councils, Newcastle.

Trist, E. L. and Bamforth, K. W. (1951) 'Some Social and Psychological Consequences of the Longwall Method of Coal Getting', *Human Relations*, vol. 4, no. 1.

TUC (1981) 'The Chip at Work', Trades Union Council Education pamphlet, London.

Turner, H. A. (1962) *Trade Union Growth, Structure and Policy*, London, Allen & Unwin.

Turner, H. A., Clack, G. and Roberts, G. (1967) *Labour Relations in the Motor Industry*, London, Allen & Unwin.

Valmeras, L. (1971) 'Work in America', *Radical America*, vol. 5, no. 4.

Wainwright, H. (1979) 'Trade Union Structures and the Fight for Full Employment: Combine Committees Versus the CSEU', CAITS Conference on Workers' Plans, unpublished paper.

Wainwright, H. and Elliot, D. (1982) *The Lucas Plan: a New Trades Unionism in the Making*?, London, Allison & Busby.

Wajcman, J. (1981) 'Work and the Family: Who Gets the Best of Both Worlds?', in Cambridge Women's Study Group (eds), *Women in Society*, London, Virago.

Walker, C. R. and Guest, R. H. (1952) *Man on the Assembly Line*, Cambridge, Mass., Harvard University Press.

Walker, P. (ed.) (1979) *Between Labour and Capital*, Brighton, Harvester.

Warner, W. and Low, J. O. (1947) *The Social System of the Modern Factory*, New Haven, Yale University Press.

Weber, M. (1964) *The Theory of Social and Economic Organisation*, New York, Free Press.

Wedderburn, D. and Crompton, R. (1972) *Workers' Attitudes and Technology*, Cambridge University Press.

Weinbaum, B. and Bridges, A. (1976) 'The Other Side of the Paycheck: Monopoly Capital and the Structure of Consumption', *Monthly Review*, vol. 28, no. 3.

Weiss, D. W. (1976) 'Marx Versus Smith on the Division of Labor', *Monthly Review*, vol. 28, no. 3.

Welch, J. (1979) 'New Left Knots', in Walker, P. (ed.).

Westergaard, J. (1970) 'The Re-Discovery of the Cash Nexus', *Socialist Register*, London, Merlin.

Whyte, W. F. (1955) *Money and Motivation*, New York, Harper.

Willis, P. (1977) *Learning for Labour*, Farnborough, Saxon House.

Wilson, E. (1977) *Women and the Welfare State*, London, Tavistock.

Women's Studies Group (eds) (1978) *Women Take Issue: Aspects of Women's Subordination*, London, Hutchinson/University of Birmingham Centre for Contemporary Cultural Studies.

Wood, S. (ed.) (1982) *The Degradation of Work? Skill, De-skilling and the Labour Process*, London, Hutchinson.

Woodward, J. (1958) *Management and Technology*, London, HMSO.

Woodward, J. (1965) *Industrial Organisation: Theory and Practice*, Oxford University Press.

Woodward, J. (ed.) (1970) *Industrial Organisations: Behaviour and Control*, Oxford University Press.

Work in America (1973) *Work in America: Report of Special Task Force to the Secretary of Health, Education and Welfare*, Cambridge, Mass., MIT Press.

Wright, E. O. (1976) 'Contradictory Class Relations', *New Left Review*, no. 98.

Wright, E. O. (1978) *Classes, Crisis and the State*, London, New Left Books.

Yarrow, M. (1979) 'The Labor Process in Coal Mining: Struggle for Control', in Zimbalist, A. (ed.).

Young, B. (1976) 'Review of Labor and Monopoly Capital', *Radical Science*, no. 4.

Young, K. *et al.* (eds) (1981) *Of Marriage and the Market: Women's Subordination in International Perspective*, London, CSE Books.

Zimbalist, A. (ed.) (1979) *Case Studies on the Labor Process*, London, Monthly Review Press.

Index